Advance Praise

This exceptionally well-researched monograph offers a groundbreaking ethnographic account of what the author compellingly terms 'visceral politics'. Viscerality offers a heuristic to explore the fusion of caste, kinship, religion, and power in south India. The result is a rare study of lineage politics alongside ritual and popular Hinduism. At a moment when Hindu nationalism and the rhetoric of Ram Rajya are shaping contemporary India, this work provides a vital contribution to the anthropology of sovereignty – by recentring the role of genealogy in everyday social life. A must-read for scholars of South Asian studies, anthropology, and political theory.

Lucia Michelutti, author of *The Vernacularisation of Democracy: Politics, Caste and Religion in India*

This is political anthropology at its best. Faithful to observed realities rather than theoretical juggling, this elegant book will take you deep into South Asian politics, where elections and pilgrimages, politicians and gods live comfortably side by side.

Anastasia Piliavsky, author of *Nobody's People: Hierarchy as Hope in a Society of Thieves*

Indira Arumugam's wonderfully written account of political life in rural Tamil Nadu starts from the premise that 'All politics is local', fleshing this out in chapter after chapter of vivid and engrossing detail. *Visceral Politics* is anthropology at its best, written with equal attention to spirit, heart, flesh, bones, and, of course, guts.

Jonathan Spencer, author of *Anthropology, Politics and the State*

Visceral Politics

When the gods stop roaming across the lands and encountering their devotees in person – what does this reveal about ongoing political upheavals? What does the insouciant trespassing of crows into human houses convey about how different kinds of kin should behave? How can offering sacrifice be tantamount to building and powering a polity? This book delineates the dynamics of a micro-polity as embodied in and made vital through the kinship, rituals, feuds, myths, and everyday lives of people in a Tamil Nadu village. Framed by caste exclusions and women's marginalization and substantiated by relations of lineage kinship, the constitutive premises of this hierarchical polity also feed into a contemporary electoral politics that claims to be more inclusive and egalitarian.

Eviscerating a body politic, this book lays bare the tissues that constitute and the capillaries that nourish the political. Power structures, political interactions, and ideals are made flesh in and animated in the persons of kinsmen, the territories in which they co-reside, and the bodies of sacrificial animals. It explores how ordinary people in the process of living their everyday lives also theorize for themselves the construction of realms and the establishment of reign. At the heart of this exploration is viscerality. Exploiting the rawness, elementality, and vitality underpinning the visceral as well as the ultimate mystery at its heart, this book goes beyond politics as ideology, interest, or instrumentality to interrogate just how it moves people and gets them in its grip.

Indira Arumugam is Assistant Professor in Anthropology at the National University of Singapore.

Visceral Politics

Imaginaries of Power in South India

Indira Arumugam

CAMBRIDGE
UNIVERSITY PRESS

Shaftesbury Road, Cambridge CB2 8EA, United Kingdom

One Liberty Plaza, 20th Floor, New York, NY 10006, USA

477 Williamstown Road, Port Melbourne, VIC 3207, Australia

314–321, 3rd Floor, Plot 3, Splendor Forum, Jasola District Centre, New Delhi – 110025, India

103 Penang Road, #05–06/07, Visioncrest Commercial, Singapore 238467

Cambridge University Press is part of Cambridge University Press & Assessment, a department of the University of Cambridge.

We share the University's mission to contribute to society through the pursuit of education, learning and research at the highest international levels of excellence.

www.cambridge.org
Information on this title: www.cambridge.org/9781009577441

First published 2025

Printed in India by Avantika Printers Pvt. Ltd.

Cover image: Horse on deity's processional chariot, Sri Kothandaramasamy Temple, Vaduvur. Image credit: Anandh Kannan, studio_we_photography, Vaduvur.

A catalogue record for this publication is available from the British Library

ISBN 978-1-009-57744-1 Hardback

For EU product safety concerns, contact us at Calle de José Abascal, 56, 1°, 28003 Madrid, Spain, or email eugpsr@cambridge.org.

For Amma and Appa

Contents

Tables

Figures and Maps

Figures

Maps

Acknowledgements

This book began with my mother's stories. Moving to Singapore after marrying my father and having me, she frequently evoked her village home. Her stories were always of her experiences growing up in Vaduvur. Stories of agricultural rhythms, childhood games, family feuds, loving kin, temple festivals, roaming gods, and haunting demons made Vaduvur appear alive, enchanting, and enigmatic. Lodging themselves in my subconscious, these stories made it impossible to see beyond Vaduvur when it came to choosing my field-site.

It takes a village to write a book. I am profoundly indebted to the people of Vaduvur. They are not only my interlocutors but also my kin. Special thanks go to my maternal uncle, Govindasamy, my cousin-sister and his wife, Samiammal (Dravidian kinship in the flesh), and their sons, Mukundan and Mukilan, my maternal aunts, Andal and Chinnappa, my cousin-sisters, Indira and Latha, and their families, as well as my cousin-brothers Sengkutuvan and Narayanan and their families. Additional thanks go to classificatory kin like Kavita, Jeyabal, and Sakthivel for the effort they made in educating me about their way of life. I owe much to the late Sevu Vanniyar – my classificatory grandfather, patient teacher, and twinkle-eyed tease – whose death has meant the demise of a living library.

This book is based on my PhD dissertation at the London School of Economics (LSE). My mother gave me the stories, but I had no idea of how to make sense of them until I met my supervisor, C. J. Fuller. After my return from fieldwork, Chris waved off my solicitations of his expertise, 'You tell me. You are the one who has done the work.' He helped me discover my own point of view and the confidence to trust it. If Chris grounded me, my other supervisor, Laura Bear, gave me wings.

Her original insights inspired my imagination to soar in wonderful directions. The careful feedback and thoughtful encouragement from my examiners, the late and much-missed Isabelle Clark-Decès and James Laidlaw, proved critical to honing my ideas.

With their genius at seminars in the Old Room and their generosity at the White Horse pub, my fellow graduate students Judith Bovensiepen, Ankur Dutta, Irene Calis, Marcello Sorrentino, Hans Steinmuller, Andrew Sanchez, Elizabeth Hull, Katie Dow, George St Claire, Marina Sapritsky, Ana Paula Gutierrez-Garza, and Elizabeth Frantz kept me sane throughout. I also thank Haripriya Narasimhan, Wu Keping, and especially Nate Roberts for their thoughtful comments and valuable friendship.

I am thankful to my friends at the National University of Singapore, especially Vineeta Sinha, Noorman Abdullah, Kelvin Low, Sidharthan Maunaguru, and Roxana Waterson for their support.

I thank my husband, Saravana Prakash for his encouragement, enthusiasm and making me laugh throughout the writing process.

I am grateful to Jeyaletchimi, not just my sister but my first and best friend. She and my brother, Muthukumar, are why the Tamil aphorism – '[she], who has [siblings], need not fear even an army' – resonates.

My father, S. D. Arumugam, is my rock, exuding great love, quiet strength, and endless support. My ever-curious mother, Jeyakody, has constantly encouraged me to dream bigger, aim higher, go farther, and know more. She impressed upon me that for a woman born on a subcontinent, an island is never enough.

Introduction
The Twilight of the Old Gods

A kinship formed in flesh and fish. 'Viranar *kari* and Senkulattu [Red Pond] *min*', explained Andal, an elderly woman, 'make us a lineage, the Sakkarei Kandiyar lineage.' Claims on the meat from the goats they collectively sponsor and sacrifice to their tutelary deity Viranar form 'temple shares' (*kovil panku*). Rights to the fish from the pond that they communally own are 'pond shares' (*kulattu panku*). Temple and pond shares, joint stakes on the agricultural bounty of their territories sanctioned by their tutelaries, make individuals into a lineage. Meat and fish substantiate a genealogical claim – a contemporary evocation of an assumed historical consanguinity. They embody the rights, obligations, and claims-making that underpin all kinship-polities from the lineage to the street to the region. This is a kinship built on bone, realized in tissue, connected by veins, lubricated by fat, and quickened by blood. One as vulnerable as flesh and as vital as entrails. A kinship vivified by the death throes of fish plucked out of ponds to flop about on the shores, writhing and gasping for breath. One instantiated in the heaps of dead fish stacked into piles and arranged in neat rows around which the bookkeeper weaved, counting the shares, matching them to the lineage-mates' names in the register, and recording those having collected their share. The blood, scales, slime, and guts – snatched by waiting crows – as women sit cleaning and cutting the fish. The tamarind tang of fish curry wafting through the air at lunch time on the day when the communal pond is harvested. A kinship that resonates with the distressed bleats of goats and the squawks of roosters about to be sacrificed. The splashes of blood spilling to the earth as the priest slices through the neck of a goat in one sure stroke. The mound of decapitated goat heads after the sacrifice. The ritual priest bearing aloft the massive bronze sabre, a lime sheathing its curved tip, dripping with goat gore. Entrails tumbling out as the butcher splits open the carcass from the goat sacrificed that morning. The piles of butchered meat, carefully weighed, uniformly divided into bowls, and equally distributed among the kinsmen with claims to it. The comparing, measuring, exchanging, and squabbling to make sure that every share of meat is absolutely identical and resolutely equal. The pile of goat bones and tough gristle spat out after a feast to be eventually fought over by dogs. A kinship substantiated by bodies, blood, sweat, toil, and tears as much as they are rooted in rights, claims, and obligations. A kinship that forms the flesh and blood of a polity and makes it visceral.

The viscera are the largely hidden, terrifically messy, but absolutely essential inner organs of an animal. In Etruscan and later in Roman religion, the viscera of sacrificed animals were considered sacred – at least while the haruspex deciphered the meanings entangled in the livers, spleens, and intestines. Disembowelled through violence, mired in blood, and reeking of faeces, the viscera nevertheless were thought to carry important messages from the gods (see Hoskins 1993 on sacrifice and divination in Eastern Indonesia). They were earthly omens to diagnose uncertain conditions and deduce indeterminate prospects. While it does not divine the future, this book too performs a kind of augury, one intimately familiar to anthropologists. It attempts to grasp the frustratingly nebulous and the intricately manifold by sifting through a few material remnants. Eviscerating a body politic, this book lays bare the tissues that constitute and the capillaries that nourish the political.

Often contrasted with the rational and the factual, the visceral is used to refer to the instinctual, emotional, intuitive, and primitive. The visceral, according to the *Oxford English Dictionary*, is defined as 'relating to deep inward feelings rather than the intellect'. This definition draws from numerous problematic dichotomies – mind versus body, reasoned versus unconscious, animal versus human, and modern versus primitive – for its contemporary resonance. Disrupting these dualisms and stagnate categories, anthropologists now see embodiment as a means to emphasize contingency, process, and permeability. Philosophical developments such as phenomenology and practice theory were sutured together with an orientation towards everyday life as the locus of social life (Carsten 1997; Das 2007), political projects (Michelutti 2008; Banerjee 2021), and moral striving (Osella and Osella 2001; Pandian 2008; Das 2012). Combining these theoretical innovations with insights from fieldwork where the ethnographer's body is entangled in the analytical process, anthropologists focused on corporeal presence in the world as a way to describe porous, intuitive, sensed, and enlivened bodily experiences in and with inhabited worlds (Csordas 1994; Farquhar and Lock 2007). Embodiment becomes a way through which to make the terrible perceptible and the visceral visible. Rosaldo (1993; also Taussig 1987) pushes this even further to argue that the visceral (and the violent) itself must be made the centre of cultural analysis so as to grapple with the complexities and potentialities of culture. Powerful visceral experiences and emotions – disruptive, untranslatable, and immune to culture – push anthropology to the limits of its capacity to represent. Upending routines of seeing culture as mere projection of our intellectual capacities, the visceral makes present and palpable what we are studying.

I return to the root of the word 'visceral' to exploit its potential to make politics not just present but also haptic. In so doing, I evoke not so much their transcendental potential but the dense juxtapositions that even the grossest materials incorporate within themselves. The visceral is used to explore the conjunction of the inner and the outer, animal and spiritual, earthly, cosmic, meaningful, and mysterious. I draw precisely from this stark contrast yet simultaneous convergence to understand the interconnections between earthly materials and their ethereal meanings that frame and feed lived politics in rural Tamil Nadu. Simultaneously, I exploit the rawness, elementality, and the vitality that the visceral involves as well as the ultimate mystery at its heart to go beyond ideology, interest, or instrumentality to interrogate just how politics moves people and gets them in its grip.

A political imaginary rendered not just visible but visceral forms the crux of this book. Visceral does refer to the blood and guts of this shared imaginary – the graphic but delicate tissues through which the imagined is made material. Concurrently, it also evokes the acutely felt sentiments and intensely experienced sensations through which this imaginary is made intimate. While not wanting to reproduce the already mentioned dichotomies, I nevertheless must insist that an emphasis on the enveloping ambience and ardent intensity of their politics does not detract from its deliberative aspects. It simply grounds erudition in the routinely done and deeply felt. Politics may be part of my interlocutors' very bones, but it is also ruminated upon, articulated, and intensely debated and contested both in private and in public. Viscerality encapsulates the immersive quality and the intimacy of a politics that is not just thought about but vividly experienced and casually lived. In Singapore, where I grew up, rather than a contest with very real stakes, politics tends to be a predictable procession inviting apathy. In Vaduvur, I was struck not just by how informed my interlocutors were but even more so by how passionate they were about politics (see Michelutti 2008; Banerjee 2020 on the singular enthusiasm that Indians have for politics with some of the highest rates of participation and contestations). Sitting on benches outside tea shops, farmers expertly dissected the intricacies of party politics. Voting for a specific party, elderly ladies explained, was a tradition passed down through their families. While their votes echoed those of their parents and siblings, the women confessed that they often voted differently than their husbands. Others cited the onscreen charisma and acting prowess of certain actor-politicians to explain their ongoing party affiliations and voting choices actualizing the symbiotic relationship with cinema characteristic to Tamil Nadu politics (see Hardgrave 1979, 1973; Pandian 1992; Velayutham and Devadas 2022).

On election day, voting stations exuded a carnival atmosphere, decorated with balloons and crepe paper festoons. White *dhoti*-clad volunteers formally greeted voters. After voting, the voters left with packets of sweetmeats, laughing, and chatting (see Banerjee 2007 on the festive atmosphere at Indian elections). Cutting across gender, age, marital status, and occupations, people not just were invested in politics but positively relished it. Politics was in the very air, and I too was caught up in its heady currents.

Place, Peoples, and Pasts

Vaduvur, with a population of 13,368, is a large village in central Tamil Nadu in what is now the Thiruvarur district (Map I.1).[1]

Muttiraiyars (previously called Valaiyars or Amblarars) (see Deliege 1996; Mines 2012) and a smaller number of Dalits (previously called Paraiyars) (see Deliege 1999), considered the lower castes, provide the bulk of the agricultural labour. From their heydays of village dominance, when nearly 250 Brahmin families were living in their own caste and spatially segregated colony (*agraharam*), now only 25 families remain. Today, the Kallars form the dominant caste monopolizing land ownership and political offices. A populous caste dispersed throughout central and southern Tamil Nadu, accounts of Kallar origins tend to be conjectural. It is generally agreed that Kallars had venerable martial and marauding traditions. Kallar is often translated as 'thief'. Their appearance in the historical record is overwhelmingly characterized by 'independence and non-submission' (Dumont 2000: 13). Many Kallar surnames to this day denote military or political titles and suggest a warrior past[2] (Karuppaiyan 1990; Venkatasamy Nattar 2005). Kallars, Bayly (2001: 285) concludes, are part of a 'title of rural groups in Tamil Nadu with warrior-pastoralist ancestral traditions'. Kallars were mercenaries and soldiers in the employ of warring chieftains as well as burglars, bandits, and highwaymen. Early Tamil literary sources do allude to the threat these peripheral castes posed to the settled and prosperous agricultural core (Pandian 2005, 2009). Through the institution of the watch (*kaval*), Kallars were able to combine the warrior qualities for which they prided themselves with lucrative practices of thieving.

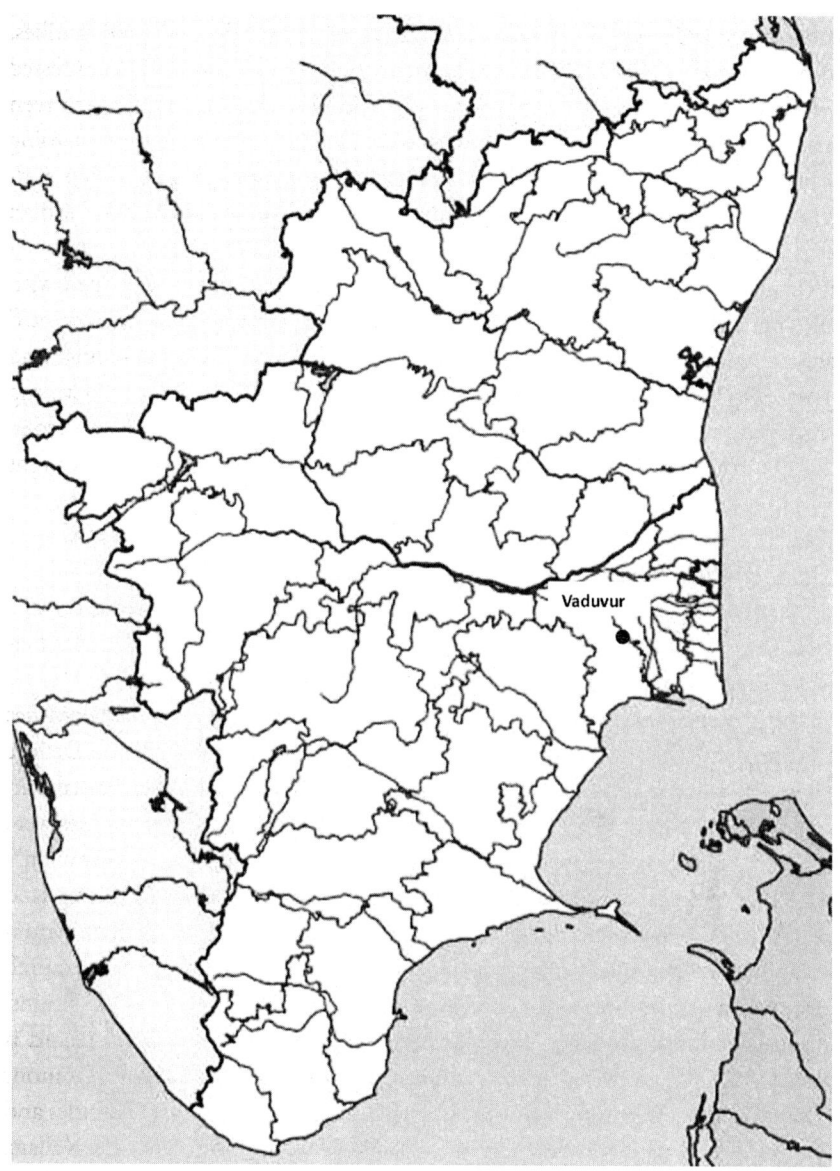

Map I.1 Vaduvur, Needamangalam Taluk, Thiruvarur District, Tamil Nadu

Source: Wikimedia Commons.

They carved a niche for themselves in the village structure as defenders of its material security even if they themselves were often the threat.

Like with protection and predation, there were structural continuities between banditry and kingship. Banditry, Shulman (1980b: 283) argues, is a 'traditional, socially recognized occupation of specific castes with its own symbolic legitimation'. Kings and thieves, as evident in the ballads surrounding a Vishnu shrine in Madurai, have been classed together and legitimized as a 'particular power structure' by the deity himself (Shulman 1980b: 285). Using their own genealogical narratives, Dirks (1982) shows how chieftains and little kings of the Maravar caste of Uttumalai, with similar histories and trajectories to the Kallars, began as bandits. The first step towards appropriating local level authority was through undertaking the rights of 'watch' as part of the village police system. These watchmen then distinguished themselves in the service of larger kings by vanquishing other bandits, in return for gifts, honours, territory, and the ratification of their authority. The Kallars thus fit into the ambiguous category of 'dangerous watchmen' and 'institutionalized bandits' (Shulman 1980b: 286). Banditry was an archetypal modus operandi for social mobility and the acquiring of political power and eventually legitimate authority.

Banditry and the watch were declared unlawful under colonial rule. In 1918, the British classified many Kallars as a criminal caste (*kuttra paramparai*) under the Criminal Tribes Act (CTA) (Mullaly 1892; Radhakrishnan 2001; D'Souza 2001). Kallars were subjected to intensified police surveillance, judicial discipline, and attempts at resettlement and reform (Pandian 2009). Defined as exemplary criminals, the Kallars were singled out as the pre-eminent policing problem in the area.[3] Kallar 'crimes' were particularly infuriating to the colonial authorities because they were often enacted in the name of policing. In his defence of the Kallar caste, Blackburn (1978) demonstrates how external pressures, particularly those related to the expansion of British rule, relegated Kallars to the 'wild *Collerie*' image that populated colonial accounts. The trope of 'criminality' as applied to the Kallars, Dirks (1993) argues, was primarily a tactic to legitimate colonial authority as it penetrated into the arid regions of southern Tamil Nadu. The British authorities did not differentiate between 'legitimate' rights of protection and 'illegitimate' forms of appropriation and intimidation. Mirroring the archetypal trajectories of pre-colonial kings, the British inserted themselves into the south Indian political landscape by defining all authorities except their own or that endorsed by themselves as criminal (Yang 1985). Classifying Kallar activities as a problem of law and order and acting to pacify them allowed the British to assert and legitimize their own authority.

The Kallars are not monolithic, and there are several endogamous sub-castes (Turnbull 1895: 5–12; Thurston and Rangachari 1909: 52–91). Converting to more orthodox, pacific, and socially prestigious Brahminical and Vellalar values, the Kallars of the wetter lowland Thanjavur regions were markedly different from their counterparts in the drier upland tracts of Madurai and Ramnathapuram. Unlike their more intractable brethren in Madurai, my Thanjavur Kallar interlocutors were settled and prosperous agriculturalists, only slightly below the exemplary Vellalars. Access to land and reliable irrigation was the key to their pacification and prosperity and their portrayal as more compliant.[4] The Thanjavur Kallars, Dumont (2000: 14) claims, 'look with scorn on their Madurai brothers, whom they consider coarse and half-savage'. Conversely, Karuppaiyan (1990) notes that the still recalcitrant upland Kallars disdain the lowland Kallars' dependence on Brahmin landlords and emulation of Sanskritic values.

Even in the more pacific climes of my fieldwork, the Kallars' willingness to resort to violence was integral to their emergence as Vaduvur's dominant caste. Vaduvur's lands used to belong predominantly to the Brahmins. Many Brahmins voluntarily sold or leased their lands to their Kallar labourers to exploit the increasing opportunities of urbanization and migration (Fuller and Narasimhan 2014). In other cases, the Brahmins had to abandon their lands due to the intimidation and intractability of their newly assertive Kallar tenants. Since 1925, Kallar social consciousness was raised by the Self-Respect Movement led by the reformer E. V. Periyar. This stressed socio-economic equality and argued that genuine political freedom was not possible without individual self-respect (see Irschick 1969; Baker 1976; Washbrook 1976; Barnett 1976). Tamil Nadu's new pro-tenant land reform legislation introduced in the 1950s and the acquiring of political power by parties founded upon anti-Brahmin ideologies since 1967 emboldened the Kallars to withhold their rents. If pressed, they threatened violence. Contemporary Kallar dominance in Vaduvur was secured partly through such unhesitating recourse to coercion.

Intimate Methodologies

At the heart of politics in Vaduvur is kinship. The logics, lived experiences, and ethics of relatedness – of lineage, clan, affines, household, street, village, and region – constitute the polity. Kinship animates citizenship, structuring the latter's political claims and also making them palpably intimate. In honing in on the relatedness upon which this polity is premised, this book makes apparent a political imaginary not just from the ground up but also from the inside out – one that includes deliberative debates and inner dispositions, feelings and fighting, love and labour. These themes also resonated through my attempts to make sense of this intricate world. Long before I arrived for fieldwork in 2005, Vaduvur was already an intimate place for me. It was where my paternal grandfather was born, and from where to escape debt bondage, he fled to Singapore. Vaduvur was also where my mother was born, had to stop schooling when her mother died when she was just seven years old, married my Singaporean father when she was eighteen years old, and was left behind for nearly four years because my father could not afford her passage to Singapore. It is also where her family – brother, sisters, nephews, and nieces – continue to live. Vaduvur was also where I was born. It was the place my mother and I left behind, when I was three years old, after my father was finally able to send for us. Since I left, fieldwork would be the first time I would be residing for so long in my birthplace and among my maternal kin.

Flesh and blood were also pivotal to my access to and understanding of the scaffolding of rights and obligations sustaining the kinship-polity. Once, I went to observe the annual harvest of fish from Red Pond. I was invited to attend because this was my own natal lineage.[5] My father is a lineage-mate. Despite living in Singapore, he tenders the requisite tax and retains his claims. Once they knew whose daughter I was, my father's lineage-mates kept asking, 'Have you come to collect your father's share?' After all, I had the rights. My supposed nativity did not give me special insights into my ethnography. Narayan (1995) disavows any epistemological distinction underpinning a so-called native anthropology. Every anthropological encounter, Shah (2017) argues, is a mixture of familiarity and estrangement in various degrees. I may have been born in Vaduvur. I may have close relatives and prior contacts there. I may be fluent in Tamil. However, I am not a native. By dint of my migration, education, class position, exposure, and everyday life, I was a stranger.

Nevertheless, my prior kinship to my interlocutors made me notice their political imaginary in the first place and framed my specific attempts to decipher it. Understanding my own rights within the polity sensitized me to the political implications of kinship positionalities and their attendant rights and obligations. It was also why my interlocutors professed to take such great pains to educate me. Ruing my ignorance, one of my many classificatory mother's brothers and neighbours explained to other villagers:

Obviously, her mother has not taught her properly. It is after all her own history, traditions, and culture. She should know about them.

While I was interviewing Sevu Vanniyar, the advisor to the headmen, he interrupted his accounts of the regional polity (*natu*) to muse on our personal connections.

> Your father came to see my daughter as a prospective bride. The match very nearly came to be. However, astrological prognoses for the union were negative. Your father then married your mother. Otherwise, I could have been your actual grandfather.

Along with forming my field-site's ambience, my own kinship with my interlocutors vivified their polity for me.

Even before I stepped foot in Vaduvur, I already had a position within the village social hierarchy. A latent one – which I would have to activate through my presence and active engagement – but one which I did not have to create anew through my own efforts. I already had claims upon and obligations to kinfolk as they did to me. I already had rights, albeit mediated by my gender, to a tutelary deity, a sacrificial cult, and shares of sacred fish and meat. Simply by virtue of my descent, I was thrust into the heart of the polity from the outset. I made sense of this polity's musculature in the usual way, through poking my nose into everything and pestering people with questions. Its marrow, however, I got at through my personal connections to it. When the headmen's advisor described how headmanship was inherited, he added that my paternal grandfather also belonged to one of these 'headmen's families'. A headman described how certain rituals conferred and signalled political distinction using examples from my family history:

> When the water is released from Mettur Dam for the year, the gates must be opened so that the water flows into Vaduvur's irrigation ditches. This is an honour – given to your [maternal] grandfather, Palaniappan Vanniyar. In recognition of this, when the *natu* goddess, Selli Amman, goes on her annual procession – she tarries in K. K. Vanniyar street where your grandfather is from. She stops in front of his house to receive offerings.

These personal glimpses – the enfolding into and unfolding of my own genealogy as part of the history of Vaduvur – grounded this political imaginary not just in the material but also in the intimate. All ethnographic research is contingent on producing intimacy, and often with strangers. This, Shah (2017) argues, is precisely what gives it its revolutionary potential – to unsettle our theoretical assumptions and produce knowledge from perspectives that had been marginalized. Intimacy, in my case, was also grounded in claims of genealogical kinship, idioms of flesh and blood, and the emotional resonance of familial connections. Unravelling my own rights within (and also marginalization from) it made this political imaginary visceral for me.[6]

Ailing Body Politic

Given this book's focus on the vital organs and life blood of a political imaginary, it is uniquely appropriate to begin with decay. Of utmost concern is the slow demise and seeming descent into irrelevance of a polity.

> A large Banyan[7] tree grew by the Pidari temple. In the day time, the headmen gathered under its branches for their *natu* assembly. All the *natu* gods also gathered here. But only at night. They sang and danced. You could hear the bells on their anklets. They bathed and washed their clothes. All temples have ponds. You could hear splashing water and pounding wet cloth on a wash-stone. The gods sang, danced, played and then went to sleep. They liked it here. This was a secluded place. They were not disturbed by the sounds of pounding grain (*ural-ulakkai*) [human habitation]. You cannot hear the echoes of the deities anymore ... the trees have been cut down ... electricity is everywhere. There are just too many houses and people.

So reminisced an elderly woman living near Pidari's temple in Vaduvur's commercial district. Pidaris are boundary goddesses. Through their annual processions, they map the contours of territories. They also protect local polities against the forces of chaos and evil that threaten their integrity. Delineating territories and defending their boundaries, Pidaris constitute vernacular polities such as the inter-village regional polity called the *natu*. Their sharing of a locus made the imbrications between tutelary deities, *natu* temples, and sacrificial rituals as well as traditional headmen, *natu* government, and deliberative assemblies explicit. The banyan tree where the deities congregated for pleasure is also where the headmen who govern the *natu* meet for politics. However, this tree – where divine pleasures and vernacular politics had once converged – is no longer standing. The deities' presence can no longer be sensed. The power of the *natu* and its headmen is no longer what it was. In Vaduvur, the vernacular polity is in crisis – a crisis of presence, power, and authority.

However much its exact configuration and the hierarchies of precedence within it are disputed, there is remarkable consensus that the Vaduvur *natu* is in decline. Netttaiyar, a headman, was so convinced that the *natu* was currently irrelevant that he saw no point in even enumerating Vaduvur's headmen, let alone relating the polity's history, structure, and functions.

> Why are you asking these questions now? What is there to know? What are you going to do with this useless information? No one listens to headmen these days. Nobody bothers to ask us anything. Everyone dances to the tunes of the politicians and political parties!

Some, like the *natu* deities' Brahmin priest, blamed the headmen themselves.

> At one time, the headmen did work for the good of the *natu* and its temples. Now, they are only interested in looking out for themselves. Why else are they wavering about renovating the Kailasanathar Temple? Many donors have volunteered the necessary funds. Instead of organizing the renovations and making detailed budgets, the headmen are only interested in getting their hands on the money. Meanwhile, the roof of the temple is practically collapsing, the supporting pillars have fallen, the floor is just sand and there are thorny weeds everywhere.[8]

Others, however, cited the deleterious effects of post-independence democratic politics. Sevu Vanniyar, advisor to the headmen's council, blamed the machinations of political parties and politicians' avaricious intrigues for undermining the *natu* government and the headmen's authority.

> The headmen themselves heed the political parties that foment dissent. They refuse to cooperate with each other. Thenpathy's (South Vaduvur) headmen are opposed to and refuse to come together with Vadapathy's (North Vaduvur) headmen. So, for the past three years, there have not been many *natu* assemblies.

The headmen's diminishing authority coincides with the tutelary deities' declining presence and prowess.

The immanence of the tutelaries has been the core indicator of divine potency. *Natu* deities are not confined to sacred sites and bound by regular rituals. Instead, they wander. They delight in the landscape – singing, dancing, bathing, and even doing laundry. They manifest themselves directly through possessing people, appearing in dreams, judging, punishing, and sometimes even killing them. They do not wait to be represented by human systems of signification but outrightly thrust themselves into this world (Arumugam 2023). Or at least they used to.

Ritual specialists and older villagers concede that the old gods' intercessions in human affairs have waned (see Obeyesekere 1977 on the rise and fall of deities' cults in Sri Lanka). These village deities are no longer encountered on their nightly patrols around their jurisdictions. They are seldom seen riding their horses, accompanied by their guardians, and policing the boundaries of their territories. They no longer appear in dreams as often as they had in the past. They do not possess as many people as they had been wont to. Those who appeared to be possessed by these deities were most probably pretending. I myself have seen Val-Muniswarar's god-dancer (*cami-ati*) – the medium who temporarily

manifests the deity – become ostensibly possessed. At the lineage sacrifice in
2007, the god-dancer drank the blood from the sacrificed communal goat. He ran
frenziedly across the fields, leaping over irrigation ditches, outrunning all the men
trying to catch up with him. Three times, he leapt up to run across the fields,
evading all attempts to stop him. In the end, he was drenched with sweat, and
appeared absolutely drained as he lay slumped against a pillar. If possession was
pretence, I asked headman Nettaiyar, what explained the god-dancer's frenzy and
subsequent exhaustion?

> There is no longer any such thing as real possession. This god-dancer was not
> even given any blood to drink. We stopped this practice. Ever since the previous
> one drank all the blood, suffered a heart-attack and died. The blood is too rich
> to be digested. We do not even allow a few sips. We simply touched the vessel to
> the current god-dancer's lips. Purely as a gesture. For tradition's sake. He did not
> drink the sacrificial blood. So how can he be really possessed?

The headman reiterated his scepticism:

> I rent part of the lands belonging to the Val-Muniswarar Temple. I often work
> in the fields next to the complex. I lay down to take naps right by the temple.
> And in the middle of the day [mid-day with the sun at its zenith is when spirits
> are most likely to seize the unwary]. But I have never been troubled by anything.
> Only those who have a nervous disposition and are already frightened will claim
> to be affected by the spirits nowadays.

The tutelary deities were no longer cavalierly roaming around Vaduvur's landscape.
More ominously, they were not attending the ceremonies that were specifically
organized in their honour and to which they had been expressly invited. Even
at their own worship, the deities were not heeding their devotees' repeated and
impassioned invocations. They were not letting their approval or disapproval of
the ritual enactments and therein their judgement of their congregation be known.
   The first goat sacrificed to Val-Muniswarar – the Southern Mannaiyar lineage's
tutelary deity – was, as always, the common one, paid for and sacrificed on behalf of
the entire lineage. Only after this communal goat is offered can all other individual
and/or household sacrifices proceed. Some blood from this communal sacrifice
was mixed with cooked rice, rolled into three big balls and thrown up into the
branches of the surrounding trees. The bloody rice balls had not fallen back down
to the ground. The *minis* – fertility spirits kept in check by Val-Muniswarar –
had swooped down from the trees, caught, and consumed the gory rice.

The disappearance of the bloody rice balls – in an apparent defiance of gravity – was evidence that the deities continued to roam among mortals.

Or at least it used to be so. This was when this lineage worship was held in the dark of night, lit only by flickering oil lamps and camphor flames. This was before electricity became ubiquitous in Vaduvur (only in the last thirty years). This was when the shrine itself was located in the middle of rice fields, amid a grove of massive tamarind and Peepul trees.[9] This was when agricultural fields (*vayal-katus*)[10] – wavering between the domesticated and the wild – were haunted by ominous beings that could only be banished by daylight. When night itself was frightening, the bloody rice balls were caught by the *minis* before they fell to the ground.

Nowadays – to facilitate the feasting and hospitality that follows – the sacrifice is held in the afternoon (see Osella and Osella 2003 on the commoditization of sacrifices in Kerala). The shadowy sacred grove, the perfect locus for the uncanniness of Muniswarar worship, has been cleared for agriculture. There are no massive trees in which the *minis* can shelter (see Parry 1980, 2005: 279 on the adverse effects of habitat destruction on spirit manifestations and epidemic diseases in Benares and Bhilai respectively). Exposing what had always been unfathomably eerie to stark daylight has inevitably transformed the ambience. The enigmatic has become prosaic. Today, this lineage's headman, after much demurral, sheepishly admitted, 'The flung bloody rice balls just fall back down and smash to the ground.' 'The old gods', he disclosed, 'no longer had any power!' (Arumugam 2015).

This elegiac juxtaposition of the headmen's fading authority and the old gods' waning potency alludes to the Vaduvur polity's intricate density. Ritual and politics, kinship and citizenship, cosmos and carcass, profundity and brutality – they had all mingled and settled together to wrought a subtle, intricate, and erudite political imaginary. Similarly, in ethnography, experience, observation, autobiography, imagination, and interpretation jostle against and bleed into each other. This allows ethnography to grasp the osmotic nature of the world, offering the closest approximation of how our interlocutors imagine, experience, and understand it. Viscerality offers a similar scope that allows us to grapple with how the very cosmos is entangled with a scrap of sacrificial meat.

Political Entrails, Ritual Infrastructure

Ritual killing, Valeri (1985: 69) observes, dramatizes the experience of transformation or transition from presence to absence. 'Sacrificial death and destruction ... represent the passage from the visible to the invisible and thereby make it possible to conceive the transformations the sacrifice is supposed to produce.' This is echoed in Vedic conventions framing orthodox Hindu sacrifices where the focus is on the transcendent, on reaching the gods. The material is merely a vehicle. The journey is all. The tangible fragments left behind are merely inert husks, carcasses left to decompose (Calasso 2014). In this case, however, the carcasses cannot just be discarded. They are the very foundations upon which the body politic itself is built. A sacrificed goat is not simply a sacred vehicle to communicate with the tutelary gods. Neither is it only a medium to appease their wrath or solicit their blessings. Nor is it merely a means to forge atomistic individuals into a collective lineage. It is definitely not just meat. It is all these. But above all, the sacred carcass is a political artefact. It materializes the rights and obligations of citizenship within a kinship-polity. It makes starkly tangible the staunchly egalitarian ethics framing Kallar political membership. It embodies the privileges of Kallar male political subjectivity and the marginalization of women and youths and especially the exclusion of non-Kallars. The sacrificial carcass is a political imaginary made flesh.

This centring of its meaty viscera rather than sacrifice's transcendental intent is echoed in my focus on the infrastructure of rituals. Anthropologists have long theorized rituals in terms of their productivity as sites where meaning is crystallized and cathected. Distilling and dramatizing customarily veiled and diffuse social experiences and thoughts, rituals render a culture's intrinsic subtext into overt texts to be read and interpreted (Geertz 1973a, 1973b). Critiques of such frameworks for presenting rituals as affirming an vital cultural essence led to analyses of rituals as sites where shared assumptions about society are not simply affirmed but actually produced, reproduced, and legitimated as elemental (Bloch 1986; Ortner 1989). This linking of ritual and ideology allowed for explorations of ritual's interpenetrations with power. Rituals' internal machinery, Bloch (1992) argues, integrates singular events into a timeless order and allows the denial of not only the transience of life but also the vicissitudes of human institutions. Serving as a vehicle for breaking away from everyday existence to plunge into an otherworldly ideal, ritual symbolically denies the validity of the former. Nabokov (2000: 151–170) elaborates that such rituals involve the symbolic sacrifice of individual participants so they may be part of a perpetual and harmonious collectivity. In these readings, rituals locate productivity and potency in a 'world beyond process' external to socio-political relations.

In other words, power is both constituted and made durable by the denial of politics – through ritual. Given that it is from an other-worldly source and attained through techniques that strive to transcend earthly vagaries, legitimate authority is stable and therefore recoverable by one type of authority from another. In transformed, fluctuating, or uncertain political circumstances, such rituals can be appropriated by aspirants to power to avow an apparently unchanging order

(Feuchtwang 2008, 1998: 38). This promise of endurance makes rituals valuable for claiming and asserting political power. The deference to a rigid ritual core and therein the appeal to an older, essential, and transcendental authority deny political contingencies to claim continuity and justify hierarchy (Bloch 1992). Here, rituals may be used to author and authorize power but are in themselves apolitical.

Such arguments can only be sustained through a narrow definition of ritual. In the case of tutelary sacrifice, only if we restrict ritual to its penultimate stage – the actual dedication and decapitation of the animal – can we make the argument that ritual is an instantiation of such an apolitical ideal. Through focusing exclusively on this core, we can argue that ritual represents a transcendence of not just politics but life itself. However, to merely concentrate on the killing of the animal would be to severely underestimate the polyvalence of the tutelary sacrifice. Not only that, but it would be to miss most of its political implications.

The killing itself is no doubt vital (see Keane 2018 on how killing effects transformations from presence to absence, also Singh and Dave 2015). Equally essential, however, are the pre-sacrificial logics of ritual organization and the post-sacrificial ethics of distribution. Killing the animal may be the core of sacrifice. However, it is also merely the spectacular tip of a subterranean bulk of prosaic discussions, casual meetings, routine tasks, hard work, heated arguments, and violent confrontations. This, more than the killing itself, is actually where polities are produced. Deciphering the proprieties governing the acquiring of the sacrificial animal and attending the sacrificial worship, as well as the routine logistics directing the disposing of the post-sacrificial meat, are just as essential to unravelling the workings of these polities and the politics they embody. Who can sacrifice? What type of sacrifice? How can they sacrifice? Who can fund the goat to be sacrificed? Who can attend the sacrificial ceremony? Finally, who can claim shares of the now transubstantiated meat from the post-sacrificial carcass? Which parts of the goat can they have the rights to? How much of the sacred meat can they claim? The assertions of and contestations over these issues are integral to the construction of polity and power.

The promise of a durable authority is predicated upon demarcating a space, time, and practice as significant, sequestering it from the mundane, and ultimately sanctifying it as ritual. Politics can be arbitrated through and resolved by ritual precisely because of the latter's presumed capacity to be abstracted from and transcend the former (Humphrey and Laidlaw 1994; Bell 1992, 1997). In an intricately wrought body politic where ritual and politics bleed profusely into each other, ritual cannot be starkly separated from, let alone resolve, politics. Several anthropologists have demonstrated how rituals are not just sites of cultural constructions and legitimation of authority but also arenas of intense political contestations. 'Rituals themselves', Geertz (1973a: 167) argues, 'become matters of political conflict.' In exploring the political implications of temple worship under the hybrid colonial legal system, Appadurai (1981) grapples with the problem of authority as a cultural rubric and an administrative reality (also Appadurai and Breckenridge 1976). Mines (2005) demonstrates how access to temples and enactments of rituals underpin village hierarchies and caste domination. In his theorizing of an Aiyanar worship that had not been performed for more than seven years, Dirks (1988: 487–488) demonstrates how rituals involve 'both claims about authority and struggles against (and within) it'. Indeed, rituals often occasion more 'conflict than consensus, and that each consensus is provisional'. In other words, rituals are liminal moments in which all relations of power and powerlessness are up for grabs. Privileging their inherent risk (Howe 2000) and the real possibility of failure (Chao 1999; Hüsken 2007), these readings fracture depictions of rituals as complete, coherent, and innately conservative. Moreover, rituals cannot simply be seen as opposed to the everyday. They are themselves produced by everyday practices of production, reproduction, and manipulation. Following these precedents, my treatment of sacrificial ritual privileges not their transcendent aims and their elegant claims but their messy, even ugly innards. While I do discuss ritual killing, I begin with the bloody butchering of the sacred carcass and the seemingly petty squabbling over the meat. Dwelling on the choosing and paying for the animal, the funding and organizing of the ritual, and even the disputes over the place and time for holding the meeting to discuss when and how to enact the sacrifice, I repeatedly juxtapose attempts to evoke the sublime with the routine hierarchies from which they emerge. Ritual poesis, however myth-patterned and deity-propelled, is inextricable from its material ingredients and political mechanics. To transcend through ritual is always a struggle – one that can and often does fail. This struggle and frequent failures are what drive this book.

Amid these socio-political constraints, that these sacrifices happen at all is what is extraordinary. Given the numerous threats to its very performance – most of which come from the sponsors themselves as they persistently resist the rituals' incorporative logic to assert their individual rights and autonomy – it is clear that the ritual does not just grapple with risk but is itself always at risk. The transcendental claims of rituals do not triumph over but are always threatened by the immanent realities of politics. Since the requisite kinsmen do not and cannot converge long enough to perform them, sacrifices are often abandoned at the last minute. Rituals do not resolve but themselves often succumb to politics.

Brutal Underbellies and Blunt Selves

Highlighting the struggles, clashes, and failures inherent to ritual enactments showcases the sinews through which bodies and imaginaries are sutured together and their continuous potential to unravel. Privileging the precarity of rituals reiterates the vulnerability of this polity. Concurrently, it lays bare the callousness, casual cruelty, and brutality underpinning these polities and their politics. Kinship connects. But it is also used to divide. Allied with gender and more significantly caste, it discriminates against, marginalizes, oppresses, and excludes. It can also harm, maim, and even kill. Even as I document the unassuming lives of ordinary people – their unheralded successes, humble pleasures, and persistent struggles – I also confront the uncomfortable realities and the casualties of these political projects.

Colonial prejudices and naked self-interest may be blamed for the classification of the Kallar caste as congenitally predatory, the criminalization of their hitherto legitimate political roles, and the brutal disciplinary reprisals that followed. However, pre-colonial sources and the Kallars' own genealogical texts do attest that violence was a vital tool in their political arsenal. Dirks (1993: 203) argues that their kinship- and territory-based social organization and their 'cultural valuation for heroism and honour' proved to be highly advantageous for 'the corporate control of violence and coercion'. Most Kallars were agriculturalists, notes Blackburn (1978: 44), but he nevertheless concedes that they 'were undoubtedly involved in cattle raids and possibly formed a reservoir of warriors for local military chieftains' in the medieval period. That Kallars are violent by nature was colonial propaganda. But the Kallars have used violence as a strategic component of their politico economic projects.

Subjects of several major ethnographies, the Kallars have sparked important debates that continue to reverberate through anthropology, specifically of South Asia. Dumont's[11] (2000) pioneering ethnography among the Piranmalai Kallars laid the foundations for discussions on the interactions between sacred authority and secular power in Hindu India. Contrary to his own ethnographic evidence in *A South Indian Sub-caste: Social Organization and Religion of the Pramalai Kallar*, Dumont privileged Sanskritic texts and Brahminical exegeses to insist on the primacy of ritual status over politico-economic power, which provoked rigorous challenge (Marriott 1959, 1976; Hocart 1969; Appadurai 1981; Daniel 1982; Shulman 1985). One of the most persuasive critiques was Dirks's (1993) analysis of the little kingdom of Pudukkottai, where Kallars were kings from the end of the 17th century until India's independence in 1947. Disagreeing with caste being represented as 'fundamentally a religious system', he instead argues that it is embedded in a political context shaped by royal authority and gift transactions. In Dirks's schema, the political is an absolutely central component of Indian society[12] (see also Raheja 1988). Along with Dirks's interrogations of kingship apparatuses, Kallar histories, experiences, and exegeses have also inspired Blackburn's (1978) explorations of the interactions between violence and statesmanship, Shulman's (1980b) interrogations of criminality and the dependence of its definition on legal systems, and Headley's (2011) mapping of the articulations between collective memories and caste construction.

The Piranmalai Kallars have also provoked Pandian's (2009) investigation of the effect of colonial governmentalities and enduring mores on contemporary ethical projects of self-formation. Against a history during which Kallar persons were defined as congenitally criminal and irredeemably immoral, Pandian interrogates their conscious projects of self-cultivation in the present. These ethical projects are not just circumscribed by the colonial inscription of criminality but also grounded in archaic Tamil mores glorifying the cultivator. In these evocations, the Kallars are continually subjected to power. They rarely appear as wielders of power either over themselves or over others. Pandian highlights their subordination, more so than their citizenship and sovereignty, and even less still their coercive oppression (Pandian 2005). This may be a consequence of this specific Kallar group's more prolonged and onerous subjection to colonial governmentalities However, such a reading also emerges from their depiction as having internalized the external and colonial evaluations of themselves as marginal and criminal. However, Headley (2011) argues that the Piranmalai Kallar's own oral narratives have produced caste identities that depart from tropes of post-colonial predicaments. When I evoked the chequered history of Kallars to gauge their contemporary resonance, a young woman retorted angrily, 'What are you saying? How can you call our caste criminals? Who told you so? How dare you? Who are you to say this?' I replied that it was not my personal judgement but a British colonial imposition, a historical fact. However, she remained angry. An apprentice priest reassured her, 'She is from Vaduvur. She is Govindasamy Vanniyar's niece. She was born here. She is one of us ... a Kallar.' The angry woman reluctantly backed down. Most of my interlocutors do not even make the etymological link between Kallar and 'thief', let alone know that their caste was once condemned as criminal. In contrast to Pandian's (2009) description of the Piranmalai Kallars continuing to be troubled by their colonial subjection and struggling with its contemporary implications, Vaduvur Kallars are almost unaware of this traumatic past. This despite the fact that while the Criminal Tribes Act (CTA) was first applied to the Kallars in Madurai district in 1918, it was extended to the Kallars in Thanjavur in succeeding years. The Thanjavur Kallars continued to be subject to the act until at least 1933 (Blackburn 1978: 48–9). However, colonial condemnation is not part of popular Kallar consciousness in Vaduvur today.

Only the headmen knew of this history. Sevu Vanniyar, the headmen's advisor, related an incident told to him by his father.

> The British defined all Kallars as a criminal caste. But we were peaceful and prosperous cultivators. Not criminals. So, a group of prominent Kallars from Thanjavur, including Poondi Vandayar,[13] registered their complaint. They drew up a petition protesting our inclusion into the criminal caste category. They inscribed it on a thin sheet of gold. They sent it to London.

A petition written in English and on gold. One that was initiated and executed by wealthy, educated, and politically active Kallar elites. The petition's form – materializing their advancement, literacy, and prosperity – was as important as the content itself for substantiating their cause. Colonial evaluations were not simply internalized but also actively resisted. More significantly, they were resisted not simply through violence but also through self-conscious and erudite protest.[14] This anticipates what I explore throughout this book – Kallar assertions of their own competing political imaginaries, practices, and ethics are attempts not just to be part of but also to capture and manipulate the nation state and its electorally legitimated powers. Kallar political projects are premised on their own enduring theorizations of polity, power, and sovereignty that both emerge from and feed into their lived politics. Viscerality facilitates grasping not just the often-hidden mechanics of exercising power but also its gritty and sometimes grotesque pragmatics that do not disdain and sometimes even relish violence.

Nevertheless, Kallar hegemony has never been total. It is also being increasingly challenged as the lower castes' economic circumstances improve and they become more politically voluble. Their wielding of power is nevertheless real and remains a dominant component of Kallar self-definition. While not above evaluations of their caste or abashed about pointing out their moral failings, they also cherish their reputation for inducing fear among their opponents and subordinates. Faults such as their quickness to anger, hypersensitivity to insults, and aggression are the attributes that, in a different context, underpinned their local dominance. These Kallars' ethical projects are not of self-flagellation but of power accretion and localized state formation. The self being fashioned is neither contingent on colonial assessments nor subject to external evaluations. This Kallar self is the locus of jural rights, legitimate authority, and, above all, sovereign. It lies at the heart of the alchemy of kinship, sacrifice, territory, gifting, feuding, adjudication, and cohabitation that constitutes their polity. Girding with bones, offering flesh, saturating with blood, and infusing with breath, this laden self is what gives life to a political imaginary.

Imagining the Political

Cleaving closely to interlocutors' imaginaries, this book offers an expansive sense of the political. Rather than being restricted to prescribed concepts such as the nation state, nationalism, and democracy and narrowly focused on explicit and entirely expected political activities, politics is understood as inescapably porous. My ethnographic scrutiny ranges widely from the cosmos to the polity, the village to neighbourhoods, kitchens to bodies. The stark distinctions between the political, kinship, kingship, and the religious, characteristic to normative understandings of politics, are deliberately blurred and sometimes even dispensed with. Politics consists of ideas about, actions within, and also bodily experiences in and with inhabited worlds, both thought and felt. Drawing correspondences across seemingly disparate fields such as anthropology, history, and theology and frames of reference from myths, rituals, memories, anecdotes, proverbs, and gossip to peruse the links between personality and potency, I unravel a metaphysics of power that is susceptible to but also reshaping a changing political landscape in India. Political imagination can be capacious and reflect thoughts and values but is also deeply entrenched in the social and the cultural.

In his germinal article, 'Postcolonialism and the Political Imagination', Spencer (1997) advocates departing from political anthropology's use of idealized concepts of politics to privilege experiences and everyday articulations of 'the political'. The 'political', Spencer insists, is not concentrated in or confined to state institutions or an 'apparently bounded and structured social unit' (1997: 9). Rather, the political is to be found in the cultural arena. While foregrounding the cultural (and historical) core, I simultaneously evoke economic, juridical, territorial, corporeal, caste, and gender domains, which may seem unconnected to the traditional political field but are nevertheless pivotal to imaginaries, experiences, and articulations of the political. This book focuses on how kinship, kingship, myths, rituals, and plural sovereignties articulate and coalesce with modern forms of governance and their attendant notions, such as the nation state, political parties, and democracy.

Contemporary political ethnographies tend to focus on how caste is an 'electoral cleavage' and an 'instrument of political mobilization' (Michelutti 2019: 199). Here, however, how a specific caste thinks about and does politics, both within and beyond the nation state, is the object of scrutiny.

How do kinship, caste, and ideas of personhood shape how people govern and perceive the link between themselves and leaders who venture to rule over them? How does a caste claim sovereignty? Interlocutors continue to resort to embodied representations such as kinship, caste, class, ethnicity, and nativity to render their political intentions, actions, strategies, choices, and modes of governance not just legible but also legitimate (see Chandra 2016; Michelutti 2004, on the vernacularization of democracy). Sifting through how such notions have become part of democratic experimentations and populist nationalisms, I engage also with how these processes serve to entrench some existing but also produce new hierarchies, inclusions, marginalizations, exclusions, and oppressions.

Just as significantly, I return the disciplinary gaze to what anthropologists understand as the original political organization, kinship. Kinship is the first arena for grappling with the primary questions of politics: who gets what, when, where, and how. For these Kallars, the kinship that constitutes polities and structures political subjectivity is explicitly jural – a lineage of inalienable rights, claims, obligations, and responsibilities (cf. Michelutti 2008, where the Yadavs of north India conceive of political prowess as a natural substance shared with fellow caste-mates and a patrimony from their tutelary deity, Krishna). Despite the shifts in disciplinary interests, resources, and fashions, even today kinship remains an constitutive domain throughout life which cannot be completely discarded. Additionally, the construction of much larger and higher-level organizations like corporations, political parties, and the nation state appropriates and builds upon illusions of kinship claims, practices of caring (and cruelty), relations of exploitation, and ethics of reciprocity and is therefore vital for understanding politics. Understanding the links between kinship and corruption, electoral candidates and nepotistic authority, and the distinctions between us and ours as opposed to them and theirs, strangers, and others attunes us to the shaping of and shifts in political subjectivity.

Viscerality is a means to substantiate abstractions such as religion, politics, and indeed theory itself through the starkly material, vitally socio-cultural, and thrillingly enlivened. More importantly, it makes clear how these abstractions are derived not simply from academic impositions but primarily from the quotidian realities and affective theorizations of interlocutors themselves. Anthropology is the most revelatory mode of enquiry for uncovering how the intimate and intuitive expands into and simultaneously grounds the immense and ineffable. This visceral political imaginary, I describe, could have only been captured, and made not just present but also palpable, by such an intimate ethnography.

Overview of the Book

Chapter 1 examines how political subjectivity is produced through inter-subjectivity – relations between kinspersons. It suggests that a personhood, premised upon an understanding of rights in and obligations to kinspersons, is at the heart of an intimate citizenship. The tense dynamic between inalienable rights (*urimai*) and obligations (*katamai*) frames both the intimate relations between kinspersons and their citizenship in kinship-polities. Overall, this chapter delineates a genealogy of political subjectivity rooted in lineage relations.

Chapter 2 explores the productive connections between the activity of rituals, specifically sacrificial worship to a tutelary deity, and an imaginary of power and citizenship. It grapples with how citizenship within a kinship-polity is quite literally made flesh. Those denied participation at the sacrificial feast and a share of the sacred meat are also not considered citizens of the polity. Contrary to theories that privilege ritual's incorporative ethic and transcendental intent that seeks to separate and quarantine ritual from politics, this chapter focuses on the logistics and the labour undertaken to produce the sacrifice. In the process, it unravels the messy politics within which rituals are inevitably and inextricably mired. Overall, it discusses how rituals do not simply constitute political authority but are in and of themselves inherently riven by politics.

In Chapter 3, I examine how conflict, even violent ones, generate lineage sociality. Contrary to the pre-occupations of anthropologists of south India, it is not so much the substance of soil that defines a kinship-polity. Rather, it is soil as territory – where rights are asserted (and contested) and power exercised, as a jurisdiction – which governs its political valence. This chapter discusses how a clear notion of territory, despite imprecise, overlapping, and/or contested boundaries, constitutes a kinship-polity. Chapter 4 follows the thread of disputes, this time towards their possible resolution through arbitration. However, it does not focus on successful dispute settlements but chronic failures. This chapter suggests that the very defiance of such authorities is indicative of competing assertions of sovereignty, which is in turn what animates these kinship-polities. Overall, this chapter explores how aggression is a medium for the conduct of political relations. It also considers how the very mechanisms set up to temper agonistic drives are themselves implicated in this political project.

Against a narrative of gradual dissolution, Chapter 5 explores the contours of the Vaduvur regional polity (*natu*). Describing how Vaduvur's very being is fundamentally imbricated in the locations, mythologies, and histories of its key temples, it delineates how the mortal struggles over who participates in and/or leads these temple rituals dramatize the polity's agonistic structure. The governing of this *natu* is inextricable from the operations – both ritual and logistical – of these temples. Moving to a discussion of the workings of the polity, it demonstrates how Vaduvur had not been subject to oversight from a central authority but had been sovereign. Overall, this chapter charts the state of the *natu* amidst increasing threats to its sovereignty from competing sources of local political authority in democratic India. Chapter 6 disrupts the elegiac narrative attached to the traditional polities. It examines the electoral landscape of Vaduvur that has been shaped by not simply democratic politics but also older traditions of vernacular authorities. It concludes with a discussion of how the headmen, despite their pessimism, are ensuring the viability of the vernacular polity and the validity of their own roles. Overall, this chapter explores the framing of newer electoral polities also within intensely local contests and in terms of idioms and mediums familiar from vernacular polities such as the gift, rituals, patronage, and kinship.

Examining the palimpsest of polities – vernacular and electoral – that continue to govern people's lives, this book unravels the conflicting political and ethical practices of governance that frame them. Even as the political defines its domain by excluding certain integral aspects of human life, such as kinship and religion, this book maps a much more expansive political universe that includes everything from the body to the nation state to the cosmos and everyone from animals to people to gods. Simultaneously, this political imaginary also excludes based on gender, age, caste, and descent. I explore both human potential and powerlessness against a milieu of gradual political decline. However, even as the polity is afflicted by and ails in the face of socio-political transformations and cosmic-ritual threats, it refuses to go gently into the night but rallies itself to continue to matter in contemporary electoral politics. Fighting against its imminent death, this kinship-polity strives to extend its own life by penetrating and appropriating newer bodies as well as haunting the realms of political modernity.

Notes

1. Thiruvarur and Nagapattinam were once part of the Thanjavur district. In 1991, Thiruvarur and Nagapattinam districts were carved out from Thanjavur to form the Nagapattinam district. In 1997, Thiruvarur was carved out of Nagapattinam to form a distinct district.
2. These include Kalapadiar (Battlefield Bard), Jeyamkondar (Victorious), Kalathil Ventrar (Victorious on the Battlefield), Vandaiyar, originally Valludaiyar (Sword Possessor), Sethuraiyar (Ruler of Territory), Arasandar (Monarch of State), and Kotaiandar (Ruler of Fort).

3. Deemed docile and productively supportive of the British Raj, the Vellalars, by contrast, were cast as the exemplary cultivating caste.

4. Mentioned in Tamil literary sources, this development is succinctly captured in the aphorism 'Kallar, Maravar, Agambadiyar gradually became Vellalar' (Stein 1999: 304).

5. Several lineage segments from the Kandiyar clan have claims on the fish from these ponds. My father is also a Kandiyar, specifically from the Mela Kandiyar lineage.

6. My prior kinship with/in Vaduvur means that the access to my field and my associates therein were not entirely up to me to choose or curate. Since I was known to be part of the dominant Kallar caste and was introduced to them as being related to a Kallar landlord, the 'lower' castes, especially the Dalits, were hesitant about talking to me. When we did talk, they were wary about my loyalties and vigilant about not critiquing the Kallars, extant hierarchies, or caste oppressions. Our conversations rarely ventured beyond the proprieties into the revelatory. Given their evident discomfort, I did not want to impose further and force them to talk to me. Therefore, most of my investigation necessarily revolved around the Kallars.

7. Ficus Benghalensis.

8. At the time of fieldwork, the delays and disputes were ongoing. However, the temple has since been renovated, and the consecration ceremony was conducted in 2009.

9. *Tamarindus Indica* and *Ficus Religiosa*, respectively. Tamarind trees' large spreading branches have been the loci of suicides by hanging and therefore restless ghosts. *Peepul* trees are sacred and typically host shrines and meditating ascetics.

10. This literally translates into 'field-forests'. While products of human culture, agricultural fields are also abodes of dangerous entities to be avoided, especially at night and specifically by women (Mines 1997: 175).

11. In 1949–1950, Dumont (2000: 10) chose to study the Pramalai Kallars of Madurai because they were 'relatively impervious to Brahmanic customs and ideas'. As part of a 'conservative Tamil-speaking milieu', they fit his objective of researching the 'civilization of Dravidian South India' (4). He notes that 'there is very little here that is peculiar to this group' (5). They were chosen simply as 'a microcosm in which the elements of the macrocosm would be seen in their living relations' (2).

12. Dirks's (1993: lii) is a 'study of the political history of Indian society or rather, social history of the Indian state'. Statecraft was demonstrated, royal authority was secured, and a political community was objectified through the giving of gifts. The substance of the royal gift was partially compounded of the sovereign

substance of the king. Acceptance of the gift meant incorporation into the king and the kingdom (Dirks's 1993: 128–138). The hollowing out of the crown – the de-legitimizing of pre-colonial state-forms and the marginalizing of the king – and the conception of Indian civilization as an overwhelmingly religiously oriented one were part of the colonial enterprise to assume control and legitimate their own competing authority. Ultimately, the opposition between purity and pollution and hierarchy are not the only or even the encompassing bastions of value in caste society. Caste cannot be divorced from 'indigenous conceptions of polity, sovereignty, dominance and kingship' (Raheja 1988: 519). Accordingly, Raheja redefined dominance in a Rajasthani village in terms of the centrality of the dominant caste and their transactions as opposed to that of Brahmins and their rituals.

13. Poondi, in Thanjavur, is a permanently settled *zamindari* estate. The *zamindar* is a Kallar and Vandayar is his surname. A. Veeriya Vandayar (1899–1970), popularly known as Poondi Vandayar, was a philanthropist, founder of a college, and the leader of the Kallar Mahajana Sangam (Kallar Great People Society). To this day, he is the epitome of wealth in the popular imagination.

14. I was not able to personally corroborate this narrative. However, the publication of several caste histories by the Thanjavur Kallars in the 1920s, Blackburn argues (1978: 50), was part of efforts to differentiate themselves from their Madurai brethren and protest the application of the Criminal Tribes Act to them.

Part I
Constituting Vernacular Polities

1

Genealogies of Political Subjectivities

Eswari watched a crow saunter into the cooking hut and grab a piece of dried fish. Boldly. Right in front of the eyes of several conversing women. She grumbled:

These crows are behaving like our *pankali*s [lineage-mates]. These crows come and go into our houses as they please. As if they have a right to do so. Coming right into our kitchens, without a by your leave....

Puzzled, I asked her to elaborate.

*Pankali*s come and go whenever and take and eat whatever they want because they have the right to. *Urai-murai* [affines], however, stand outside, only coming into the house if they are invited to do so, eating only what is given to them.

In her exasperation with the audaciousness of the thieving crows, Eswari offered an elegant conceit for expressing what it means to be agnatic kin – fellow members of a patrilineage (hereafter lineage-mates) – and how markedly this differs from being an affine. The crow is 'a scavenger bird and is everywhere associated with death and accordingly is impure' (Srinivas 1952: 106). In Indian folktales, the crow is often associated with untouchability – an ascribed and inescapable impurity (Dundes 1997). Crow symbolism is premised on an almost entirely negative portrayal through showcasing the bird's associations with death, impurity, and untouchability. In Vaduvur however, crows are esteemed, albeit reluctantly.

Crows haunt this chapter – alerting us to the rupture of death, the trauma of loss, and the burden of remembrance. In their temerity, they embody the discriminations between different kinds of kin and how they are expected to act. Above all, they foretell the persistence of kinship and especially the insistence on lineage among the Kallars. Here, I trace how political subjectivity is produced through kinship between persons. Unravelling the intricacies of a funeral complex and its aftermath makes clear how fundamental lineage is to definitions of Kallar personhood. Just as the crematory fire disintegrates a dead body into ashes, a funeral ritually decomposes a socially complex and relationally extensive person down to their elemental core. Counterintuitively factoring out competing loyalties, a funeral ritually returns a person to their primordial source, the lineage, and their essential self, as a lineage-mate. What a funeral is doing through ritual is what I am doing anthropologically – demonstrating the essential edifice upon which lived understandings of more intricate polities (including the Indian nation state) and wider political subjectivities are built. A personhood premised upon conceptions of rights in and obligations to kinspersons is at the heart of understandings of an intimate citizenship. The tense dynamic between inalienable rights (*urimai*) and obligations (*katamai*) frames both the intimate relations between kinspersons and their citizenship in these kinship polities. Overall, this chapter delineates a genealogy – rooted in lineage relations – of political subjectivity.

The crow is a particularly apt metaphor for expressing what it means to be a lineage-mate and the ethics framing this relationship for two reasons. First, Tamils admire crows for their solidarity. A well-known film song advises humans to learn from crows, which are naturally cohesive:[1]

> We should learn to be united.
> We should accept this truth.
> Look at a flock of crows.
> Who taught them to be united?

This philosophy was brought to life when Samiammal, an Upputanni lineage-wife caught and killed a crow. A murder of crows flew in from all directions and gathered in the nearby tamarind tree. A cacophony of shrill but sorrowful caws ensued for nearly an hour until she removed the carcass from their sight. Samiammal said this was typical:

> When one crow gets injured or dies, all of them gather to mourn their comrade. I have even seen them peck at the dead body and devour it. This way, they ensure that their dead comrade is never separated from the clan.

This ideal of corvine unity reverberates through everyday village life and the villager's repertoire of metaphors for solidarity. Only a few days into my fieldwork in Vaduvur, I asked a neighbour (and former *panchayat* president) the meaning behind the name of the street where we were both living. Why was it called K. K. (pronounced as Ka Ka) Vanniyar (K.K.V.) Street? *Ka ka* is the Tamil name for the crow and its distinctive caw. This local politician said that the street's name signified the exemplary solidarity of its residents. It only took a few days for me to grasp the irony of this statement as I became privy to the deep rivalries and fierce feuds that underpinned life on this street. K.K.V. Street, I eventually learned, is named after one of the first settlers on this street.

Secondly, crows are extremely bold. They are audacious enough to dart into houses to steal food right in front of people. Most other animals are reticent about trespassing into human habitations. Even when threatened, crows dart a little distance away, only to quickly return. Crows take liberties like lineage-mates should and do and affines cannot and must not. Affines must be diffident, while lineage-mates are free to be audacious.

At the heart of such differential expectations of agnatic kin and affines are the classificatory differences between various kinds of kin. Even more significantly, they are based on the categorical distinction between self and other. Lineage-mates (*pankalis*) are defined as 'others of the same sort' or of like 'kind, species' (*vagei*), as evident in the etymology of another term for lineage, the *vahaira* (Dumont 2000: 185; Nabokov 2000: 155, 175). They claim descent from a common male ancestor. Lineage-mates are defined as being of *oru rattam* (one blood) or, at some now-forgotten historical point, *oru tai vaittu makkal* (born from the same mother's womb). They are therefore substantially the same and ontologically self. Affines may be related but they are qualitatively different and categorically other. They are kin but not kind (Fruzzetti, Ostor, and Barnett 1982; Kapadia 1995: 13–45; Trawick 1992: 132–135). This also underpins their suitability as partners for marital exchange (Trautmann 1981; Busby 1997: 38). Affinal reticence is framed by their elemental difference. Lineage-mates, by contrast, are allowed and indeed expected to take liberties because they are substantially equivalent to the self, as evident in the following example.

Sivalingam belongs to the Upputanni lineage but now resides in Tamil Nadu's capital city, Chennai. On a visit to Vaduvur, Govindasamy, his lineage-mate, asked him why he had not returned to the village to attend Govindasamy's niece's wedding. They had sent the wedding invitation to Chennai through another lineage-mate. Sivalingam replied that he had not received the invitation. Others muttered about the emissary's envy of Sivalingam's success, which probably led to his deliberate withholding of the invitation. Govindasamy refused to accept this ostensibly valid reason. He blamed Sivalingam himself:

> You do not need an invitation. You are neither a stranger nor an affine. You are our *pankali*, one of us. A marriage in my family is like one in your own. Your lineage-mate's daughter's wedding is akin to your own daughter's wedding. You should be handing out invitations yourself, not waiting for one. You have the right to attend this wedding without any invitation. As a lineage-mate, you are supposed to direct the preparations and ceremonies yourself. The success of the ceremony was your responsibility. Even if I didn't call you, you should have been one of the first ones to be there.

Affines have to be formally invited even to a funeral. Lineage-mates do not have to be invited, even to weddings. Even if they are kin, affines are always guests. Not exactly strangers, affines are also never completely integrated into the kin group. Even at funerals, let alone weddings, affines are primarily guests and gift-givers.[2] The onus on lineage-mates, by contrast, is not to tender gifts but to ensure their presence. They should be there to assume their lineage-mates' responsibilities as their own, thereby sharing their burden. A host's lineage-mate is himself a host, never a guest. Affines must always be governed by protocol and are defined by formality. Lineage-mates, on the other hand, are vested with rights and therefore expected to behave with a casual temerity.

This question of rights (*urimai*) – as defined by the idioms, practices, and ethics of kinship itself – is at the heart of the constitution of local polities and definitions of political subjectivity. Kallar lineage-mates trace their descent to a common male ancestor. They are defined by their shared and equal inherited rights – to a tutelary deity and sacrificial cult, to a territory, but, above all, to each other based on claims of common descent and shared substance. Rights are an elementary jural and ethical component of definitions of lineage membership. There has been a tendency in the anthropological literature to analyse rights largely in terms of claims to property and land, natural resources (Subramanian 2009), family businesses (Rudner 1994), the lineage cult (Dumont 2000), and temple honours (Dirks 1993). These are indubitably important, and in subsequent chapters, I will address rights in these very terms. However, these are but partial and essentially derivative definitions of rights. At a more fundamental level, rights are constituted in terms of claims to and upon persons, specifically kin. Claims in and through kinship form the prototypical and the exemplary understanding of rights. It is the foundation upon which other forms of rights, such as to properties and distinctions, are built. It may even be a means through which other configurations of rights are acquired in the first place (Sahlins 2013). In his ethnohistory of Kallar monarchs in the neighbouring state of Pudukkottai, Dirks (1993: 143) attributes the Kallar's dominant position in the regions in which they have settled to their martial prowess and their 'strong territorial clan organization'. Their kinship configurations enabled them access and the means to mobilize allies and labour. This has also been key to Kallar efforts to acquire and control land in Vaduvur (see also Beck 1972: 266 for the Gounders in the Kongu region in Tamil Nadu). Extensive lineage and clan organizations are also part of an intimidatory structure to claim, maintain, and defend power, property, and position. Their rights to their kinsmen have allowed the Kallars to weld themselves together into an effective corporate body and to efficiently wield power. These kinship-framed rights are the basis of their political structure. They are also the source of the power that the Kallars have been able to accrue and continue to exercise.

These rights – their conception, their exercise in everyday life, and their idealization as an ethical force – are at the heart of specific (*a*) constructions of local political communities and (*b*) understandings of political citizenship. Political communities in this case refer to what I call kinship-polities, such as the lineage, the street, and the region. Premised upon kinship (lived understandings of lineage and caste), rituals (enactments of tutelary sacrifices), and the juridical (adjudication of disputes), these micro-polities are edifices of self-government, political authority, and sovereignty. They are rooted in territory, with their jurisdiction not extending beyond a small and intensely local ambit. However, this does not necessarily mean that they are parochial or simply entwined with the lifeworld of a single group. Rather, they are at the heart of local state formations that not only articulate with but often overlap and even compete with the Indian nation state (see Chapters 5 and 6).

The ontologies operationalized by such kinship-polities – the nature, categories, relations, and hierarchies of rights and obligations of political belonging – are the foundations of a local political imaginary. Specifically, the dilemmas – between the ideal and the actual, collective and individual, and ethical and political – provoked by the often-contested definitions and fraught applications of these rights fuel an everyday theorizing of politics. At the heart of this everyday political theorizing is the lineage – the nucleus of a nested conception of progressively larger and more socially complicated political structures and forms of citizenship. Political subjectivity is built upon the logics of lineage membership. Lineage ethics form the illocutionary force that animates political citizenship, including that within the Indian nation state. This requires deciphering what membership within a lineage entails.

Lineage Architecture

In Tamil, a member of a lineage is termed a *pankali*, or shareholder. Its etymological root is *panku*, or share. At the heart of the lineage is patrimonial inheritance – an equal share in the lineage cult and more rarely to any lineage-owned territory. This share, and membership within a specific lineage, is premised upon claims of shared patrilineal descent. Only males are acknowledged as lineage-mates. Only they enjoy the rights and suffer the obligations that underpin lineage membership. Given the rules of patrilineal descent and patrimonial inheritance, women cannot be lineage-mates. Women do not inherit; they are dowered. When I refer to lineage-mates, I refer exclusively to men, just as my interlocutors do.

Women who are married into a lineage (to *pankalis*) are almost totally subsumed by the lineage membership of their husbands and sons. In the absence of a local designation, I refer to women married into a lineage as lineage-wives. Although they are indispensable to the practices of lineage, lineage-wives are rendered structurally invisible. They do not have a formal or ritual role in their husband's lineage. However, this does not mean that all women are similarly excluded from the lineage. Women who are born into the lineage (*poranta-ponnus*) may not have rights to a *panku* but the very fact of their birth into a particular lineage gives them a special status. As lineage-wives, women are defined only through and by their husbands and sons with regard to their married lineage. As *poranta-ponnus*, however, women are not defined relationally but in and of themselves with regard to their natal lineage. While not on par with the rights and privileges of their fathers and brothers, *poranta ponnus* are not only structurally legible but also have significant claims to and roles within their natal lineage. A relatively unacknowledged fact, even in studies focusing on the classificatory and institutional aspects of lineage in India (Gough 1956; Beck 1972; Dumont 2000), is that birth, more than gender, defines the patrilineage (Ortner and Whitehead 1981).

The fundamental kinship ties, according to which lineages are defined and classified, are that of biological parent–child and sibling. Parents, progeny, and siblings who are related to one by 'blood' are one's own (*conta*) kin. Members of one's lineage are the classificatory equivalents of one's parents, children, and siblings. Lineage-mates are the succeeding (*atutta-atutta*) branches of what were originally 'sons born of the same womb'. Villagers readily acknowledge that their current lineage-mates were at some distant point related by blood and are descended from their own ancestors. Contemporary classification is founded upon presumed historical consanguinity. This underpins some of the ethical force surrounding lineage membership. Such classificatory kin warrant the same terms of address, treatment, and respect as one's own biological kin of an equivalent standing. They also merit similar, if not the same, ritual and kinship obligations as one's own kin.[3] However, what is owed to one's own kin is 'obviously' always greater.

The Kallar lineage structure is nested and segmentary; *pankali* is therefore a super category. When dissected further, there are different categories and levels of lineage kinship. This classification hinges on the quantity of segmentation (*pirivu*) or distance from the foundational procreative ties – biological parent, child, and siblings. These segmentations are premised on

1. 'blood' or consanguinity and descent
2. generation or age-cohort
3. social proximity and distance

A socially proximate kinship tie is a direct one, with the least number of intervening segmentations. A socially distant tie, however, is a mediated one, with several segmentations in between. In Tamil society, social structure is often mapped onto spatial structure (Beck 1972; Daniel 1982; Rudner 1994). Therefore, proximity and distance in terms of kinship often correlate with near and far respectively in spatial terms. These classificatory divisions are articulated using the idiom of 'immediate' (*utan*) and 'distant' (*turam*). Lineage-mates are classified according to a continuum flowing between the poles of 'immediate' and 'distant'.

In Vaduvur, four levels of lineage kinship are recognized, in accordance with proximity to the foundational patrilineal tie. First, there are immediate (*utan*) *pankali*s, who form the core of the entire lineage structure. Immediate lineage-mates are a man's biological father, brothers, and sons. Second, there are the 'once-removed' (*onnu-vitta*) *pankali*s, who are his father's brothers and his paternal cousins. They are still related to him by blood. However, it is no longer a direct or immediate tie but extended and mediated by generation. These 'once-removed' lineage-mates are actually one's father's immediate lineage-mates. Third, there are his 'twice-removed' (*rentu-vitta*) *pankali*s, 'thrice-removed' (*muntru-vitta*) *pankali*s, and even further segmentations in this fashion. These are paternal grand-uncles and their sons. The segmentations from the core biological paternal and fraternal bond are now not only those of a waning blood tie but also an increasing generational one. The levels of lineal kinship enumerated above constitute a Kallar lineage.

A lineage is also termed a *kulam*. Along with presumed claims of shared blood, lineage-mates have equal rights to a common tutelary deity (*kula-teivam*) and ritual cult. Another name for a lineage is a house (*vitu*). Lineage-mates are shareholders in a joint estate. In Vaduvur, this is largely confined to the remnants of what had been jointly bought land parcels. Therefore, lineage-mates also tend to be neighbours, co-residing in and owning adjoining lands. The houses and yards of the lineage-mates concerned lie either next to or across the street facing each other (see Dumont 2000: 351 on 'residential clusters'). There are strong indications that the imbrications between social organization and territory used to be even deeper. Although they now live in separate households, many lineages in Vaduvur had begun as extended families in large joint households. Given the correspondence between social and spatial structures in rural Tamil Nadu, referring to a lineage as a house is highly suggestive.

Even within the lineage, the knowledge as to how exactly each member is related to one another is vague. Compared to the hitherto impoverished Piranmalai Kallars of Madurai (Dumont 2000), let alone the Kallar kings of Pudukkottai (Dirks 1993), genealogical memory is shallow among the Kallars in Vaduvur. Outside of the lineage, knowledge of exact kinship ties is even more nebulous. This brings us to the fourth and last level of lineage membership – the distant (*turattu*) *pankalis*. Exactly how distant lineage-mates are related to each other is unclear. Segmentation from the common progenitor is supposed to have occurred so long ago and on so many subsequent occasions as to be virtually untraceable. As per anthropological conventions, distant *pankalis* are actually members of a common clan, 'a non-corporate descent group in which genealogical links to a common ancestor are assumed but cannot be actually demonstrated' (Fox 1967: 49) rather than a lineage per se. Unlike more immediate lineage-mates, these clan-mates do not share a known ancestor or traceable bio-genetic links. Neither do they worship the same tutelary deity nor have rights in the same ritual cult. They also do not tend to live among each other, although they may live on the same street (*teru pankalis*) or village (*ur pankalis*).

What denotes kinship among clan-mates is their common surname (*pattai peiyar*). What is shared is the self-avowed agnatic ties among themselves, which underlies their clan exogamy. All Kallars who have the same surname are considered part of the same patri-clan. Those with a different surname from one's own are classified as actual or potential affines (*urai-murai*). Common clan names in Vaduvur Vadapathy include Vanniyar, Kandiyar, Pullavarayar, Ontiriyar, and Mannaiyar. These surnames are also martial titles that allude to the Kallar caste's history of marauding, kingship, and military service under pre-colonial kings (Dumont 2000; Venkatasamy 2005; Dirks 1993, 1986, 1982).

Several lineages with the same surname may live on a particular street. The proliferation of separate lineages with the same surname is largely the result of processes of segmentation. According to Cheran, a Sakkarei Kandiyar lineage-mate residing on Middle Street:

The Kandiyars of Middle and neighbouring East Street are actually one big lineage. Our lineage deity, Viranar is the same as the Viranar of East Street. When we split from them, we duplicated him where we lived. I don't know why we split up and moved away. It happened too long ago for anyone to remember.

From the literature, it is evident that such splitting off occurs for two reasons. First is migration to a distant location, which makes travel to worship at the original temple burdensome. So, the lineages ask to participate in the worship of another lineage's deity in a temple close to their current residence. Second is disagreements within the original group that can lead to splinter factions who choose to have their own exclusive versions of the original lineage deity and cult. This is what happened to the aforementioned Sakkarei Kandiyar lineage.[4] In K.K.V. Street, where I lived, there were three distinct lineages with the Vanniyar surname. So, each one was differentiated with an additional designation, such as the name of their founding ancestor, their ancestral occupation, or even on which end of the street they lived. The Upputhanni lineage, who reside on the southern end of K.K.V. Street form the backbone of this ethnography. Their name originates from their ancestors' good deed. At the outset of their migration into and settlement in Vaduvur, this lineage's communal house used to be at the junction of K.K.V. Street and Mannaiyar Street. On their way to other villages further south, travellers used to pause to rest at this house. This lineage took to leaving a terracotta pot of sorghum or millet gruel on the porch with which passers-by could refresh themselves. Grateful for this sustenance after the exhausting heat and arduous journey, a traveller blessed the lineage members for giving them essential salt (*uppu*) and water (*tanni*). Thereafter, they came to be known as the 'Salt-Water' or Upputanni lineage. To underline just how vital lineage kinship is to Kallar definitions of personhood, sociality, and ethics, we now turn to the symbolic implications of their funerary rituals.

Funerals: Ritual Decomposition, Distilling Subjectivity

Social life in Vaduvur, as is common across Tamil Nadu, is framed by kinship relations. Social occasions are divided into two types: the auspicious or 'good' (*nallatu*) and the inauspicious or 'bad' (*kettatu*). The auspicious include births, ear-piercing, puberty, wedding, and house-warming ceremonies. The inauspicious primarily refers to funerals. The hyphenated *nallatu-kettatu* (auspicious-inauspicious) encapsulates all the life crisis rituals and ceremonies that constitute the village social calendar (Good 1991). Rural sociality revolves around hosting, helping in, and attending these life-crisis ceremonies. Attending these rituals organized by one's kin, neighbours, patrons, and clients is the mark of any properly socialized villager. However, attending the 'auspicious-inauspicious' occasions of one's lineage-mates – one's closest kin after one's own family – is absolutely essential. As the villagers insisted, 'Lineage-mates are for *nallatu-kettatu*, but especially the *kettatu*.' Apart from one's nuclear family, one's lineage-mates must be the first ones to attend one's life crisis rituals. To partake of the joys of one's lineage-mates is well and good. To share in their sorrows demonstrates the depth of one's ethical commitment to one's lineage-mates. The latter is far more important. Missing a wedding is not ideal, but it is a forgivable lapse. *Deliberately* missing a funeral, however, is a diplomatic statement.

Deliberately foregoing a lineage-mate's funeral is tantamount to breaking off of all lineage ties and declaring war. One's lineage-mates are supposed to remain with one till the end and carry the palanquin that ferries one's corpse to the cremation grounds. Along with one's own sons, one's lineage-mates ensure that the proper mortuary rituals necessary for transforming one's ghost into an ancestor are performed. To be an orphaned corpse – with no one to perform the final rites – is a 'bad death' (Parry 1994). In light of the anathema that this represents for Kallar individuals, repudiating lineage ties is equivalent to renouncing elemental sociality. The funeral of a Kallar person is the quintessential manifestation of Kallar lineage practices. It is the distillation of the lineage's significance to Kallar definitions of personhood and ethics of sociality. Only sacrificial worship to the lineage deity is comparable. To the Kallars, the funeral is the very apotheosis of a lineage's social meaning and ethical consequence.

Since Parry's *Death in Banaras* (1994: 212), analyses of funerals in India have focused primarily on how mortuary rituals mark the 'proper transformation' of the deceased, from 'ghost to ancestor' and the 'proper recycling of the soul' (also Uchimayada 2000; Hertz 1960). Mortuary rituals are typically concerned with neutralizing and transforming the potentially malevolent threat of a ghost into the generalized benevolence of an ancestor (Gold 1988: 91). While the analytical emphasis on the dead at the funeral is understandable, simultaneously, it is decidedly partial. In her study of funerary practices among women and men of lower-caste Dalits, Clark-Decès (2005) returns to an older anthropological tradition (Dumont 2000; Mines 1989; Nicholas 1981) to focus almost entirely on the bereaved social body. However, Clark-Decès does not simply recount the ritual obligations of the bereaved, which would once again privilege the deceased. Inspired by the 'creative functionalism' of Bloch and Parry (1982: 6), who argue that death is a catalyst for creative or reproductive processes so that social order is not reasserted but is a product of funeral rituals, Clark-Decès (2005) demonstrates how mourning behaviour is not so much about grieving over the dead but imparting meaning to the gender, caste, and personal experiences of the mourners. Through mourning behaviour and mortuary rituals, the normally amorphous fundamentals of a society are explicitly articulated and thereby crystallized. Similarly, the Kallar mortuary complex is about arriving at and articulating the essence of what it means to be a Kallar person, in which the lineage plays a constitutive role. The lineage is unusually isolated, made singularly prominent like at no other life crises ceremonies, and persistently reiterated at and through Kallar funerary rituals.

We can divide the Kallar mortuary sequence into three ritual stages to grasp corresponding transitions in the status of the bereaved social body (Van Gennep 1960 on rites of passage; Uchiyamada 2000). These are:

1.   dis-embedding and retrieval
2.   pollution and consolidation
3.   re-embedding and return

The first two stages are concerned with retrieving the deceased for the originating lineage, isolating this lineage, and asserting its solidarity, respectively. In the last stage, both the deceased and the bereaved lineage are returned to their customarily complex sociality. In the process, the absolute centrality of the lineage to the definition of Kallar personhood and sociality is distilled and made visible.

The Kallar mortuary complex is elaborate. At each stage, there are different obligatory mourning behaviour, ritual enactments, and practical assistance required from different categories of kin. My focus is on how affines and marital kin are deliberately effaced from Kallar funerary rituals in order to render the lineage more prominent – or rather to make the lineage appear complete unto itself and therefore autonomous. In *The Fame of the Gawa*, Nancy Munn (1992: 163) argues that affines in a Melanesian community take centre stage at nuptials. Weddings are essentially amalgamative, 'aimed at forming a [wider] connectivity built upon a marital couple'. Each member of the marital couple is a compound of the substances and bonds from previous generations (ancestors), their contemporaries (existing kin), and the potential for new kin connections (descendants). Through the marriage (and subsequent procreation), the individual becomes enmeshed in further kin connections, accrues even more substances, and is composed of ever-greater social complexity. This incorporative logic also applies in the final stages of the Kallar funerary complex when mourning restrictions have largely ceased, the deceased has been processed into benign ancestors, the bereaved have been reinstated into the social body, and customary life is resumed. As the funeral concludes, affines once again assume their prominent role.

Death (and funerals), however, represents a rupture. In the initial stages of the funeral, affines (and their amalgamative resonance) are counter-intuitively de-emphasized. Their constitutive significance to biological fertility and a dense sociality is deliberately underplayed. Mortuary exchanges centre on the disintegration of the substantially and socially totalized and therefore holistic self (see also Thune 1989 on death and matrilineal reincorporation among another Melanesian group). At the onset of death, the affines are marginalized in order to recover the deceased for the lineage – the source of a Kallar man.

Death initiates the decomposition of the corporeal body. Mortuary complexes assert the decomposition of the social being. Munn (1992: 164) argues that the initial stages of a funeral in Massim are aimed at

> factoring out the marital, paternal and matrilineal components, which have been amalgamated to form the deceased's holistic being, and with returning this being to a partial, detotalised state – an unamalgamated matrilineal source.

The aim of Kallar mortuary rituals is to similarly dis-embed the deceased from all other and subsequent social bonds and recover them for the originating patrilineage. Therefore, it is at funerals and through mortuary rituals that what is conceived as the fundamental constituents of a body, a self, and a social is asserted. Kallar funerary rites and behaviour presage the decomposition of the intricately interwoven Kallar social self into its fundamental and original constituent – as a lineage-mate. This social decomposition takes two forms – (*a*) the ritual pre-eminence of the lineage (and concurrent marginalization of affines) and (*b*) the lineage's exclusive assumption of the duties of caring for the bereaved.

Funeral: Disembedding from Sociality, Retrieving for Lineage

As soon as a death occurs, the deceased's lineage-mates undertake the funeral's logistics and ensure its smooth operations. After prolonged ill-health, Ramasamy Vanniyar of the Upputanni lineage passed away in October 2005. His lineage-mates made the funeral announcements. They informed close relatives and friends. They hired workers to construct the awning out of tarpaulins stretched over bamboo scaffolding. Another tarpaulin was spread on the earth floor for female mourners to sit. Garlands of folded coconut leaves, bunches of mango leaves, and the leafy tips of banana plants were suspended from the bamboo framework. Plastic chairs were lined up in front of the house for the important guests and male mourners. The Upputanni lineage-mates engaged the barber to shave the corpse and the head of the chief mourner[5] and act as the 'funeral priest' (Hocart cited in Dumont 2000: 46). They notified the washerman, who provided the white cotton *dhotis* that serve as the shroud and the collection plate. They fetched the Dalit musicians, who have traditionally accompanied funerals with their drums and conches. Workers constructed the ladder-like bier on which the body would be laid and the palanquin to convey the bier to the cremation grounds out of green bamboo strips. They elaborately decorated the palanquin with garlands of marigolds, paper flowers, folded coconut leaves, the tops of banana saplings, and tinsel.

Meanwhile, Ramasamy's lineage-mates bathed his corpse and dressed it in a white shirt and *dhoti*. They poured a mixture of kerosene and sesame oil into the deceased's mouth to obviate any smells. They placed betel leaf, areca nut shavings, and tobacco in the mouth and bandaged the jaw shut. They tied the thumbs together and the big toes to each other. They seated the body on a chair. To keep the body upright, they tied it to several sugarcane stalks arranged behind the chair. They suspended a bunch of limes from the sugarcane over the head of the deceased. Sheafs of coconut blossoms were planted into bowls of unhusked paddy and placed on either side of the body. A steel platter of husked rice grains with a coconut on top was placed under the chair. Lighting two brass oil lamps, the lineage-mates placed them on either side of the body. A terracotta bowl filled with glowing coals was placed beside them. They affixed eye-guards of beaten silver to the eyes. They placed a 1 rupee coin on the forehead. They dotted the forehead with saffron and hung a flower garland around the neck. Thus titivated, the deceased was arranged as the guest of honour at his own funeral. He was set up to survey the scene and receive the full complement of mourning rituals that were his due by dint of his full life involving marriage, children, and grandchildren.

Having thus far stood on either side of the body, a representative from both Ramasamy's lineage and affines initiated the proceedings. Incense sticks were lit and stuck into the usual makeshift holder of a single banana. Frankincense was sprinkled onto live coals smouldering in a brass vessel. The vessel from which fragrant smoke was billowing was lifted and waved in a circular motion before the deceased. The coconut was split open with a machete, its husky beard pulled off, and the resulting halves placed on either side of the body. Camphor was lit on a tray, and the flame circled before the deceased. The flame was then brought to the praying men, who cupped their hands over the flames before touching their fingertips to their eyes. They took holy ash from the pile beside the flame with the tips of their fingers and daubed it on their own foreheads. This standard process of worship is termed 'strewing frankincense' (*camprani potutal*) and 'praying to deities' (*cami kumpitutal*). It forms the crux of Tamil worship, be it at a domestic altar or at a large temple, where it is further elaborated upon (Fuller 2004: 57, 62–69). This prayer process was repeated numerous times during the mortuary rituals. Whenever I mention that they worshipped, I refer to this four-step process.

Along with being primarily responsible for the mortuary logistics and labour, lineage-mates also assume ritual prominence during the initial stages of a funeral.[6] Even for mourning practices, the deceased's lineage-mates' wives take the initiative. Numerous women arrived, each as part of a band of wives married into a particular lineage (lineage-wives). They clustered to cry also as a kin group – the wives, mothers, and daughters-in-law of a group of lineage-mates. As Ramasamy's widow, Manimammai sat by the feet of her husband's body, a cluster of kinswomen encircled her. Each woman entwined her arms around the shoulders or across the backs of the women on either side. Including her within their collective embrace, they swayed back and forth with the widow as she shouted and whimpered her pain. The eldest among them sang a few mournful verses lamenting the fate of the abandoned wife. Tears glinting in their eyes, the other huddled women repeated after the leader or simply punctuated her chanting with elongated wailing, quiet weeping, or outbursts of distress. 'Crying in clusters' (*katti alutal*) and 'funerary songs' (*oppari*) are characteristic of Tamil mortuary customs, especially in villages (Clark-Decès 2005). As each new cluster of female mourners – the widow's consanguine kin, her neighbours from the street she had married into, those from her natal street, or other fellow villagers – arrived, they immediately enfolded the widow in a crying cluster. After several minutes of dirges, each crying cluster disbanded to make way for new arrivals, who reignited the flagging crying. The first women to envelope the widow in such a mourning cluster will always be her fellow lineage-wives. Other kinswomen will come, lament, and leave. Only her fellow lineage-wives will stay throughout the funeral, always ready to assist with the funerary rituals, necessary logistics, and the dirges.

As soon as all the expected mourners had arrived, the funeral ceremony proper began. The body was detached from the seat, the fabric tied around the thumbs and toes was unwound, and the body was undressed till only the *dhoti* remained. The body was laid on a wooden bench, and the 'women's ceremony' (*pompala catanku*) began.

I am Ramasamy's classificatory granddaughter – my mother is born into the Upputanni lineage. Along with the other actual and classificatory daughters and grandchildren, of both sexes, I formed a queue in front of the body. I scooped up some sesame oil and some oil-removing herbal paste (*araippu*). As directed by the barber, I smeared them on the deceased's forehead and that of the widow seated near the deceased's head. Meanwhile, the lineage-mates went to fill pots with water from the communal pipe. They blended turmeric powder into the water and poured it onto the body, systematically proceeding from the legs up to the head. What water remained in the pot was poured over the widow. The dead man and his now bereft widow were deliberately and symbolically associated.

After this second bath, the body was completely encased in the white *dhoti* provided by the washerman. The lighted oil lamp that had stood at the head of the body throughout the funeral was given to the deceased's eldest daughter-in-law. This lamp, along with some milk, flowers, a few coins, husked rice and unhusked paddy, was to be placed at the family's domestic altar. This is the 'placing the auspicious lamp' ceremony (*nalla vilakku vaikkiratu*). Given the widow's inauspicious status, the deceased's eldest son and his wife are now the new heads of this family. They are charged with the responsibility for its continued reproduction, auspiciousness, and well-being. The transfer of the lamp symbolizes the deceased's final blessing – that his descendants' auspiciousness is not cremated along with his body but continues under the auspices of his living successors. Mourning should eventually cease and normal life resume.

Even as these hopes for future auspiciousness were being transferred, the widow was ceremonially denuded of her own auspicious married status (*cumankali*). This was the logic behind the heart-rending 'confiscation of the nuptial symbol' ceremony (*tali-pariccu*). The widow's earrings were removed. Her nose stud was unscrewed. Her gold bangles were removed. Glass bangles she wore for the occasion were violently smashed. Flowers, she had worn in her hair, were torn away. The red dot of vermillion on her forehead was smeared. Crucially, her nuptial symbol (*tali*) was confiscated and placed in a bowl of milk to be placed at the domestic altar. The symbolic force of this ceremony must be understood in terms of the ideal Hindu woman's life revolving around marriage, giving birth preferably to male children and crucially dying before one's husband. Auspiciousness, prestige, privileges, and actual material support are attached to the marital status as opposed to the inauspiciousness, physical and behavioural circumscription, and economic dependency associated with widowhood. For the widow, the funeral signifies the death of both an other (the husband) *and* a self (Clark-Decès, 2005: 38).

The lineage-mates carried the body further out into the tented front yard for the 'rice for the mouth' (*vaikkarici*) ceremony. The lineage-mates and affines ensured that they had a few coins in their hands. The barber went among them distributing small fistfuls of rice from the pile, to which each group of affines had contributed upon their arrival. One by one, we touched the rice to the mouth of the deceased. We 'fed' him one last time to sustain him on his final journey. We then dropped this rice and the coins onto the *dhoti* spread on the other side of the body.[7] Preceded by all the grandchildren bearing lighted torch (*pantam pitikkiratu*), the shrouded body was placed on the bier and carried out onto the street. The pallbearers consisted only of the deceased's lineage-mates. Shouldering their kinsman for one last time, they accompanied him right to the end.

They circumambulated the funeral chariot parked at the junction of Ramasamy's front yard and the street. They placed the body within the chariot. Her brother's funerary gift – a new *sari* – draped around her shoulders and supported on each side by two fellow lineage-wives, the widow walked under the funerary chariot held aloft by the pallbearers. She circled the funeral chariot thrice. Finally, she bowed to the body, touched her palms to the head, and touched her eyes with her fingertips in the classic pose of prayer. The other female mourners copied her gestures. A cacophony of drums, brass horns, and exploding firecrackers ruptured the air. Preceded by two of the all-male mourning party tossing and catching a ball of flowers between themselves and showered by the petals torn from the funeral garlands, the funeral chariot proceeded to the cremation grounds.

A great wave of anguished moans arose from the women as they followed the chariot to the street junction. They soon had to stop and turn back. Women are forbidden from the cremation grounds. The female mourners left behind formed a circle at the crossroads. One woman chanted a lament. The other women repeated the line, collectively hitting their chests with their fists. After a few verses, the chanting stopped, and all the women simultaneously squatted on the ground and then got up immediately. This coordinated but abrupt motion signified the conclusion of the funeral ceremony (Table 1.1).[8] Most of the attendees immediately went to bathe to rid themselves of the temporary ritual pollution (*tittu*) attendant to proximity with a corpse. They had to ensure that they did not touch anything or anyone so as not to contaminate those not similarly polluted. The widow's fellow lineage-wives, however, returned to the bereaved household to clean the detritus from the rituals. The deceased's lineage-mates' and especially their wives' work was not yet over.

This brings us to the second means through which the lineage is made central via a funeral – life-sustaining nourishment and routine care work. For the other castes in Vaduvur (Acari [artisans], Muttiraiyars, Dalits, and Brahmins), the affines are responsible for the post-funerary cooking and caring for the deceased's family. For the Kallars, their affines do also provide nourishment given the ritual proscriptions on the bereaved lighting a fire – but only during the fast[9] in force while the corpse is still in the house.[10] Before the cortege leaves, the bereaved will not eat rice – the prototypical food and that which constitutes a proper meal. After the cortege has left, the lineage-wives prepare the first proper post-funerary meal. Unlike all other castes in Vaduvur, for the Kallars, the first rice-based meal consumed immediately after the funeral must be provided by the lineage.

For Kallars, the lineage nurtures the bereaved after the funeral by providing the exemplary sustenance, rice. During the 'Rice for the Mouth' ceremony, the corpse may have been ritually fed rice by both affines and lineage-mates. The bereaved,

Table 1.1 Stages of a Funeral

Ceremony	Rituals	Actors
Decorating and Displaying the Body	Bathed and titivated body awaited the arrival of the mourners	Lineage-mates (if male) and lineage-wives (if female)
Crying Clusters	Mourners encircled the widow, cried, and lamented	Female kin
Women's Ceremony	Daubed sesame oil and herbal paste on the body	The deceased's daughters and granddaughters
Bathing the Body (and the Widow)	Poured pots of turmeric-stained water over the corpse and the widow	Lineage-mates
Placing the Good Lamp	Gave the blessings of the dead to the daughter-in-law so that life may continue after this death	Lineage-wives
Confiscating the Nuptial Symbol	Denuded the widow of her marital auspiciousness and signified the inauspiciousness conferred by her now widowhood	Lineage-wives
Rice for the Mouth or Feeding the Corpse	Rice placed in the body's mouth and together with coins strewn over the corpse	Lineage-mates, women born into the lineage, and grandchildren
Bearing Lighted Torches	Preceded the corpse being carried to the funeral palanquin with lighted torches	Grandchildren
Circumambulating the Funerary Palanquin	Circled the palanquin, crying and lamenting	Widow, lineage-wives, women born into lineage, granddaughters, female affines, and female kin
Transporting to the Cremation Grounds	Carried the palanquin bearing the corpse to the crematory grounds, tossed a flower ball and chanted	Sons, grandsons lineage-mates, male affines, male kin

however, are fed, at least initially, exclusively by their lineage. Cooked food, in particular, is pervaded by the qualities of the cook which are then consumed by the eater (Parry 1985). That the first proper meal after the cremation that the bereaved eat must be prepared by 'others of the same kind' means that substance exchange is restricted to the narrowest unit, the lineage. This singularly Vaduvur Kallar variation on the customary Tamil mourning customs underlines the overwhelming importance that Kallars give to lineage. These ritual means – through the separation from and continued exclusion of all other kinship ties (except for the immediate family) – are part of the consolidation of the lineage, as the source and sustenance of a Kallar person. This is amplified by the post-funerary period of ritual pollution that applies exclusively to the deceased's lineage.

Ritual Pollution, Lineage Consolidation

Like the other mourners, the lineage-mates and their wives had bathed after the funeral. Daubing their forehead with sesame oil and herbal paste, they had rid themselves of the immediate pollution arising from their proximity to the corpse. Unlike the other mourners, however, the lineage was subject to further ritual pollution – a sixteen-day[11] period of relative isolation and restrictive taboos. The obligatory period of seclusion, prohibitions, and expatiatory rituals vary according to the category and closeness of kinship. The weaker the kin tie to the deceased, the briefer the mourning period and the lesser the restrictions. The more and deeper the substance shared with the deceased, the more extensive the mourning period, the more the ritual pollution, and the more onerous the mortuary taboos. During the sixteen-day mourning period, the affected lineage-mates and their immediate families tended not to socialize but kept to themselves, as per standard Hindu post-funerary prohibitions (Dumont 2000; Clark-Decès 2005; Parry 1985, 1994). They did not attend any auspicious occasions such as weddings. Any such occasions that they themselves had proposed to host should be postponed, if not as is ideal until the next year, then at least until after the sixteen-day mourning period. They did not celebrate any intervening festival occasions like the Harvest Festival (Pongal) or Deepavali. They did not go to the temple. Neither did they worship at their household altar. During the mourning period, the lineage should be strictly vegetarian. Sumptuous consumption is eschewed in favour of a more austere fast. Oil, formerly a scarce commodity, especially in large quantities, is one of the substances prohibited. While sautéing with oil is allowed, deep-frying, with its implications of abundance, luxury, and celebration, is eschewed. They cannot even anoint their hair with oil. They should also abstain from elaborate personal adornment.

Social relations between members of the bereaved lineage and those who were not similarly affected by ritual pollution were severely curtailed. Just as the diet and personal grooming were pared down to the absolutely necessary, customary social interactions were similarly distilled to the basic. Consequently, the bereaved lineage became necessarily restricted unto itself. This mortuary ritual pollution is one of the main indices of immediate lineage-hood. Death (and birth) pollution is spread through 'shared body particles' (Parry 1985: 622). Those subject to death pollution are immediate lineage-mates (and their nuclear families) considered to be of 'one blood'. Due to their ongoing disputes over land, Govindasamy did not attend his paternal uncle's funeral in 2009. But like the rest of the Upputanni lineage, he still observed the funerary taboos for the full sixteen days. As Govindasamy's wife, Samiammal, opined, 'How could we not? We are still, after all, of one blood.' Despite their personal animosity, they had done their duty as members of the same lineage.

Unlike their male counterparts, unmarried daughters and sisters – though they tend to – do not have to observe ritual taboos for deaths in their natal lineage. Since they will marry out and become permanently absorbed into their marital lineage, they are considered to be only temporarily and incompletely part of their natal lineage. They must, however, observe these restrictions for deaths in their marital lineage. Women observe death taboos as lineage-wives, not as women born into lineages. Men observe them as lineage-mates. To refuse to observe these mortuary taboos is to reject lineage kinship. Citing the ongoing enmity between themselves and several members of their lineage, Chidambaram and his family did not attend his lineage-mate Ramasamy's funeral. Unlike the aforementioned Govindasamy, Chidambaram and his family also chose not to observe the taboos. Funerary taboos are not just mediums for asserting the lineage but can also serve as arenas for its rupture. Nevertheless, mourning restrictions remain an important means through which to not just reckon but also experience lineage kinship. Disembedded from other competing social and kinship association, during funerary rites and through their attendant ritual taboos, the lineage assumes an almost unprecedented prominence. Only on one other occasion does the lineage become as central as it does here (see Chapter 3).

As extra-lineage commensality is restricted, the separation and social seclusion of the lineage is reinforced through commensality within the lineage and with the spirit of their recently deceased lineage-mate. Not eating with those who are not of one's lineage during the mourning period represents the temporary 'repudiation of kinship' (Parry 1985: 614) outside of the lineage while simultaneously reinforcing lineage solidarity. Food is a vector not just for the transfer of dangerous substances but also for nourishing kinship and caregiving, as evident in a series of feast-offerings (*pataiyal*) following a funeral.

The day after Ramasamy's cremation, the ashes and bone remnants were retrieved from the now cooled funeral pyre (*elumpu allutal*). Offerings and prayers were made at the cremation ground itself. The deceased's lineage-mates cast the ashes and bone fragments into a designated river.[12] The corporeal aspects of the deceased were now fully disposed of. Similar feast offerings and worship were made on the 8th, 10th, 15th, 16th, 22nd, and the 30th days after death, but these were performed at home.

Fruits, flowers, and food were arranged on a banana leaf and offered to the deceased's spirit. Funerary offerings tend to be vegetarian. Sweetmeats and savouries, rather than full rice-based meals, form the bulk of post-funerary offerings to the deceased. Given the injunction against the use of oil, these snacks were not cooked by the bereaved. The lineage-wives made or bought them. Directed by an elderly lineage-wife, each of the adult participants followed the four-stage rituals of worship. Once everyone had had their turn,[13] they waited for several moments. This was for the deceased spirit to partake of the feast dedicated to him. When the spirit had had his fill, as indicated by the dying down of the camphor flame, the ritual director dipped her fingers in a tumbler of water placed by the side of the banana leaf. She waved her hand thrice around the offerings, ensuring that some water droplets fell on the food (*nir lavutal*). This indicated the conclusion of the spirit's consumption of the offerings. Humans could now begin eating and distributing them. Such feast-offerings (which can also include meat and fish) are an integral part of Tamil worship practices, including tutelary sacrifices and especially post-funerary and ancestor worship (Arumugam 2021). In the first and second stages of the mortuary ritual complex, the deceased is disembodied and becomes a spirit. Simultaneously, the bereaved lineage becomes disembedded from other social relations, and via social seclusion is delineated as a lineage. This is reinforced through the lineage-mates eating the offerings already consumed by their deceased compatriot's spirit. Sharing the consecrated leftovers from the worship with their lineage-mates reiterates the lineage as a group.

Funeral: Re-embedding in Complex Sociality, Return to Routine

The first two stages of the mortuary ritual complex marked the transition of the deceased into a disembodied spirit. These rituals also served to disaggregate the socially embedded deceased man, retrieve him for, and return him to his perceived origins, his lineage. Simultaneously, the lineage was earmarked as not only a Kallar man's most fundamental social body but also his source. Lineages observe almost the same mortuary rituals for their lineage-wives as they do for their lineage-mates. For a woman, however, her marital lineage, into which she becomes absorbed, rather than her natal one, assumes centrality. The initial rituals are concerned with singling out, secluding, and consolidating the lineage. The last stage of the mortuary ritual complex, however, marks the transformation of this spirit into a benevolent ancestor, a type of deity. Simultaneously, the socially dis-embedded and self-focused lineage is re-embedded into their customarily complex social relations and returned to their full sociality. The lineage members take a backseat. The affines are the ritually prominent kin so much so that these rituals are termed 'customs/prestations of the affines' (*cammanti murai*).

The affines' ceremonies occur on both the 15th[14] and 16th days after death. The 16th day is when the final funeral obsequies are performed (*karumati*). This is when the deceased is inaugurated into the pantheon of benevolent ancestors. A photograph of Ramasamy, swathed with a piece of cloth, was set up at a makeshift altar on which were placed an unlit oil lamp, a platter of fruit, and flowers. The deceased was now a revered ancestor. Subsequent prayers and offerings will be made to this photograph.

The *karumati* is also when affines tender prestations and gifts of money (*moi*). As the chief mourners, Ramasamy's sons sat in a row. One by one their affines presented them with gifts of money or gold jewellery depending on the closeness of the kinship tie. Gifts are always presented by affines at the end of ceremonies to which they are invited, be they on auspicious or non-auspicious occasions like this. As the exemplary affine, the maternal uncle initiated the cycle of gift-giving. Immediate affines (their mother's brother, wife's father and brothers) presented them with gold rings of half or one sovereign or gold chains, new clothes, and money. The lineage-mates of these immediate affines, also affines but more socially distant ones, presented only cash gifts.[15] The *karumati* was concluded by a vegetarian feast for all the guests, paid for by the bereaved household. This signalled the resumption of the normal relations of commensality that had been suspended over the mourning period. The bereaved recommenced their totalized sociality after its temporary disaggregation and proscription. In the evening, the bereaved went to the temple where the priest performed the *karumati* prayers for their departed family member. This was also part of their return to customary life as the prohibition against their entering a temple was lifted.

The 17th day is when the family of the deceased and their immediate lineage-mates can add meat to their diet after abstaining throughout the mourning period. This non-vegetarian feast is called 'cook and leave' (*akki vitutal*) or 'cooking by the affines' (*cammanti camayal*). All the expenses for this meat-based feast must be borne by the affines. Where once all their affines would come together and cook for the bereaved household and their lineage-mates, now they purchase the ingredients and pay a caterer to do so. What is significant is affines still ensuring that they paid for everything without taking or borrowing anything from the bereaved household. For the first time in sixteen days, Ramasamy's sons' and grandchildren's hair were anointed with oil by each of their maternal uncles. The maternal uncle's wives similarly anointed the hair of Ramasamy's daughters-in-law. This signalled the lifting of yet another mourning restriction. The maternal uncles presented the wife and sons of the deceased with new clothes. Similarly, the natal family of the deceased's daughters-in-law presented them and their children with new clothes. This is the only time over the mourning period when meat and fish constitute the feast-offering. Goat curries, sautéed chicken and fried fish were poured over mounds of steaming white rice on a banana leaf. The usual rites of worship were enacted. All the deceased's lineage-mates and the invited affines sat down to a carnist feast.[16]

Mourning restrictions were then completely lifted for the lineage-mates and almost fully lifted for the bereaved household. The immediate family itself is considered to be in partial mourning until the first anniversary of the death (*tevacam*) which represents the end of the journey from disembodied 'spirit' to revered ancestor (Parry 1994: 204). The widow herself continues to be subject to various restrictions, some of which are permanent. Her situational ritual defilement may have been lifted but her inauspicious status has become permanently ascribed. The deceased's widow should restrict her society to that of her immediate household at least until the *tevacam* is over. She should not visit other houses so as not to communicate her inauspicious status and therefore taint anyone not similarly affected with her ritual pollution. However, there are ways to circumvent these taboos that are onerous for everyday life. The widow may be able to avoid associating with most of her street and her village for an entire year. However, she cannot avoid her husband's lineage-mates and fellow lineage-wives. Consequently, once the sixteen-day mourning period was over, Ramasamy's widow, Maniammai, was invited to the houses of her husband's lineage-mates.

The lineage-wives at each of these houses had set out bowls of water, rice, oil, and salt. Clad in the *sari* that was gifted by her brother and supported by her fellow lineage-wives, the widow dipped her fingers into each of the substances in turn. She then left to repeat the procedure in yet another lineage-wife's house. The widow was now free to visit her husband's lineage-mates without fear of contaminating them before the one-year seclusion period was over (Table 1.2). Ostensibly, the widow touching the elemental substances of Tamil food, domestic economy,

Table 1.2 The Kallar Mortuary Sequence

Day	Logic	Rituals	Rites	Ritual Actors
1st	**Dis-embedding and Retrieval**	Cremation	Cremation ground rituals and beginning of ritual pollution	Sons, grand-sons, lineage-mates, male affines
2nd or 3rd	**Pollution and Consolidation**	Gathering the Bones and Ashes	Disposal of the corporeal effects of the body in a river	Sons, lineage-mates
8th		Eighth Mourning	Feast-offering of sweetmeats and savouries, prayers	Bereaved, lineage, women born into the lineage
10th		Tenth Mourning	Feast-offering of sweetmeats and savouries, prayers	Bereaved, lineage
15th		Fifteenth	Wake, Feast-offering of sweetmeats and savouries, prayers	Bereaved, lineage, women born into the lineage
16th	**Re-embedding and Return**	*Karumati*	End of mourning restrictions, prestations by affines	Bereaved, lineage, affines
17th		Cook and Leave	Feast given by affines, resumption of consumption of carnist diet	Bereaved, lineage, affines
22nd		Twenty-Second	Feast of sweetmeats and savouries, prayers	Bereaved, lineage
30th		Thirtieth	Feast of sweetmeats and savouries, prayers	Bereaved, lineage, women born into the lineage
1 Year	**Complete End of Mourning Restrictions**	*Tevacam*	Prayers and vegetarian feast	Bereaved lineage, women born into the lineage

and social life would seem to pollute them and by extension the members of her husband's lineage who would consume them. However, this controlled exposure to ritual pollution inoculates her husband's lineage-mates and their families. In the process, it insists that substances and sociality are shared between herself as a lineage-wife and her marital lineage. The only other kin group to which such premeditated contraventions of strict funerary taboos are similarly applied is the widow's natal household. This again underlines the tremendous importance Kallars give to the lineage.

Crows, Death, and Kinship

The crow, with which I began, is also an omen of death, mourning, and remembrance in Hindu cosmology. Their inky colour, their mournful hoarse cries, their haunting of rubbish dumps and cremation grounds, their consumption of carrion – these are why crows tend to be despised. The crow is the vehicle of the planet-deity Saturn, whose malefic gaze can reduce empires to rubble and render even mighty gods powerless. The crow is the messenger of Yama, the God of Death. And yet crows are also revered. Women and children ardently cry 'ka, ka, ka, ka' to invite crows to eat before humans themselves sit down to eat. Crows are supposed to represent the ancestors – they are invited to consume the balls of rice offered to the deceased during funeral rites and ancestor worship. In connecting the worlds of the living and the dead, crows are kin (our ancestors) and yet not kind (estranged by death and species). Crows allude to the traumatic rupture of death. But they also signify the insistent ties that continue to bind and which not even death can completely sever.

At death and through the rituals processing mortality, what a society conceives as being the fundamental constituents of a body, a self and a social are asserted. I have delved in great detail into the death of a lineage-mate and its aftermath to describe how the funeral is a process of social decomposition that shadows the corpse's biological decay. This was critical to reiterating how absolutely fundamental the lineage is to the constitution of a Kallar person. Through rituals, an intricately woven social self is broken down into its most primary and elemental constituent – a member of a patrilineage. Symbolic pollution and the prohibitions that follow exclude or marginalize other kin ties to further reinforce the lineage as the most important social relationship of a Kallar person. The lineage assuming primary responsibility for the routines of care that nourish the bereaved consolidates the primacy of the lineage in defining Kallar personhood and society.

Their symbolic resonances allow crows to embody kinship. However, it is their temperament – their audaciousness – that allows them to encapsulate the unique significance of lineage-mates. Lineage-mates are equal to each other for they are substantially the same. Affines on the other hand are not. Asymmetry defines the relationship between affines. One must behave in a more circumspect, diffident, and even obsequious manner, especially if one is a wife-giver. If one is a wife-taker, one is free to behave in an imperious fashion. However, their behaviour must still conform to protocols that govern their interaction. Affines are governed by rules (*murai*). Lineage-mates, however, do not stand on ceremony with regard to each other. They take what they want for themselves. Lineage-mates are invested with rights (*urimai*).

This distinction recalls Schneider's (1980) thesis regarding American kinship where consanguine relationships are perceived as defined by nature (substance) and affinal relationships by law (code). However, this proffered distinction becomes untenable when we interrogate the definitions, everyday practices, and ethics of lineage more assiduously (Carsten 1995). Blood and law are mutually imbricated as we see in subsequent chapters. A Kallar man can take certain liberties with his lineage-mates precisely because they share substance. While they may all be separate bodies and selves, they are of the same kind. However, such liberties (or contraventions of protocol) are overwhelmingly framed in terms of rights. Rights are a politico-jural concept. This jural and ethical definition of rights, rooted in substance and derived from kinship, lies at the heart of a Kallar personhood. It is also the genealogical edifice upon which a political subjectivity is built, which in turn frames their understandings of citizenship – not just in their own kinship-polities but also in the wider nation state.

Notes

1. From the song 'We Should Learn to Be United' for the 1965 film *Loving Arms*.
2. Except for the mother's brother, his wife, and his sons who have significant ritual obligations as befitting their status as not only the primary but the exemplary affines.
3. Lineage-mates are classificatory fathers and sons and elder and younger brothers to each other. Mothers and elder and younger sisters of one's lineage-mates are one's classificatory mothers and sisters. Women who marry one's lineage-mates are addressed as sisters-in-law since they correspond to one's own brothers' wives. The children and grandchildren of one's lineage-mates are one's classificatory children and grandchildren.
4. Methods of duplicating lineage shrines vary, but the most common one is taking "a handful of earth from the original site and carry [ing] it to the new one" and building the new temple on this older foundation (Dumont 2000: 371,

Nabokov 2000). Given that soil bears and transmits substances and qualitative essences, it a particularly apposite medium for this purpose (Daniel 1982).

5. If the deceased is the father, then the chief mourner is the youngest son. If the deceased is the mother however, then the chief mourner is the eldest son.

6. Having said this however, affines are not completely side-lined but have their own comparable value (Dumont 1983). The funeral may not begin without the new *sari* that is the 'brother's gift' (*porantavan koti*). If the deceased is his sister, this *sari* will clothe the corpse and be burned on the pyre. If the deceased is his sister's husband, this *sari* will clothe the widow. Preceded by the discordant sounds from a Dalit band of drummers and horn-blowers and exploding firecrackers, the brother, his lineage-mates, his street-mates, and their wives will form a ceremonial procession to bring the *sari* and a flower garland for the corpse. Women married into this lineage, or lineage-wives, will carry a deep bronze vessel filled with unhusked paddy, collected from their lineage's constituent households, topped by a coconut. This paddy will be added to the pile that had already been collected by the bereaved household. Some of it forms the basis of the 'rice for the mouth' ceremony. The leftover grains are retained by the mourning household to be consumed throughout the duration of their ritual pollution and therefore seclusion. These grains, which have been polluted through their association with death, will not be kept in the house after the mourning period. All funerary proceedings must wait till the woman's brother brings his gift. Other affines like those who had given their daughters and sisters in marriage to a man from the bereaved household or even if either the deceased or the widow was born on their street will arrive with similar fanfare. This is termed *cammanti murai*, or 'affines' customs'.

7. At the conclusion of this ceremony, the barber and the washer-man share the collected money and any leftover rice.

8. Since women were not allowed onto cremation grounds, I could not personally observe the cremation itself or the rituals preceding and succeeding it. From subsequent interviews however, it is clear that they do not significantly deviate from those described by Dumont (2000: 275) and Clark-Decès (2005).

9. A fast does not mean an abstention from all food, but only from food eaten every day, specifically rice, which is the prototypical food.

10. When one of their *poranta-ponnu*'s father-in-law died, the Upputanni lineage-wives prepared coffee and sweet mung dal porridge to distribute to the mourners. This was part of their obligations as affines.

11. Sixteen days is the ideal, but for the sake of convenience, some villagers are opting to observe only ten days of ritual pollution.

12. Tiruvaiyar.

13. Who had a turn and when was calibrated according to a number of social and status indicators. These include gender (men first, then children and finally women), seniority (oldest to youngest), precedence in terms of marriage (which of the women first married one of the relevant lineage-mates), birth position and the closeness of the kinship tie to the deceased (consanguineal kin take precedence over classificatory ones).

14. Affines and women born into lineages are responsible for the offerings to the deceased. They, with the assistance of their fellow lineage-wives, used to personally make the huge quantities of savouries and sweets that formed part of the offerings, although nowadays they are bought from specialists. While all the affines will bring snacks, women born into the lineage must ensure that she also brings some form of flavoured boiled rice (*ponkiya coru*) such as sweet rice pudding or curd rice. For the deceased Ramasamy's ceremony, his daughter and all the members of her marital lineage arrived in a group bearing snacks, flower garlands, and fruits. She then proceeded to invite neighbours residing on the same street. After following the four-stage worship process, the daughter distributed betel leaves, areca nut shavings, and snack packets to all the attendees, especially the neighbours. On the night of the 15th day after death, lineage-mates, women born into the lineage and close affines stayed awake for the entire duration. Women stayed in the house, conversing and assisting with the preparations. Men remained outside the house, playing cards and gossiping. At intervals of three or four hours, three more worship ceremonies were performed throughout the night.

15. Information about gift-givers – who they were, the village or street they were from, and the quality and quantity of their gifts – was meticulously recorded in a notebook so that an equivalent amount may be reciprocated at the giver's own future ceremonies. Not only reciprocity but the absolute equivalence of the gift to be returned (with adjustments made for inflation) underpins these prestations.

16. There are supposed to be two more such worship ceremonies with vegetarian offerings on the 22nd day and 30th days after death, but these may not necessarily be observed. If they are observed, then attendance is often restricted to the immediate family and the lineage-mates. Again, snacks are made and offered to the now-deified ancestor and then distributed to the attendees.

2

Animal Sacrifice and the Body Politic

Kavya, an Upputanni lineage-wife, tried cajoling her husband and brothers-in-law to enact a worship during the 2007 sacrificial season:[1]

> What is the point of spending so much money and effort to build a temple if we then go back to neglecting our lineage deity? What was the point of the consecration ceremony if we are not going to have a sacrifice every year? We might as well not have bothered at all.

Another lineage-wife, Malar, tried shaming the men into action:

> Even the artisan caste (poorer than their Kallar neighbours) can manage to come together to host a lineage ceremony every year. If they can do it, why can't we? We should be ashamed of ourselves.

They tried to rally their men right up till the very last Tuesday and Friday of the month. But to no avail. The women were disgusted, most particularly with the behaviour of the lineage headman, Ayyakannu.

> He should be the one rallying everyone, making sure that we stage the lineage sacrifice. But he is only concerned about sacrificing goats for his personal use. For his son's wedding, he sacrificed two goats to our deity [Ravuttar] and served them as *biryani* at the post-nuptial feast. The very same goats he had kept aside for the proposed lineage sacrifice. Since we did not have that worship he used the animals for the wedding ... two mangoes with one stone.

Again in 2008, the men began to demur as soon as the sacrificial season came around. A lineage-wife again tried shaming the men to rouse them to action.

> After such a lengthy lapse, even the K. K. Vanniyar and Tontani lineages [their neighbours] have managed to become organised enough to stage a lineage sacrifice. If 20–25 households can come together, why can't our 10 households unite? The entire K.K.V. Street is going to look down on us.

Sacrifice is an essential part of the ethical covenant between a lineage and its tutelary deity, the withholding of which invites terrible retribution. Sacrificial worship is the very apotheosis of the lineage ritual cult. Along with the funeral, it is through this sacrificial worship that the lineage is made material. Through funeral rituals, the densely woven person is unravelled, and the lineage is posited as the first and most fundamental element of the Kallar self and society. In its sacrifice to its tutelary deity, the lineage is posited as the source of fertility – both procreative and socio-economic. The life that such sacrifice promises is a permanent and perfect one uncompromised by the messiness of sexual reproduction, decay, and death. Above all, the efficacy of lineage sacrifice is contingent on the renouncing of individual lineage-mates and their nuclear households for the collective lineage. It is premised upon the sacrifice of the self for the lineage. Focusing almost exclusively on the enactment of the sacrifice itself has allowed anthropologists to privilege their incorporative ethic premised upon the sublimation of individual interests. Honing in on the symbolic logic of ritually killing an animal enables them to showcase the transcendental intent of sacrifice which seeks to separate and quarantine ritual from politics. And yet, very often sacrifices do not happen at all. Each sacrifice that is actually performed is an achievement, against overwhelming odds. Almost a miracle. Why is this so?

This chapter reeks of blood, throbs with violence, resounds with dissent, and is rife with marginalizations and exclusions. Here, sacrifice is not primarily a symbolic vehicle for transcending the chaos of life and the anarchy of politics to assert a sublime authority. The ritual itself is riven by politics. Focusing on the logistics of organizing a sacrificial worship, the labour involved in its enactments and the practices of processing the post-sacrificial meat – I unravel the sinews by which rituals are inevitably and inextricably bound to politics. Rather than resolving politics by transcending it, rituals themselves have become overwhelmed by politics enough to be abandoned.

Acutely sensitive to sacrifice's viscerality – flesh, blood, bone, guts, and fat – I explore how the sacred carcass of the sacrificed animal quite literally makes flesh a polity and the political rights embedded within. Who is allowed to offer sacrifice?

Who has rights to the post-sacrificial meat? How much and what parts of the sacrifice can they claim? Answers to these questions make visible the assertion of citizenship within the kinship-polity. Who cannot tender sacrifice? Who is denied the sacrificial meat? Who is merely given the bony, gristly, and fatty leftovers? These are the ones marginalized or excluded from the polity. Sacrifice forms the very meat from which a polity is built, a political community defined, and sovereignty asserted.

Sacrificed Carcass, Corporate Lineage Estate

The sacrificed goats' headless carcasses hung from the eaves. The Upputanni lineage-mates surrounded the butcher. Bowls in hand, they waited to collect their share of the meat from their first sacrifice to their lineage deity, Ravuttar, in more than sixty years. As his assistant held onto the swinging carcass, the butcher carefully snipped the sinews to detach the black pelt, which would add to their remuneration. He made a large slit in the torso and removed the stomach, intestines, liver, heart, lungs, kidneys, and pancreas. These were washed and kept aside. The butcher set about expertly chopping the meat into cubes and piling them onto mats. The second goat was also dispatched summarily.

Sizing up the quantity of meat and knowing there were fourteen shares in total, the butcher estimated that there would be slightly more than 1 kilogramme of meat per share. He piled meat onto the weighing scales. When it reached the designated weight, he dumped it into a waiting bowl (Figures 2.1 and 2.2).

Figure 2.1   Weighing the Shares

Source: Author.

Figure 2.2 Apportioning the Shares

Source: Author.

After each bowl had the allotted amount, he divided the pieces that were left over and added another equal portion to each container. The gathered lineage-mates watched carefully. They protested if there appeared to be more or less meat in a share. They also remonstrated if one pile seemed to have more of the desired flesh as opposed to another with more of the less desirable offal, bone, or fat. The butcher then adjusted the quantities. He substituted a smaller piece for a bigger one, exchanged a piece of meat for a piece of offal or fat or subtracted from one pile to add to another. The aim was to get each share of meat as equal as possible, at least to the satisfaction of the gathered lineage-mates (Figure 2.3). On more than one occasion, the butcher even weighed the disputed portions again to demonstrate equivalence. Once parity was achieved, or rather accepted by the gathered throng, the men brought the meat home.

Houses and land are individually owned. This leaves the sacrificed goat as the only actual communal lineage resource. The portioning of the carcass is the culmination of the lineage's most significant corporate activity, the worship of their tutelary deity. It is an explicit manifestation of the principles of the lineage. The entitlement to a share (*panku*) of this sacred carcass identifies men as shareholders (*pankalis*) and therein lineage-mates. Kallar lineage-mates are in essence joint shareholders. However, the joint estate of the Kallars now primarily involves just the cult of their lineage deity and the carcass of the sacrificed goat.[2]

Figure 2.3 Individual Shares of Meat

Source: Author.

The prescriptions governing the sponsoring and division of the sacrificed goat materialize the premises and claims of lineage membership.

At a lineage sacrifice, there must be at least one goat paid for by and sacrificed on behalf of the entire lineage. This communal goat (*potu keta*) must be sacrificed first, before any private sacrifices on behalf of individuals or households (*conta keta*), reiterating the pre-eminence of the lineage. What determines whether a sacrifice is communal or private is, first, the sponsorship of the live animal and, second, the distribution of the sacrificial meat. Animals for private sacrifice are paid for entirely by the individual donors. The animals for communal sacrifice, however, are paid for through a tax (*vari*) on all the members of a lineage. Designating each lineage-mate's financial contribution to the sponsorship of the sacrificial animal as tax has political overtones. Taxation is compulsory, signifies representation, and, above all, encapsulates rights.

Only the members of a lineage tender this tax. All the lineage-mates tender the same amount of tax. Wealthier individuals may volunteer more but this does not translate into differential rights to the cult or the sacrifice. Women do not tender any tax. Women born into the lineage may donate money to the more expensive religious endeavours of their natal lineage, such as the construction and consecration of a new shrine or the refurbishment of an old one. However, this is a voluntary gift, not a compulsory tax. Their donations do not entitle them to the same rights as their fathers and brothers. However, the fact that their donation is accepted and even solicited, as opposed to the disdaining of donations from outsiders, does indicate that they do have some rights. These are simply not equal to those of male lineage-mates. This initial collective tendering of tax is what renders the sacrificial goat into a corporate estate to be publicly divided among the lineage-mates rather than an individual asset to be privately consumed by the individual or their domestic households.

The head, legs, liver, and skin of the sacrificed goat form the *caruvatai*. It is only the *caruvatai* and not the whole animal that forms the share of the lineage deity and the lineage as a whole. The head is given to the professional priest who decapitates the animal, as part of his remuneration. The skin goes to the butcher. The legs and the liver go into a curry (*vippuli racam*),[3] which is mixed with rice and offered to the deity. After the worship, this now-sanctified offering of curried rice is distributed to the congregation as a part of a feast. If the animal is individually paid for by a lineage-mate, then the entire decapitated carcass is returned to the sponsor. If the animal is communally sponsored by the entire lineage, however, the remaining carcass is either consumed as part of a communal feast the night of the sacrifice or chopped up to form equal shares to be distributed to each lineage-mate the next morning. These rules are particularly illuminating about the place of women in the lineage cult.

When a male lineage-mate sponsors an animal for sacrifice, the parts of the animal that form the *caruvatai* are retained and eventually distributed to the lineage as part of a cooked feast and/or as a share of raw meat. However, if a woman born into a lineage sponsors the animal, the entire carcass is always given back to her. The head may still go to the priest. However, the rest of the *caruvatai* is returned. None of its parts are retained either for consumption as a communal feast or for distribution as shares – for the *caruvatai* is what encapsulates shares in and rights to the lineage. If the *caruvatai* from the animal sponsored by their daughters and sisters was retained, then it would mean giving women a share and accepting that they have the same rights in the lineage and to the lineage deity as the men do. It would effectively mean accepting women as shareholders in the lineage cult. It entails recognizing the women as being equal to the men. 'And we can't have that,' Sevu Vanniyar, an advisor to the Vaduvur regional polity, chuckled mischievously.

Women and Sacrifice: Scapegoats, Subsumed Associates, Sponsors

Women born into a lineage do partake of the sacrificed animal after the sacrifice and even take some of the meat home. More significantly, they can also sponsor a sacrifice to their lineage deity whenever it is calendrically appropriate to do so. Pregnant women sponsor sacrifices to their natal lineage deity to seek protection during pregnancy and for a healthy child. They do not have to seek permission from the male lineage-mates. This is a right only available to those who, regardless of gender, are born into a particular lineage.[4] Lineage-wives cannot initiate or sponsor a sacrifice to their marital lineage deity, except through their husbands and sons, who are lineage-mates. Lineage-wives have *no* rights – to their marital lineage cult – unmediated by their men. Their membership to the lineage itself is through marriage and motherhood and always through a man and thus indirect. Any rights they may have in their marital lineage cult are subsumed so totally by that of their husbands and sons that there is no term even to refer to this category of women participants. For women born into a lineage, their membership to a lineage is conferred by birth and is thus direct. Their rights to their natal lineage's cult are unmediated even by their fathers and brothers.

Their right to sacrifice (on their own and at their convenience) is an admission that women born into a lineage have some inherent rights to and prior claims on their natal lineage's tutelary cult. All women born into the lineage have the same rights to the lineage into which they are born and its attendant lineage deity. Nabokov (2000: 175) argues that the primary purpose of women's presence at lineage sacrifices is to be demonstrably excluded. Excluding women from the lineage's sacrificial rituals expunges the domesticity, putrescence, and transience they symbolize. This in turn affirms the 'perpetuity' guaranteed by the lineage deity uncompromised by 'decay, impermanence or replacement' and sustained by the 'sameness, unity and corporateness' of the lineage. The lineage deity promises a life premised on death (sacrifice), but this is a 'permanent' life that transcends the imperfect and chaotic actuality of sexual procreation. This resonates with my own findings. Women do not attend any of the lineage meetings to determine the date, duration, and financing of the worship. They do not contribute to the financing of the sacrifice. Until recently, most women were not even allowed to attend the sacrifices. Women themselves were too afraid to be anywhere near the lineage deity or its shrine. Some may be stricter in their enforcement than others, but all lineage cults do impose exclusions on the presence itself, let alone the participation, of post-pubertal but pre-menopausal women. Most women know the rules and adhere religiously to them for fear of being possessed and/or smote by a wrathful deity.

As Bloch and Parry (1982) and Nabokov (2000) attest, the natural fecundity of women is an obvious threat to the ritual appropriation of fertility and counterintuitive positing of a male-centred, perfect, and perpetual generativity. However, such a reading also glosses over an important point made by Ortner and Whitehead (1981). First, all women are not equally excluded from the lineage cults. Severe prohibitions apply only to women who are in their reproductive prime. Pre-pubescent girls are treated just like men and allowed unlimited access, while post-menopausal women can approach as close as they dare. Second, women married into the lineage – wives and mothers upon whom the reproduction of the lineage directly depends – are who are most expressly excluded. They are so completely subsumed by their husbands' and sons' status as lineage-mates as to be rendered structurally invisible.

The fruits of their reproduction (their daughters) – women born into the lineage as sisters and daughters of the male lineage-mates – are also excluded. But not to the same extent that women married into the lineage are. They have a singular status with regard to the lineage into which they are born. They are singled out with the specific term of *poranta-ponnu* that refers to their natal distinction. Women as fertile reproducers rather than women per se are at the root of lineage prohibitions. Birth into the lineage is still singled out and valued, not to the same extent as for the men, but still to a significant degree. Women born into a lineage have some rights, albeit less than that of their fathers and brothers, to the cult. Despite their birth into the lineage, women can never be lineage-mates having equal rights and responsibilities as the men. This is illustrated by the rejection of the *caruvatai* from the animals that they sponsor. Women-sponsored sacrifices are always individual, never communal. The access of all fertile women to such tutelary deities is similarly restricted. This does not mean that they are merely exemplary scapegoats to be expunged in order to assert male solidarity and lineage continuity. Women's role as fertile reproducers (wives and mothers) is ritually denied and devalued while their status as kinswomen (sisters and daughters) is recognized and valued. This is materialized in the differential access (inclusion versus exclusion) and rights (direct versus mediated/subsumed) that different categories of women (fertile and non-fertile) have to their natal and marital lineage cults, respectively.

Sacrifice: Logistics, Labour, and Rites

As the sole remaining material basis to corporate lineage membership, the sacrificed animal, its offering and the protocols governing the disposal of the sanctified carcass are fundamental to grasping the constitutional premises of lineage membership.⁵ This recalls the abiding concern with the political ramifications of south Indian temple rituals that had been developed to counter the privileging of a discrete religious sphere in the analyses of India and especially the characterization of rituals as apolitical (Appadurai and Breckenridge 1976; Dirks 1993). The distribution of post-worship offerings (*pracatam*) and honours (*mariyatai*) is a means to establish and publicly signal differential socio-political rank. Whoever receives the consecrated offerings first or if they receive the honours at all is judged to have precedence in terms of their proximity to the deity. They are styled as the first worshipper with 'superior status and authoritative rights' within the temple (Fuller 2004: 80). Contestations over precedence may be so intense and protracted as to threaten the very occurrence of worship ceremonies (Dirks 1993: 254–255). In lineage worship, the body of the sacrificed animal is the primary sanctified offering, the substance transmuted by being in contact with the deity to become the 'material symbol of the deity's power and grace' (Fuller 2004: 74).⁶

In lineage sacrifices, what is at stake is not the confirmation of precedence and differential rank through the distribution of transubstantiated offerings. More relevant is the materialization of citizenship within the given kinship-polity and the equality of socio-political rights that said citizens are able to wield. The focus therefore is, first, on the inclusion of lineage-mates and the exclusion of non-members from receiving the lineage deity's power and protection. This divine grace is localized to the lineage's territory and restricted to the lineage-mates and their immediate families. Second, the emphasis is on the equality of rights to the lineage cult and the deity's grace for all lineage-mates. Every lineage-mate has exactly the same rights. No lineage-mate has precedence, and none of them is superior or inferior to each other in their standing with the lineage deity. The ranked difference established within a lineage cult is framed by two other principles, birth (women who are born into the lineage have more authoritative rights than lineage-wives who are married into the lineage) and gender (male lineage-mates have more authoritative rights than their female counterparts). Women born into a lineage have superior rights when compared to women who marry into a lineage, but they have inferior rights when compared with lineage-mates.

Before pursuing the political ramifications of the tutelary cult, we must first understand its theological resonances. What is the typical sequence of a lineage sacrifice? How do sacrificial rituals manifest the rapport between a lineage and its tutelary deity?

Lineage ceremonies vary in terms of the nature of the worship (sacrificial versus non-sacrificial) depending on the nature of the deity and the cult (carnist versus vegetarian). Most lineage deities are vegetarian. Neither the sacrifice nor the sanctified cooked meat is offered to the deity itself. The animal may be sacrificed in the name of the lineage deity, but it is not sacrificed directly to or even within the god's sight. The meat offerings are never made to the lineage deities (*kula-teivam*) themselves, only to their guardians (*kaval-teivam*). In Vaduvur, guardian deities such as Munnadiyan and Pecchi Amman are the ones who observe the sacrificial animal's killing and to whom the cooked meat is actually offered. Only the living animal is presented before the lineage deity. The killing, however, takes place elsewhere or after a curtain is drawn across the deity's shrine. Lineage worship ceremonies also differ in terms of the frequency of their staging. Not all of them are staged annually or even at all. In 2007, the Mannaiyars staged an especially grand sacrifice to their Val-Muniswarar after a gap of fourteen years. Being unable to afford an annual worship, they have decided to hold one every five years instead. As for the Tontani and the K. K. Vanniyar lineages of K.K.V. Street, they had not sacrificed to their Viranar for decades. They always planned to sacrifice but had never been organized enough to actually do it.[7] However, the sacrifice of goats or roosters to the tutelary deity is actually obligatory.

The first task is to locate a suitable animal, especially if they are to be sacrificed to Viranar and Ravuttar, who can be quite particular. It must be a male goat with large horns to emphasize its virility. The goat must also be completely black without any white or rust-coloured patches. With the sacrifice season imminent, ad hoc committees made up of senior lineage-mates contacted those rearing goats. As they sourced suitable candidates, they carefully inspected the specimens for physical handicaps or colour blemishes. Second, they must find a priest to perform the necessary rituals and decapitate the goat on the day. During sacrifice season, both goats and ritual specialists are in demand. Third, they must hire butchers to skin, clean, and portion the sacrificed animals according to the number of shares.

On the morning of the sacrifice, all the lineage-mates cleaned and decorated their lineage shrine. Lineage deities may not be housed in permanent human-constructed structures. They may not even be represented anthropomorphically or even with icons. Instead, lineage deities may be represented by a terracotta urn with an opening for an oil lamp (the K.K.V. Street artisans' Viranar), an overturned brass water pot (Serrukkan Vanniyar Street Vanniyar lineages' Naccimuttal Amman), or a particular tree or a mound of earth or a slab of granite (East Street Kandiyar lineages' Viranar). Through processes of adornment, these seemingly pedestrian objects are iconicized for worship. Artful arrangements of garments, particular placements of sandalwood, turmeric, and vermillion pastes, hanging of flower garlands all contribute to the implication of a body, face, and neck (see Flueckiger 2020 on 'the agency of ornaments'). Conjuring the deity is completed through the rituals and invocations of worship.

Lineage deities are usually housed under trees or along thorn fences in yards and open fields that are the communal property of their respective lineage congregations. They prefer to dwell outdoors, open to the elements, thereby reiterating their connections with nature and fertility. Thus, it would normally be difficult for an outsider to even recognize a lineage shrine or deity. Such shrines only come alive during lineage worship. With already constructed temples, however, the animation efforts of lineages are less elaborate. However, lineage-mates must ensure that their temple is clean and their deities garlanded and clothed with new silk garments (Figure 2.4).

The next step is the worship itself, which has a tripartite structure. All lineage worship ceremonies draw from the same basic ritual repertoire. The following description is a composite of the ten rituals that I have witnessed. First, there was the ritual of requesting the attendance of the deity to its own worship and subsequent feast (*varuntutal*). The deity does not readily consent to appear and must be persuaded over a period of time through invocations, songs and poems of praise, and sometimes music. *Varuntutal* means suffering or exerting tremendous effort, suggesting that considerable effort is warranted to conjure the deity.

A feast-offering (*pataiyal*) is laid out. The lineage deity is ultimately responsible for the fertility and success of its respective lineage. Therefore, the deity should be thanked and should also partake of current prosperity to ensure further success. Hence, the offerings are presented like an abundant feast for an honoured guest. On a huge banana leaf are piled mounds of the prepared food offerings.

Figure 2.4   The Upputanni Lineage's Ravuttar Temple

Source: Author.

These include rice pudding, sweet gruel, curd rice, dried rice flakes mixed with sugar and lentils, a sweet relish of mashed bananas, jackfruit slices and jaggery, and a sweetened beverage (*panakam*), particularly beloved of the mother goddesses (*amman*). There are plenty of fruits, especially bananas, jackfruit segments, and halved coconuts (Figure 2.5).[8] Enough quantities of food are prepared to feed all the worshippers and for them to take home. Any meat offerings will be made at the end to the lineage deities' guardian deities. Animal sacrifices are offered in addition to rather than as a substitute for vegetarian offerings.

When everything is ready, the typical worship sequence is enacted. Then each lineage-mate lines up in front of the deity's enclosure. Shirts off, eyes closed, they clasp their palms together in prayer. While they do hire professional priests to perform the rituals, sometimes they make do with a senior member of the lineage.

This priest stood in front of the shrine with a terracotta vessel filled with glowing coals that he presents to the deity. He circled the vessel clockwise in the air three times. He occasionally sprinkled the coals with more frankincense to produce a thick fragrant smoke. Meanwhile, his assistant rang a brass handbell. The fragrant smoke was wafted in front of the lineage-mates' faces so that they could inhale it. The priest presented the vessel to the deity again and then wafted even more smoke at the lineage-mates. The deity and its lineage were repeatedly associated with each other through the medium of the smoke. The smoke and

Figure 2.5   Ravuttar with Feast Offerings
Source: Author.

the rhythmic tolling of the bell were to induce a trance in the worshippers, in the hopes that one of them might become susceptible to manifesting the lineage deity through his mortal body – an ephemeral apotheosis. The priest looked out for the swaying and the body tremors that are the preliminary symptoms of possession.

This is a serious moment when direct communion was to be established between a lineage and its deity. However, the solemnity was often punctuated with mockery, jovial laughter, and even doubt as to actual possession.[9] Despite the lengthy wait, sometimes no one ever gets possessed as was the case for the Upputanni lineage at their sacrifice to Ravuttar. This was attributed to a number of factors: the novelty that the lineage sacrifice had become for the Upputanni lineage, which were staging one for the first time in more than sixty years, the insufficient purity of their preparations for possession, and the deficiency of their faith. However, the failure of this testament to the communion between a lineage and its tutelary deity did not disrupt the ritual proceedings.

One purpose of this ritual is to satisfy the lineage that their deity was pleased with their preparations thus far and permitted them to proceed. Their deity's presence – through the possession of one of the lineage-mates – would signify divine approval. Any swaying and moaning person is assumed to be possessed and often bombarded with the following questions: 'Are there any deficiencies (*kurai*)? If there are, open your mouth and tell us!' This is an opportunity for the deity to communicate their pleasure or displeasure at their lineage's general conduct and the preceding ritual procedures. Quite often there is a lot of moaning and grunting but no articulate answer. The priest repeats his question a number of times. If there was still no coherent answer, then he pragmatically concludes with, 'Please forgive us our trespasses, we will try not to make any mistakes next year!' He then continues with the rest of the ceremony.

The second stage is the sacrifice itself. The sacrificial goat was brought in with a garland around its horns. It was presented to the deity. If the lineage deity is vegetarian, then the goat is led away to be sacrificed elsewhere so that the deity is spared the sight of bloodshed. Otherwise, the priest splashed turmeric water onto the goat's head to purify it. The sacrificial goat was worshipped as a camphor flame was waved before it. The massive bronze sabre – the instrument of sacrifice – was also garlanded, and a lime stuck onto its sharp end. The sabre was similarly worshipped. The goat's head was held down to signify its consent to be the sacrifice. The bleating goat was pulled by a couple of lineage-mates at each end in order to stretch out its neck (Figure 2.6). The priest brought down the sabre to sever the goat's head from its body in one stroke (Figure 2.7).

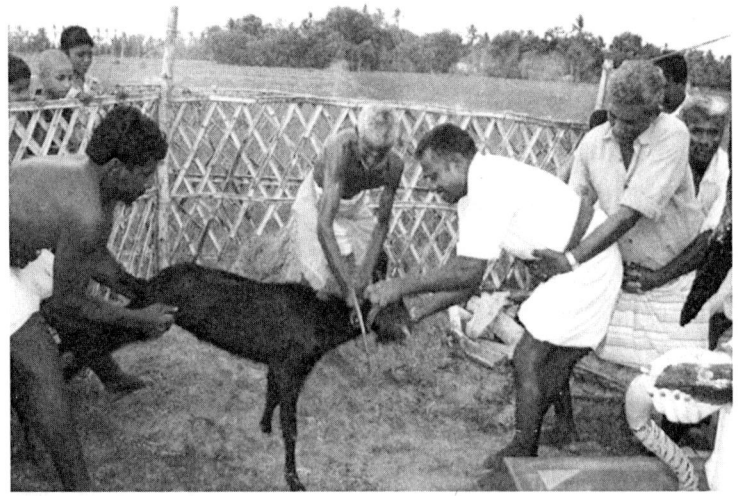

Figure 2.6   Sabre Slicing Through Stretched Neck

Source: Author.

Figure 2.7   Sacrificial Decapitation

Source: Author.

The convulsing, bleeding torso was flung away to avoid getting blood on everyone (Figure 2.8). Then it was onto the next animal. The garlanded head was presented before the lineage deity's guardian deities (Figure 2.9). This head was given to the religious specialist performing the decapitation.[10] The torso was then passed onto the sponsors of the ritual, the lineage. Finally, the priest dipped his fingers in and sprinkled water around the feast-offerings three times. This signified that the deity had finished partaking of the offerings and departed. The leftovers were now consecrated and could be distributed to the worshippers. The ingestion of these offerings would allow worshippers to partake of the deity's power and grace.

The third stage of the worship involves the processing of the body of the sacrificed animal. The sanctified carcass may be dealt with in two ways: as shares of meat and/or as part of a communal feast. The shares of meat are consumed by the lineage-mates, their families, and guests. There are also rules as to how any meat not consumed immediately should be handled. These vary according to the cult. The Southern Mannaiyars' Viranar cult demands that while non-lineage members can consume the sacrificed meat, it must be consumed within the lineage territory itself. None of the meat can be gifted to family living outside the territory concerned. There are contradictory accounts about whether the meat can be

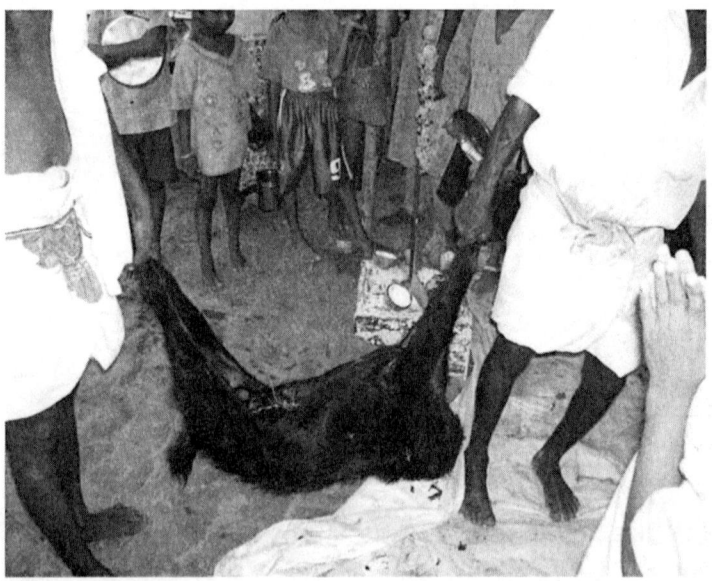

Figure 2.8   Decapitated Carcass
Source: Author.

Figure 2.9 Disembodied Heads
Source: Author.

dried and kept aside for later use. The Viranar and Ravuttar cults expressly forbid this. The Northern Mannaiyars' Val-Muniswarar cult only forbids the drying of the meat out in the sun in full sight of everybody. The meat can, however, be dried out of sight, in the shade. Such prohibitions and prescriptions denote that the meat from the sacrifice is sacred and must not be treated like any other meat.

Sacrifice is the primary way in which lineages transact with their lineage deity. Fuller (2004: 84–85) argues that in Hindu sacrifice, the animal victim is both an 'intermediary between the deity and the human sacrificer' and a 'substitute for the latter'. Sacrifices are the primary means to dissolve the normally prevailing boundaries between the human and the divine, in this case the lineage and its tutelary deity (Fuller 2004: 87). The deity absorbs the sacrifice, not through the ingestion of the sacrificed animal's lifeblood and/or its cooked meat but through the purely visual apprehension of the sacrificial animal before it is killed. The worshippers in turn absorb some of the divine essence through their own visual apprehension of the deity. Such ocular transactions (*darshan*) have been described as the fundamental currency of Hindu worship (Babb 1975; Eck 1998).

Consumption of the sanctified offerings by worshippers facilitates the further, albeit temporary, assimilation of the deity's more purified and powerful essence into the worshippers' own bodies.

The relations created between a deity and its lineage in this way may be asymmetrical and even hierarchical (Fuller 2004: 69–73). Simultaneously, such connections also produce ontological transformations as the boundary between the devotee and the divine is temporarily breached (Marriot 1976: 111–112). Accounting for such ontological transformation is even more pertinent, Nabokov (2000) argues, when we consider that lineage rituals also involve the invitation for the deity to possess the lineage-mates. 'Trans-possession often becomes the means by which participants assimilate supernaturals into their bodily persons' (Nabokov 2000: 9). These attempts are not always successful. Often, the deity does not possess any of its congregation. This is considered a judgment on the staunchness of the lineage-mates' faith and the parlous state of their relationship with their deity. However, this setback does not stop the ritual. The lineage's personal rapport with and confidence in their deity's mercy is more important. The priest apologizes for any wrongdoing and the ritual proceeds as normal. What is significant is that lineage deities are not as 'fierce' (Mines 2005) or as erratically perilous (Masilamani-Meyer 2004) as usually portrayed. Their fierce countenance – bulging eyes, protruding canines, and weaponry – is an iconicization of their prowess against demons, ghosts, and evil spirits. Their fearsome appearance serves as visual representation of their tutelary duties rather than as commentaries on their character. Lineage deities may have fierce responses, especially if the rituals due to them are flouted or neglected. However, this fierce reputation does not manifest itself unless the covenant between a lineage and its deity is *severely* compromised. The violence of lineage gods may be retaliatory or punitive but never gratuitous. They may act if their lineage members are not as devout in their attentions as they should be or have committed grievous offences. However, they are not wantonly bloodthirsty. If one's lineage god is 'acting up', this is not simply an expression of the deity's fierce nature. Rather, what this denotes is that there is something seriously amiss in the constitutive covenant between a lineage and its deity.[11]

Neglecting the Sacrificial Covenant, Dire Consequences

The covenant between a lineage and its tutelary deity comprises two aspects. First, one must respect one's own lineage god as one's original and paramount deity who should be worshipped before and above all others. Failure to do so can impede the effort and efficacy of worship dedicated to other deities. This is evident in the decision of a member of the East Street Kandiyar lineage to resume participating in the sacrificial worship to his lineage deity, Viranar. Having moved to the neighbouring district of Tondaiman Pudukkottai, Raju had stopped attending the Viranar worship. Although he had to rush off to work early in the morning, he ensured he attended the 2008 ceremony precisely because of what happened when he undertook a pilgrimage to the Ayyappan temple in Sabarimalai, Kerala.

> Despite having observed the strict fast, I could not climb the steep hill to the temple. Ayyappan would not allow me to ascend to see him. I had to abandon the pilgrimage which I had tried so hard to fulfil; Ayyappan was telling me to worship my lineage deity first.

The lineage deity is charged with only one responsibility: protecting the interests of the members of its lineage. Approaching one's lineage god before embarking on any major endeavour ensures that one has that deity's permission, cooperation, and protection so that obstacles are removed and success facilitated. When Upputanni lineage-mate Govindasamy bought a new tractor, he had 'With the Protection of Sri Ravuttar Ayyan' inscribed on the name plate. Furthermore, the first stop in Vaduvur on the tractor's long voyage from the sales lot was Ravuttar's shrine. Only after prayers were conducted there was it driven home.

The second aspect of the covenant is sacrifice and, at the very least, worship. According to Hubert and Mauss (1964: 52–57), there are two categories of sacrifice: 'the sacrifice of desacralization' and 'the sacrifice of sacralisation'. The former are piacular sacrifices aimed at divesting the sacrificer of unwanted supernatural elements such as demons and ghosts. The latter revolve around allowing the sacrificer to partake of the powerful and purified substances of the divine. The goal is to establish relations between the divine and the worshipper. Through his concepts of 'negative sacrifice' and 'positive sacrifice', Fuller (1988: 23–24) elaborates on this delineation by grounding the distinction on consumption. Where the fruits of the sacrifice are not cooked and consumed, it is a negative or expiatory sacrifice. Where they are consumed, it is a positive or consecratory sacrifice. Lineage sacrifices are primarily sacralizing, with the express intention of imbuing the lineage with some of the lineage deity's sacred substances.

Failure to offer sacrifice can have severe consequences. A crisis prompted the Upputanni lineage to build their own lineage temple and hold a consecratory sacrifice. Thus far, their lineage god, Ravuttar had been represented by a large rusty tin can with a hole cut in it, in which a lighted lamp was placed. Ravuttar's shrine consisted of this can and a small trident (representing Durgai Amman) propped up against a tree in the lineage's common territory. Individual lineage members would go to the makeshift shrine and worship Ravuttar from time to time. However, no collective worship had been staged by the whole lineage for more than sixty years. Ravuttar and his dormant worship were increasingly on their minds.

The tree under which the tin-shrine stood had fallen down during a storm. They had rescued the lamp and the trident, but the shrine was no more. Then, the Upputanni lineage's headman, Ayyakannu, recounted a dream where he was approached by a man on a white horse. This apparition told the headman, 'While you are all sleeping peacefully indoors, I am being burned by the sun and buffeted by the rains!' The headman ignored this and sank into deeper slumber. The man on the white horse returned and roared, 'I keep trying to tell you and you dare to continue sleeping!' The headman sat up straight. He realized that he had been visited by their lineage deity, Ravuttar. This dream initiated the Upputanni lineage's temple building. Asked why the Upputanni lineage had decided to build a temple in 2005 and organize a consecration and sacrifice in 2007, another Upputanni lineage-mate, Surendran, recounted a number of disconcerting dreams[12] that he had had. More importantly, he related how the lineage-mates had been troubled by misfortune for some time.

> Marriages that had been more or less finalized broke down at the last hurdle. Crops failed. Livestock died unexpectedly or did not multiply as they should. The lineage-mates themselves suffered health problems or had business failures and debt problems....

They consulted a number of astrologers independently and as a group. The diagnoses were all startlingly similar. They had a powerful lineage god in the form of Ravuttar who continued to be by their side. However, he was on the verge of abandoning them due to their neglect. This explained their numerous setbacks. Problems in their relationship with their lineage god were diagnosed upon the basis of lineage-mates not enjoying the desired outcomes of marriages, parturitions (both human and animal), harvests, and businesses. This decline in productivity was symptomatic of deeper problems in the bond between a lineage and its deity. Therefore, in 2005, the Upputanni lineage-mates began building their own lineage temple.

Political Clashes, Ritual Predicaments

Dire omens and especially various fertility crises instigated the Upputanni lineage's temple-building project. The immediate prompt, however, was a violent dispute with other lineages living on K.K.V. Street, over curry. The street temple (*teru kovil*) dedicated to the elephant-headed god, Pillaiyar, is common to all the lineages living on K.K.V. Street. Every Panguni (mid-March–mid-April) Uthiram, the K.K.V. Street residents gather at the shores of the pond at the end of their street to watch some of their street-mates fulfil their vows to the deity Murugan.[13] After this worship, the entire street sits down to a vegetarian feast.

During the 2004 festival, Anandhi, an Upputanni lineage-wife, asked for some lentil curry to take home. A member of another lineage gave her some curry but also made gibes about Anandhi's ill-manners in asking for the curry before the feast was over. Sethu, a Upputanni lineage-mate, was incensed by this insult to his kinswoman. He swung a fist at his contemptuous street-mate. The lineage-mates of each disputant became involved as they tried to assist their respective kinsmen and stop the fight. This soon developed into a mêlée. Since she had already returned home, Anandhi was oblivious to the commotion she had caused. The fallout was that the Upputanni lineage considered this to be an affront to their dignity. Consequently, they refused to participate in the street festivities or even to step foot onto the street temple the next year. Their street-mates' apparent 'disrespect' persuaded the Upputanni lineage that they needed their own temple over which they had exclusive rights. Only in 2007 – after having proved their worth by completing their own lineage temple and being vindicated by the repeated entreaties from the other lineages for them to return – did the Upputanni lineage resume participating in the K.K.V. Street's temple worship.

Throughout the arduous process of building their own temple, it was the galling thought of their street-mates' scorn in the event of their failure that motivated the Upputanni lineage. Govindasamy attested to this fear of a potential loss of face.

> It was a matter of prestige. People would laugh at us, would talk bad about us behind our backs. We would never be able to walk with our heads high in the street again if we had failed.

Surendran concurred:

> Our honour was at stake. We would have lost honour if, after how we were insulted, we did not build. So even with all our numerous problems, we persevered.

However, the unity of purpose within a lineage, prompted mainly by the antagonistic actions of other lineages, is tenuous and often temporary. Temple-building and ritual sponsorship are also driven by chronic competitiveness and a heightened sensitivity towards any loss of parity. Such ritual practices are yet another arena for the playing out of fraternal rivalries and competitive politics.

The tensions between assimilation and autonomy, cooperation and competition, ethical ideals and political interests are part of the cultural schema framing kinship bodies such as lineages (see also Ortner 1989: 59 on fraternal conflicts among Sherpas in Nepal). Indeed, they constitute such polities and fuel their politics.

The lineage sacrifice is a means through which to 'transcend life – its divisions, transitions and finality' (Nabokov 2000: 178; Marriot 1976; Bloch 1992). However, the vitality it promises involves the destruction of constitutive elements of nature and culture through the omission of women and the immolation of livestock. Above all, it is based on the 'destruction of individuality'. The efficacy of lineage sacrifice – 'the human power over life and death' – is dependent on the 'total abnegation of the I'. The lineage ritual is contingent on the renouncing of individual lineage-mates and nuclear households for the collective lineage. Focusing on the structural logic of sacrifice, Nabokov argues that the lineage is made immanent and material and posited as the source of fertility through these rituals. This is indubitably the case when one focuses on the penultimate rite of the lineage worship – the dedication of the live animal to and its decapitation in the name of the tutelary deity. But if one were to consider the ritual complex as a whole – from the procuring of the live animal to be sacrificed to its ritual killing and finally the processing of the sacrificed carcass – multiple and rival ritual logics become apparent.

The logic of lineage sacrifices is premised on the assertion of an ideal of self-abnegating collective unity. However, this is precisely why the performance of the lineage sacrifice is so contentious and its successful enactment so precarious. First, there are conflicts between the ideal and the actualities of intra-lineage social differentiations and agonistic relations, which are most apparent during the organization of these rituals. Second, and even more fundamentally, there are competing logics within the structure of the ritual itself – between collective identity and individual rights. The distribution of the carcass – its apportionment into individual shares, the fixation on the absolute equality of these singular shares as evident in the constant adjustments made to the portions through adding, subtracting, and substituting and finally the recourse to technological accuracy to substantiate visual estimates – are assertions of individual (and equal) rights. These individual rights are guaranteed by but are in no way sublimated to the collective lineage and its rituals. The ideal asserted in the lineage ritual is not just a communal one. The individual is not simply suppressed and subsumed by the collective. He is also materialized and asserted through the structures of this same ritual. Evident in the ritual structure is not simply an encompassment of the individual by the collective but a productive tension between two domains, two different scales of sovereignty.

Along with the tensions within the ritual structure (individual rights and collective identity), the sacrifice also reveals the contradictions between the ideals of collective identity and the realities of social differentiations within the lineage. The lineage ritual is also an arena for contests and confrontations among the lineage-mates themselves. The ritual's ideal may be that the self be renounced in favour of the lineage. However, often it is the self that is asserted and reasserted within and through these rituals. The assertions of individual autonomy and differential status vis-à-vis the threat of encompassment by the lineage and its ideals of equality may even foil the enactment of the very sacrificial rituals that claim to be premised on their suppression.

The lineage cult is fraught with rivalries. These politics have often stymied the very rituals that claim to produce intimate communion between a lineage and its tutelary deity and solidarity among the lineage-mates. In his chronicle of a local Aiyanar festival as part of his ethnohistory of the Kallar kingdom of Tondaiman Pudukkottai, Dirks (1994: 489) describes how he had assiduously researched this festival and was looking forward to finally observing it first-hand. Having turned up at the headmen's house, he discovered that this festival had been a victim of inter-lineage conflicts. Not only had it not been staged for seven years, but no one expected it would occur anytime in the near future. Dirks understood this non-event as in itself anthropologically significant. This non-event – the failure to ritually constitute community and confirm and dramatize power and rank – demonstrates the permeability of rituals to politics. Rituals are neither insulated from power struggles nor do they resolve politics.

For the Upputanni lineage, the tutelary sacrifice was continuously threatened by the internal competition and strife among the lineage-mates. Given the disputatious planning for their temple's construction, that the Upputanni lineage-mates were able to cohere long enough to build a new temple, stage a consecration ceremony, and make a sacrifice was surprising. So heated are the internal rivalries that the Upputanni lineage-mates have not been able to cooperate long enough to repeat the sacrifice that should actually be an annual affair. Similarly, the annual sacrificial worship to the East Street Kandiyar lineages' deity, Viranar, was suspended for a decade. A legal dispute over the ownership of agricultural fields had been contested by two members of the Mela Kandiyar lineage. One claimant was the cultivating tenant, and the other is my father, the landlord residing in Singapore. Other lineage-mates kept out of the dispute or publicly supported their locally resident kinsman. Another lineage-mate who presides over Viranar's worship, Sakthivel Kandiyar, conceded, albeit long after the courts had adjudged it to be so:

The lands rightfully belonged to your father. We should have supported him.
You were all in Singapore. But because the other party lived in the village ... we
kept out of the dispute. If we had advocated for the rightful owner, perhaps the
court case would not have dragged on for so long like it did.

It was only after the court case had been concluded that the lineages could come
together to worship their Viranar. Since then, however, they have managed to
stage a sacrifice annually. In 2008, they sacrificed five male goats, which were
portioned into seventy-six shares for distribution among the lineage-mates. Only
after the legal resolving of their economic antagonisms could the Mela Kandiyar
lineages' seventy-six shareholders come together to regularly worship their tutelary
deity. However, the twelve shareholders of the Upputanni lineage are too caught
up in their rivalries and still unable to cohere long enough to offer collective
worship. The constant threats to the worship, the resultant intermittence of its
enactments, and the doubts about whether it will be staged right up to the last
minute underscore the precariousness of lineage sacrifices. The lineage sacrifice
is always at risk, primarily from the conflicting political interests of and economic
competition among the lineage-mates themselves.

To emphasize how much of an achievement a lineage coming together to build
a temple and/or stage a collective sacrificial worship at all – let alone regularly – is,
I turn to the complicated negotiations and contestations that preceded the building
of the Upputanni lineage's new temple to their deity, Ravuttar. Again and again,
the organization of the ritual evidenced the failure of the renunciation of the
interests of the individual or nuclear household for the collective lineage. Rather
than their negation, it became an arena for the assertion of social differentiation
and individual status.

Initially, not every Upputanni lineage-mate was committed to the building of
a temple. Ramanathan and the headman Ayyakannu's younger son absolutely
refused because of perceived slights to their honour. Who had initiated the idea
to build a temple, whose proposal was listened to, and whose was not became a
matter of prestige. When everyone had finally been convinced of the merits of
the idea, seemingly petty but deal-breaking obstructions kept emerging. Given the
various fissures within the Upputanni lineage, finding a neutral place to meet to
discuss the staging of the consecration of their new temple was itself challenging.
Ramanathan and his two sons would not speak with his nephew Govindasamy
due to their numerous and ferocious disputes over land, unequal inheritance,
perceived slights, and economic competition. Azhagu and his two brothers, being
the poorest members of the lineage, assumed that the others looked down on them.
This rancour informed their relationship with the rest of their lineage. They would

not speak to Rangavelu and his three sons because of a boundary dispute over their adjoining yards. Azhagu and his family were also on bad terms with Ayyakannu and his brother since they thought that the Ayyakannu family was allied with Rangavelu's family. Sozhan was not on speaking terms with Govindasamy due to economic rivalry and alleged insults. For precisely these reasons, lineage-mates would usually meet at the neutral venue of their communal temple. However, the Upputanni lineage did not yet have such a temple. Eventually, they compromised by meeting at Govindasamy's porch since he was the one who was on speaking terms with most of his lineage-mates. The lineage headman, Ayyakannu, would relate the issues of the meetings to those who would not attend any meetings held at Govindasamy's house.

To fully appreciate the nuances of the contestations within the Upputanni lineage, we must remind ourselves of the structural principles underlying lineage. With reference to non-lineage members, the rights of all lineage members to their temple and cult are defined by exclusivity. The new Ravuttar temple built by the Upputanni lineage was entirely financed by the lineage-mates themselves via a tax. Additional contributions were sought and accepted only from women born into the lineage who as such had rights – albeit comparatively secondary ones with respect to the male lineage members – to the lineage cult. According to Govindasamy, the lineage-mates were adamant about this. They could have solicited donations from local dignitaries and political elites but considered it a matter of pride to depend entirely on themselves. Restricting the financing only to the lineage-mates also ensured that they retained exclusive rights to the temple, never having to answer to anyone else. In terms of fellow lineage-mates, however, rights to their lineage temple and cult are defined by equality. Each lineage-mate has equal rights to the cult, no more and no less than any other lineage-mate. Attempts to violate this fundamental principle nearly derailed the temple-building project.

Ramanathan offered to pay for an iron fence around the new temple compound and a grand wrought iron gate at the entrance at a cost of INR 14,000. In return, he wanted his name and that of his sons to be inscribed on the gates. This did not bode well with the other Upputanni lineage-mates. They could accept a lineage-mate voluntarily contributing more than the compulsory tax to finance an expensive cause. However, they did not want this extra contribution to compromise the equality of the rights accruing to each lineage-mate. To this end, they had backtracked from their original decision to have a plaque with the names of all the lineage-mates and their contributions. Foreseeing quarrels about differing contributions being seen to lead to differential rights to the temple, they decided not to publicize the contributions. They also decided that none of their names would be inscribed in any shape or form onto the new temple.

They hoped to avoid queries about whose name was first on the list and the attendant quarrels over precedence. When Ramanathan made his offer contingent on his name being inscribed in black metal curlicues, his lineage mates tried to reason with him. They pointed out that if they were to accede to his request as the donor of the highest amount, then they would have to advertise my mother's name. As a woman born into the Upputhanni lineage, she had financed the buying of all the oil paints and other paraphernalia needed to decorate the temple and icons. Everyone else who had contributed funds would also expect their names to be inscribed. Otherwise, they would be accused of pandering to the demands of rich men and abandoning the principles of equality that must define the lineage-mates' relations to their deity and to each other. A piqued Ramanathan interpreted his lineage-mates' refusal as disrespect and rescinded his offer. However, he vented his frustrations by deliberately obstructing the rituals for the following year, even as everyone had hoped the lineage sacrifice would become an annual affair.

The 2007 sacrificial season came around and the cycle of lineage sacrifices across the village began. Some Upputanni lineage-mates discussed conducting the sacrifice to Ravuttar. Negotiations began as lineage-mates went back and forth trying to rally funds and motivations. Rangavelu's family were hesitant to spend the money as was the headman, Ayyakannu. The biggest obstacle, however, was Ramanathan, who absolutely refused to participate in the sacrificial worship. His reasons ranged from his own frail heath to that his sons, who were not residing in Vaduvur, being uninterested and refusing to join in. Other Upputanni lineage-mates speculated that he was angry at their snub regarding the gate and was exacting his revenge by rejecting their pleas. Ramanathan did, however, ask the Upputanni lineage to go ahead with the worship without him. Despite the appeals from the lineage-wives, quoted in the introduction, the already wavering motivations of the Upputanni lineage were extinguished. The proposed sacrifice was abandoned. In 2008 too, there appeared to be little chance of a lineage sacrifice occurring. Samiammal, a Upputanni lineage-wife, chuckled as she related:

> My son was so fed up with last year's disappointment that he threatened to go it alone. He said that he didn't care if none of the other lineage-mates joined in. When the time came, he would drag the goat we had set aside for the sacrifice to the Ravuttar shrine and personally saw its head off if he had to. [Not decapitating the sacrificial goat with one stroke is considered extremely inauspicious which is why a professional priest is usually engaged for the purpose.]

Given their utter frustration with the recalcitrance of the Upputanni lineage-mates, Samiammal and her son were seriously considering performing a personal lineage sacrifice. They even managed to get Azhagu, another lineage-mate, on their side. Azhagu said that he had the goat ready and waiting and would join them whenever they wanted to stage the sacrifice. However, Samiammal and her son eventually backtracked from their hitherto adamant position. As she explained:

> If it were any other month but Adi [mid-July–mid-August], we could have done it alone. But Adi is specifically for collective lineage worship, and you can't do it by yourself.... I am afraid that if something untoward or unlucky were to happen to my family, then everyone would say, 'Look at her, she was stubborn, ignored her elders and decided to strike out for herself and look at what happened. She deserves it....' A lineage sacrifice is a collective enterprise; for stressing the unity of the lineage. There is no point, no meaning to it if we break off and conduct our own. So even though I do not like it, I have to back down.

The ritual once again did not transcend but became mired in the internal tensions within the lineage and was once again abandoned.

Such frequent non-occurrence does not invalidate the reading of the logic of lineage sacrifice as being about the assertion of an ideal collectivity. As evident from Samiammal's account, the lineage-mates themselves are committed to this ideal. However, competing individual interests are why the lineage-mates cannot enact the solidary ideal through the collective tutelary sacrifice. Rather than capitulate to their own autonomous interests and enact their own private sacrifices, the lineage-mates preferred to abandon the public lineage ritual itself.

The emphasis on how the socio-political not only threatens but also often overwhelms the ritual disrupts the notion of ritual as effortless and routine occurrences. Given their choreographed, rule-bound, and repetitive characteristics, rituals can inadvertently appear to be infallible mechanisms impervious to individual motivations, politico-economic contexts, and ambivalent impulses, making them almost a foregone conclusion. Privileging performance and process, instead of simply focusing on shared meanings and synchronized social realities, has enabled anthropologists to be sensitive to the transformations, innovations, accidents, and mistakes that also constitute rituals. Going even further to focus on failure foregrounds just how risky rituals actually are given the mystery and potency of the sacred forces being engaged with. In rituals, nothing can be taken absolutely for granted; there is always something at stake. However, the risks here are not the cosmic powers but the lineage-mates themselves, their self-interests, and their politicking. In this case, ritual is part of everyday ethical dilemmas produced by the conflict between the egalitarian structural logic of the tutelary sacrifice and the realities of politico-economic differentiation within the Kallar lineage. More significantly, failures to enact the obligatory sacrifices are produced by the simultaneous but competing imperatives – the communal ideal and ethics of autonomy – embedded within the ritual itself. Rather than transcending or resolving fractious political realities, the sacrificial ritual practices embody politico-ethical dilemmas.

Spectacular Killing, Subterranean Work, Sovereign Assertions

The lineage sacrifice has been presented in an inverted manner. I began with its aftermath – the division and apportioning of the sanctified meat under the lineage-mates' vigilance. Only then did I proceed to what most other ethnographies focus on, the actual sacrificial act itself. I concluded with where it all actually begins – the social circumstances, funding, work, planning processes, and deliberations about whether even to stage the sacrifice. Through this deliberate disarrangement, I have juxtaposed the iconic with the organic and the ideal with the intimate. The apportioning of the post-sacrificial meat exemplifies the absolute egalitarianism that should characterize intra-lineage relations. The sacrificial ritual is paradigmatic of how the lineage should operate, sublimating the individual and the devotee to the lineage and its tutelary deity, respectively. This is the apotheosis of the corporate assertions of the lineage.

According to this formulation, sacrifice revolves almost entirely around the enactment of the ritual culminating in the killing of the animal. However, the sacrificial ritual itself is merely the spectacular tip of a subterranean bulk of prosaic discussions, casual meetings, routine tasks, hard work, and heated arguments. This, more than the ritual itself, is actually when and how lineage-mates interact and produce lineage. Lineage sacrifices may be intended and claim to produce integration. However, this is often only contrived for the purposes of the ritual and therefore tenuous. Much more durable are the persistent risks to the very enactment of this ritual, let alone its successful conclusion. The competing interests of individuals and households continually resist the incorporative logic of lineage sacrifices. Evident from the funding of the live goat and the distribution of the post-sacrificial meat are the assertions of individual rights and autonomy that do not deviate from but are also part of lineage sacrifices. Given these competing but nonetheless illuminating socio-political resonances, that these sacrifices happen at all is what is extraordinary. I began with the aftermath of a successful lineage ritual not so much to delineate the normative fundamentals of lineage citizenship but to foreground what an achievement enacting a tutelary sacrifice actually is. Given the numerous threats to its very performance, most of which come from the lineage-mates themselves, it is clear that the ritual does not only grapple with risks but is itself always at risk. The transcendental claims of rituals do not triumph over but are always threatened by the immanent realities of politics.

Calasso (2014: 11–12) argues: '(Only those who take part in the sacrifice can be saved) ... nothing else was as serious, for gods just as much as for men, as being excluded from the sacrifice'. In this chapter, I have demonstrated how exclusion from the sacrifice means marginalization from the polity and exclusion from sovereignty. Sovereign power, according to Agamben (2005), grows from the ability to define and draw distinctions – between those who are ensconced within the polity and those who are left out of it. Those outside the political community are reduced to *bare life* – simply biological life that cannot partake of politics oriented towards the good life. Moreover, they can be killed and punished with impunity. Agamben (1998: 14) argues: 'The problem of sovereignty was reduced to the question of who within the political order is invested with certain powers and the very threshold of the political order itself was never called into question'. Under this rubric, sovereignty is derived from the power both to define – what is simply bare life and bereft of political rights – and to determine what happens to it. Sacrificial rituals make this sovereignty not just visible, but also visceral.

The ritual killing of literal animal life (sacrificial goats and roosters) helps to constitute and define citizenship within a kinship-polity. The de facto right not just to sacrifice but also to consume the resulting sacred meat constitutes a political community. Those who cannot partake of killing through animal sacrifice or eating the sacred flesh are, if not completely outside the polity, then at least marginal to it. Their potentiality for a full political life is not recognized. They are merely subjects upon which political decisions are exerted, not sovereigns who exercise political rights. To the Kallars, the non-Kallar lower castes are a form of 'accursed' beings that cannot even be sacrificed. The ritual pollution attributed to them, within the caste hierarchy and through its theological justifications, means they are prohibited from the Kallar sacrifice. Their very presence is deemed capable of contaminating and polluting the sacrifice (Arumugam 2015). Unlike Agamben's *Homo Sacer*, the question here is not whether they can or cannot *be* sacrificed (they must not be). It is that they are not allowed *to* sacrifice.

Women, even Kallar ones, are also not allowed to sacrifice. Kallar men huddle around the altar, at the centre, fully immersed in the ritual. Women hover around the edges, not being allowed to even glimpse the sacrifice. Women may be included but are at best marginal to this polity. Prohibited from sacrificing, their political faculty is subsumed into that of their husbands and sons. In addition, as biologically fertile beings, women are themselves 'bare life'. Denied political capacity, they are debased as mere animal life. However, this is the very raw life that must also be ritually governed to channel towards the good life – through sacrifice. Unlike the lower castes, Kallar women can be and are sacrificed. They are the scapegoats sacrificed by the political actors in order to counterintuitively assert male potency and politics. Women may not be literally killed with impunity. However, as scapegoats, like the animals that are the surrogates for the human sacrificers, women may be symbolically and ritually dispensed with. Indeed, they are the ideal sacrifice. Upon these exclusions, prohibitions, and marginalizations is a polity and a privileged citizenship built. From (sacred) meat – and the rights to kill, receive, and eat – is wrought not just a political edifice but also a metaphysics of power.

Notes

1. During the Tamil month of Adi (mid-July–mid-August).
2. Along with goats, roosters are the most common animals sacrificed in Vaduvur. Rather than the main sacrifice, roosters are an addendum to the goats sacrificed to the lineage deity. Roosters tend to be sponsored by individual lineage members or households. If they are communally sponsored, they become distributed as cooked meat during a feast for the congregation. They are not distributed as shares of raw meat the next morning.
3. *Vipuli* is an amalgam of *uppu* (salt) and *puli* (tamarind or sour). *Racam* means soup or essence.
4. Normally, non-members are not allowed to sacrifice to lineage deities not their own. In extraordinary circumstances, they may be given a special dispensation, but this is entirely on the sufferance of the relevant lineage.
5. However, one cannot stretch this point too far. Fuller (2004: 81) argues that such an approach is based on a 'transactionalist, exchange model of worship'. It ignores the fact that the 'distribution of offerings and the presentation of honours' form the conclusion to the worship and not its core. His main criticism is that this approach reduces worship to its political components and fails to account for how the rituals of worship themselves represent the worshippers' relationship with the deity. Overemphasizing the relations between the worshippers themselves as mediated by the deity, it does not pay sufficient attention to the relationships between the worshippers and their deity.
6. Some lineage cults are entirely vegetarian, and no animal sacrifice is made to the deity or its guardians. As is usual in orthodox temple worship as well, the

consecrated offering in this case involves half a coconut, a banana, betel leaves, other fruits, vermilion, and holy ash. This offering is returned only to members of the lineage.

7. Until 2008, when a lineage-mate horrifically murdered a lower caste youth. The lineages interpreted this as a punishment for them not having voluntarily offered sacrifice to their tutelary deity who had reacted by taking an unwilling life for himself. They responded by organizing a sacrifice with alacrity.

8. Sometimes such fruits are piled onto the feast so as to completely cover the other food offerings beneath. This is called 'spreading the green' (*paccai parapputal*), which reinforces associations with natural fecundity.

9. The gravity of the situation is often punctured with levity as the gathered crowd enjoys the spectacle. If no one seemed about to be possessed, some playfully chided the participants for not being pious enough. If someone did seem to be trembling on the initial throes of possession, a spectator would question the authenticity of their possession. Jokingly, they threatened to light camphor and place the flame directly on the palm to test whether they were really possessed or merely pretending to get the whole enterprise over and done with.

10. If it is a large ceremony with many goats sacrificed, then the priest may decide to auction some of the heads that are his due so as to augment his payment. The gathered congregation can bid on these heads. Goat brains are considered culinary delicacies.

11. Apart from the Southern Mannaiyars' Val-Muniswarar, most of the lineage deities in Vaduvur are considered consistently benign. Lineage gods are kin and akin to one's own parents. The appellation of father (*ayyan*) or mother (*amma*) is appended to their names, such as Ravuttar Ayyan or Nachimuttal Amma. Alongside the hierarchical relationship between the divine parent and mortal child is the intentional flouting of rules governing appropriate terms of address towards superiors. Viranar may be called plain Viran and addressed in the singular rather than the plural pronoun as is appropriate for superiors. This is not a sign of disrespect but a traversing of categorical domains to signal intimacy and affection.

12. One dream involved his daughter standing at the temple and an elephant bearing down towards her. He also recounted how I was also present, and he had shouted at me to run. Meanwhile, another lineage-mate was running away from the advancing elephant. My mother is born into this Upputani lineage. Surendran is therefore my classificatory maternal uncle and has known me since I was little. Another dream involved Surendran himself cooking food and serving food in a newly built temple.

13. This vow involves balancing a *kavati* – an embellished wooden structure with brass pots filled with milk hanging at each end – on one's shoulders and walking

barefoot, under the mid-day sun, from K.K.V. Street to the Kailasanathar temple at the other end of the village. An obligatory stop is made at the K.K.V. Street's Pillaiyar temple. At the destination, this offering of milk is poured onto Murugan's icon. Family and street-mates accompany the devotees along the dampened and decorated streets, helping to support the *kavati*, cheering and singing songs to keep up waning morale. When the devotees return from their pilgrimage, further prayers are held at the street temple.

3

Territorialized Rights, Contested Boundaries

Fights over goats, fights over cows
Fights over backyards,
Fights over sweeping, fights over gathering.
Fights over fields, fights over canals
Fights over levees, fights over fences
Fights all through the year.

– Chinnappa, a women born into the Upputanni lineage on common
triggers for lineage conflicts

Two Upputanni lineage-mates disputed the boundary between their adjacent houses in 2006. Surendran contended that Mohan's fence infringed upon his plot. He had tolerated this infringement for several years. However, the escalating foul-mouthed public altercations between his female family members and Mohan's wife, Mala, were embarrassing. To demarcate precisely where the boundary between the two properties should be, he arranged for a land survey. Under the aegis of the village administration officer (VAO) and supervised by other Upputanni lineage-mates and several elders from the street, the surveyor began measuring the two plots and comparing them with the land registry records. He concluded that Surendran was right. Mohan was guilty of encroachment. Then, pandemonium erupted.

Mani, Mohan's youngest brother, lunged at Surendran, yelling, 'No one is going to tear down the fence!' Surendran retorted that nobody was asking them to do that. An unheeding Mani, however, started hitting Surendran. Surendran's brothers Sethu and Pazhani intervened. While everyone else was trying to separate the feuding lineage-mates, Mani grabbed Sethu's throat. As his head flopped to the side, Sethu's face turned blue. However, Mani would not relent. The Upputanni lineage-wives, who had been watching the proceedings from their own porches, ran onto the scene to stop their men. Mala, however, began throwing stones at them. Kavya, fearing that her husband, Sethu, might be strangled to death or, worse, suffer the humiliation of a woman striking him, rushed into the melee. As she was dislodging Mani off her husband, Mohan grabbed her hair, nearly tearing it out by the roots. Another lineage-mate, Govindasamy, forced Mohan to let go and dragged him away to the adjacent street. Thinking that Kavya was hitting his brother, Azhagu whacked her back repeatedly with a bamboo pole. Kavya did not even notice that she was bleeding from a head wound from a flying stone. Mani pushed Sethu into a nearby ditch littered with stones, thorns and glass fragments. As Surendran's wife, Vanitha, stepped off her porch to see to her husband, a missile struck her forehead, narrowly missing her left eye. Bleeding profusely, she collapsed to the ground screaming, 'My eye is gone!'

Mala flung stones and periodically sheltered behind a local politician's wife[1] believing that no one would dare go through this personage to get to her. Even so, Surendran's paternal cousin, Karmegam, warned the politician's wife to move out of the way or else he would hit her too. She immediately fled. Karmegam struck Mala repeatedly on her back until the bamboo pole broke in two. Mala barely seemed to notice. Meanwhile, Mani had been dragged away to his own house by the mediating parties. Even as his dishevelled and crying wife clung to his legs begging him not to, he insisted on returning to the fracas. As he tried to shrug his wife off, Mani shouted at her to let him go. Bleeding from the head and sporting a blood-flecked shirt, Azhagu also wrestled to get away from his pleading wife. Finally, seeing his diabetic brother itching to fight further, he calmed down and managed to persuade Mani to return home. Apart from a few shouted threats, the fight dissipated. Sethu, Vanitha, and Kavya were rushed to the government hospital in nearby Mannargudi.[2] Mani, Azhagu, and Mala left to lodge a police complaint. Warrants were issued for Sethu, Kavya, and Surendran. Surendran was arrested at the hospital. He posted bail and in turn lodged a complaint against Mala, Azhagu, and Mani. Their court cases were adjourned after one hearing. The dispute, however, was far from over – reigniting, as we will see, in 2008.

During this melee, I was crouched behind a goat-shed. Sheltering from the stones that were whizzing past my head, I was also craning my neck and peeping out to make sure that I missed nothing. This vivid fight – over a seemingly small issue – prompted me to concentrate on the visceral political imaginaries of the Kallars. Being woken on several mornings not by the rooster's crows but by screaming matches over the use of the communal tap sensitized me to just how much altercations were part of the village soundscape. Expletive-threaded threats about a long dead ancestor's transgressions. Spit-flecked roaring about insults to honour. Protracted rows over a few handfuls of earth. Violent clashes about the inches by which a boundary wall protrudes. Police cases lodged about the killing of coconut trees. This chapter explores how conflicts, even violent clashes, generate lineage sociality.

The previous chapter described how a common tutelary deity and sacrificial cult constituted the lineage polity. Here, I grapple with the final component in defining lineage kinship – rights in/to a shared territory. The violence that erupted over a boundary between two lineage-mates' houses materializes an intrinsic tension between individual rights over and collective usage of a territory. Contrary to substantialist arguments, it is not so much the substance of soil and water that defines a kinship-polity (Daniel 1982). Rather, it is soil, as territory where rights are asserted (and contested) and power exercised, or as a jurisdiction, which governs its political valence. Overall, this chapter discusses how a clear notion of territory, despite imprecise, overlapping and/or contested boundaries, constitutes a kinship-polity.

Lineage-mates are not only each other's classificatory fathers, brothers, and sons as well as members of the same congregation; they are also each other's closest neighbours. A lineage is always embedded within and bounded by a territory. This articulation between lineage and territory is manifested in two modes – constitution and contestation. First, a lineage is partly defined by its rights to and use of specific territories. Second, the interpretations of these territorialized rights are frequently contested which can fuel feuding among lineage-mates themselves and with other lineages. Not just rights over a territory but also disputes over it define the lineage and sustain lineage relations.

Lineages and their lands mutually constitute each other. Lineages are defined by their rootedness within a particular delimited territory. The deep implication of related persons and shared places in each other is articulated through two key ideas: (*a*) mutually constitutive substances and (*b*) geo-political jurisdiction. First, people and their places are made up of the same substances. Elaborating on Marriott's (1968, 1976) notion of transactionalism,[3] Daniel (1982) traced the shared substances between a place (and its soil) – the native village (*conta ur*) – and the people that claim nativity to that specific place. Shared substances help define personhood and nurture its essence as part of routine life. Everyday practices – like consuming the vegetables growing in that soil and drinking the water – solidify and further cultivate the relations between people and their places. The substances of their native place are considered the most compatible with the substances of their indigenous inhabitants. Being away from their native place for an extended period of time induces qualitative imbalances manifested as anomalies in health, fortune, morals, and temperament. Places make their people just as people make their places (see also Osella and Osella 2009, 1996). This semantic understanding is complicated by Mines's (2005) introduction of a political dimension to her analysis of how spatial distinctions underpin social distinctions in a village. The higher castes reside in the interior, the densely inhabited centre of the village. The lower castes, specifically the Dalits, inhabit the peripheries, outside the main village, in segregated hamlets. From the perspective of the centrally located elite castes, the lower castes reside in or near the wilderness sharing its feral and volatile characteristics. These peripheralized castes are seen as only partly civilized and always vaguely threatening (see also Uchiyamada 2000 on 'soil slaves' in neighbouring Kerala). Making associations between the substances of a people and a place is never purely descriptive or simply neutral. They are also the mediums of moral evaluations, ideological impositions, and power differentials that serve to reinscribe territorialized political hierarchies.

The political valence to lineage territories is even more blatant. Lineage territories are essentially jurisdictions, areas where rights are asserted and power exercised. In the anthropology of India, the political domain and therefore state, kingship, and territory have been seen as being subordinate to, subsumed by, and indeed unrecognized by the ideological one – the latter reduced to an opposition between purity and pollution underpinning caste hierarchies (Dumont 1986: 196). Territorial divisions are understood as defined in terms of groups of people rather than through geographical boundaries. This has led some scholars to contest the very validity of the term 'territory' when applied to pre-colonial political units in India (Dumont and Pocock 1957; Wink 1986; Jaffrelot 1996, quoted in Berti 2011: 22). Contrary to this underestimating of the territorial principle, Tarabout (2009: 284) argues that there has been a notion of clear boundaries between territories in pre-colonial India. Borders were not all vague, as has often been claimed, but overlapping and extremely complex. Rather than no territories at all, the problem is that there were simply too many of them. The concept of shared sovereignties underlying multiple and overlapping jurisdictions could not be accommodated into the state-making of colonial regimes and was therefore dismissed (Berti and Tarabout 2009). Wielding a localized sovereignty over a specific territory is fundamental to the definition of a lineage. Rights to a lineage territory are predicated on membership in that lineage. Lineage territory is defined primarily by the rights claimed and exercised by the relevant lineage and only thereafter by culture and/or identities. These rights are materialized in territorial terms through jural concepts such as:

1. personal property (*patta*),
2. shares in a corporately owned property (*panku*),
3. usufruct (*polanku*)
4. boundary markers (*poli*)

The jural-moral rights of lineage members to their territories and these territorial boundaries are clearly defined externally – vis-à-vis non-lineage members. However, they are more nebulous internally – among the constituent lineage members themselves. The tensions between individuals/households and lineages, sovereignty and sharing, and demarcation and ambiguity underpin the ubiquity of intra-lineage disputes. Disputes, largely over territory, are an inevitable part of being lineage-mates. Conflicts are therefore a characteristic feature of lineage life.

Territories and Their Grammars

Tamil spatial categories correlate with social structures and vice versa (Selby and Peterson 2008). Precisely how they do so have been the subject of fierce debates. Dumont (2000: 183) argues that kinship is primary and what shapes specific modes of territorial occupation: 'Territory as an objective category exists objectively only for the outsider; for the inhabitant himself it is subordinated to caste from without and kinship from within.' Leach (1961) disagrees, arguing that 'a piece of territory laid out in a particular way' is what produces the patterns of individual actions that anthropologists then abstract into social structure. Comparing changing systems of land tenure in Sri Lanka, Leach understood kinship systems not as pre-given but as ecological and administrative adaptations. Beck (1972: 266), correlating extensive land ownership and an elaborate clan and lineage structure among the Gounders in northwest Tamil Nadu, concurs. However, she also clarifies that it is not so much the control over land that underlies the Gounders' wealth and prestige as the control over people and *through* them the land. She delineates how lineages and clans are not adaptations per se to forms of land tenure but are in and of themselves political configurations (see Witsoe 2009 on 'territorial democracies' in rural Bihar).

Extensive lineage and clan organizations are part of an intimidatory structure to claim, maintain, and defend power and position as well as acquire and control land (Dirks 1987). The access and means to mobilize allies and labour that such kinship configurations enable are key to caste dominance in villages. Kallar caste dominance in Vaduvur is manifested in two ways: the monopoly of (*a*) political offices (see Chapters 5 and 6) and (*b*) ownership of fertile agricultural fields. However, this has not always been the case. Until the 1960s, the Kallars were tenants of and agricultural laborers for Brahmin landlords. Therefore, the Vaduvur Kallars' extensive clan and lineage structures precede their ownership of land. It is more plausible that their elaborate lineage and clan relations enabled these Kallars to mobilize and impose themselves onto the existing agrarian structure. Additionally, their readiness to resort to violent coercion when opposed facilitated their contemporary dominance (Dumont 2000; Blackburn 1978; Dirks 1987).

In Vaduvur, lineage kinship among the Kallars is defined by territory. Just like their individual and equal rights to the lineage cult, deity, and sacrificed animal carcass, lineage-mates (*pankalis*) have shares (*panku*) in a common territory. Rights to agricultural land are not framed in terms of shares. Under the colonial regime, the *ryotwari* system – a form of permanent tenure for each cultivator in return for payment of land revenue to the state termed *patta* – came into effect (Baker 1976; Ludden 1985, 1999). Indeed, there is no evidence to suggest that agricultural land has ever been communally owned in this region. Lineage territory does not refer to agricultural fields, orchards, or any such cultivable land. Therefore, it is not governed by legal decrees, taxed by state institutions (colonial or nation state) or subject to market transactions. I use lineage territory to refer to two specific forms of land rights and use – (*a*) 'shrine-territory' and (*b*) 'residential-territory'.

The 'shrine-territory' is where the lineage deity is located and tutelary worship takes place. Establishing the shrine is also a means for claiming rights over a specific territory in the name of a lineage. Therefore, it is part of the wielding of an extremely localized sovereignty (see Feuchtwang 2004 on shrine establishments as part of state-making projects in China). Only the relevant lineage-mates have access to and rights over their territory. Non-members cannot even enter this site unless expressly invited or permitted by a lineage-member. Rights of access underpin the distinction between the lineage's 'own' or 'private temple' (*conta koil*) and a 'communal' or 'public temple' (*potu koil*). The territory where the shrine is located does not belong to any one lineage-mate. Even if the shrine space protrudes into their individually owned plots or a lineage-mate had donated the initial site to build the shrine, the land on which the shrine sits is collectively owned. No one lineage-mate, not even the former owners, has any more rights than any other lineage-mate. Any member of the relevant lineage can access the 'shrine-territory' whenever they want. No one, not even the lineage headman, can restrict their access to the shrine. For the lineage, the shrine is a neutral territory which all lineage-mates can access without being restricted by intra-lineage conflicts (Dumont 1986; Dirks 1987; Nabokov 2000; Mines 2005).

The second type of lineage territory, 'residential-territory', is a comparatively less researched phenomenon. Large, elongated houses – subsequently divided into separate small apartments for each inheriting son – had characterized Vaduvur's traditional architecture (see Reiniche 1979 on Tamil houses in Tirunelveli). Even within a single house, separate doorways delineated individual ownership and defined discrete nuclear households. Since residence and filiation flow in the same direction among the Kallars, lineage-mates tend to live among each other and be each other's closest neighbours. This correspondence had once been even more intimate. Currently, lineage territory does not encompass house sites. However, when they had first migrated to Vaduvur, the Upputanni lineage-mates could not afford to build individual houses. According to Upptanni lineage-wife, Samiammal,

> We lived, all together, in a single long house. This communal house was located on the first plot of land that we bought in Vaduvur. It is our old (*palaya*) share.... Our ancestral ... original (*purvika*) share. Our first share (*ati panku*).

Those who now have a share in this primordial plot are the direct descendants of the Upputanni lineage's first migrants to Vaduvur. Many contemporary lineage-mates still have fond memories of the ruins of the large communal house that represented the Upputanni lineage's settlement in Vaduvur. This house had also materialized the lineage's communal ideals as the lineage-mates shared their resources and helped each other to alleviate their mutual poverty. This is the territory where it had all begun. This is also the territory now subject to such frequent and intense intra-lineage disputes.

Such 'residential-territories' are termed *kollai*s. These are communal spaces that surround the lineage-mates' individual houses, flow in between, and also divide them into discrete households. *Kollai*s are the interfaces between private houses and the public street, between domestic households and the wider socio-political organizations of the lineage and the street. By lineage territories, I mean these *kollai*s that surround, flow between, and connect each lineage-mate's house, the uses of which are not strictly private and whose borders are subject to frequent intra-lineage contestations.

Kollai Topographies

*Kollai*s are nondescript places. Consisting mainly of a few square meters of scrub land dotted with some trees; *kollai*s seem to be unlikely catalysts for such fervent intra-lineage disputes. They scarcely seem worth the physical injuries, medical and legal costs, and efforts of a protracted feud. However, this instrumentalist perspective entirely misses the point. Much more than money, meaning is at stake in these feuds (see Geertz 1975b on cockfights among the Balinese). While the use of resources is never other than rational, what constitutes a resource is culturally specific (see Mosse 1998, 1999 on tank irrigation systems in southern Tamil Nadu). Despite their unremarkable appearance, *kollai*s are resources absolutely vital to rural life.

A *kollai* is partly a garden plot and a mini orchard. Herbs and vegetables intended for domestic culinary and medicinal purposes are planted. Flowers and leaves are plucked to offer to the household and temple deities or to adorn women's hair. Fruits are harvested directly from the trees or collected when they fall to the ground. Branches, fronds, and twigs are collected for use as firewood. Trees themselves are hewn to be used as timber for building houses or making furniture.

A *kollai* incorporates yard space where the everyday tasks integral to the subsistence of agricultural households are performed. Plant detritus from the harvest such as stalks and husks are piled up into haystacks to feed milking cows, calves, and draught oxen. Cattle are housed under sheds located therein, watered from troughs and milked by the women. *Kollai*s house goat pens and chicken coops. Organic waste – animal dung, crop debris, and garden pruning – are composted in the rubbish pit dug in a corner and used as premium fertilizer for the crops. Dry palm fronds, kindling, and logs for wood fires are stacked there. It is where the storage shed for the tractor and other farming equipment is located. Still verdant *mung* and *urad* dal plants are spread out on tarpaulins to dry so that the pulses can be easily removed from their pods. New harvests of groundnuts or tamarind pods are piled onto the ground so that kinswomen or hired labourers can shell them.

A large proportion of the village domestic economy involves the preservation of garden produce during the hot months for use over the rainy months. These stored foods must be periodically sun-dried to preserve them and prevent spoilage and infestations by vermin and mould. Spiced ground rice is piped onto mats spread out in the sun to dry into crackers that will be deep-fried into accompaniments for a bland starch-based meal. Goat meat or fish marinated with spices are threaded onto twine and hung out in the fierce sun. Boiled and salted vegetables from a garden glut are laid out on mats draped over bedsteads to be dried. These will form the basis of warming curries during the monsoon season. Spicy mango and piquant citrus pickles bask in the sun as do vats of freshly pressed coconut, peanut, and sesame oils to concentrate their flavour and preserve them. Seeds, spices, pulses, and grains are dried so as to obviate musty smells, weevils, and mildew before they are put away for storage, ground into powders, or pressed into oils.

A *kollai* is also an extension of the house. An outdoor cooking area or shed is constructed there. Equipped with a make-shift wood stove and heavy granite spice and grain grinders, these outdoor cooking facilities are where most of the heavy cooking, especially for feasts and festivals and for the agricultural workers is done. Women and girls rinse and dry the dishes and pots used for cooking and serving at the outdoor pipes or wells. The washing water is not wasted but channeled to the plants cultivated in the area. Clothes are washed and dried out there. People brush their teeth, wash their faces and legs before heading into the house, and bathe themselves and their children there. It is the site of an outdoor toilet although more often than not people retreat farther into the bamboo thickets surrounding *kollai*s for this purpose.

A *kollai* is a recreation space. Women pause to engage each other in conversation during the course of their domestic duties. Adults tarry to sit on the benches placed under the trees and converse. On humid nights, men opt to sleep in the open, dragging their rope bedsteads outside to catch the intermittent breeze. Children play cricket, 'run and catch', or hide and seek there. Neither the semiotic complexity nor the functional density of *kollai*s are quite captured by conventional terms such as house sites, gardens, yards, or waste spaces.

Kollai Politics

A *kollai* and its uses must also be understood in terms of Vaduvur's wider political, economic, and social hierarchies. Owning *kollai*s also contributes, in quite unexpected ways, to Kallar dominance in Vaduvur. The transfer of ownership of agricultural fields and houses from the departing Brahmins to the resurgent Kallars in the 1950s and 1960s was the most visible manifestation of the shifting power dynamics in Vaduvur. However, this dominance was also underlined by Kallar acquisition of yet more *kollai*s. K. K. Vanniyar (K.K.V.) Street is the only street in Vaduvur's Kallar neighbourhoods to have a significant cluster of non-Kallar residents. Most *kollai*s (and several of the large houses) on K.K.V. Street had been given as remuneration to the artisans (*acari*s) for their services as carpenters and blacksmiths when constructing Vaduvur's main temple, the Kothandaramaswamy temple. Due to their alcoholism and the resultant debts, these once prosperous artisans lost their wealth. To service their debts, they had to mortgage their *kollai*s. This was exacerbated by the fraudulent tactics of land-hungry Kallars. Each household on a street has to pay a small amount of tax every month to the street council. This tax funds the organization of social and religious activities by and for the street's residents (see Chapter 4). An artisan interlocutor, Subha, raged,

My grandparents fell behind on these taxes. They owed the street council a paltry INR 100[4] in total. But they had no ready access to cash. Their debts kept mounting. One of the Kallar neighbours[5] offered to pay these debts on our behalf.

But he wanted our *kollais* in exchange. We lost our lands for the price of *murukku* and *vatai* [cheap snacks]!

The artisans felt that they had no choice. They were few and the Kallars were many. Furthermore, the Kallars had a reputation for violent retaliation if they were thwarted. Kallar dominance, in K.K.V. Street at least, was at the expense of the artisan castes. It was underscored by the acquisition, fraudulently or otherwise, of valuable *kollais*.

The ownership and access to *kollais* continue to reinscribe Kallar dominance. A Dalit agricultural labourer, Kani, conceded her caste's improving social possibilities.

We are no longer entirely dependent on the goodwill of the Kallar landlords. Our children now go to school and out of the village to work. We do not drum and dispose of dead people and cows [their traditional but socially ignominious and ritually polluting occupations] unless we want to.

Agriculture has been intensified to up to four plantings and harvests a year. This has resulted in increasing competition for agricultural labour. So, the asymmetrical social structures that had been overwhelmingly in favour of Kallar landlords and against lower-caste labourers are being undermined. This is being exacerbated by government initiatives such as the Mahatma Gandhi National Rural Employment Guarantee Act (MGNREGA) whereby a villager is guaranteed at least a hundred days of work on infrastructural projects during the agricultural off season and the '1 Kg of Ration Rice for 1 Rupee' scheme. Along with the greater opportunities offered by urban work, the possibilities of regional migration have reduced Dalit labourers' reliance on local landlords and on agriculture itself. Nevertheless, there remain certain dependencies that constrain the choices of Dalit labourers and keep them tied to specific Kallar landlords. Dalits live on the outskirts of Western Vaduvur (Vadapathy) in relatively congested colonies with small houses linked by government-built cement streets. As Kani elaborated,

We only own our houses. The rest of the land still belongs to the Kallars. If we refuse to come to work for them then the landlords will not let us use their *kollais*. They will shout at us. You didn't come when I call you for work but still want to use my *kollai*? If we don't heed them, then we won't have pastures for our cows and goats ... no place to store our hay or gather firewood. We won't even have a place to go to shit!

Like temples (Appadurai 1981; Dirks 1987; Heitzeman 1991) and water tanks (Mosse 1998, 2001, 2003b), *kollais* are embedded in the wider set of transactions and social relations that frame Tamil Nadu villages. *Kollai*s are political assets in that they are 'underpinned by caste [and class] based authority and involve social exclusions and forms of dominance' (Mosse 1998: 9). Land ownership continues to be the basis for the entrenchment of caste dominance in rural India. Land and tenancy reform laws are at the heart of the measures to transform inequitable agrarian structures and remove institutional barriers to more egalitarian socio-economic configurations. The slew of post-independence land reform legislation passed by the Tamil Nadu state were aimed at breaking up monopolies over the primary means of production (land), enjoyed by a particular caste or class and their resulting inordinate power vis-à-vis their tenants and landless labourers. The aim was to abolish intermediaries and return land to the tillers themselves. Such laudable initiatives, with their instrumentalist aims, have focused almost exclusively on cultivable land and to a lesser extent house sites. Indeed, the 1961 Fixation of Ceiling on Land Act granted exemptions to house sites, plantations, orchards, gardens, and land used exclusively for growing fuel, all of which are essentially *kollai*s. The 1970 Amendment did close these loopholes. However, vague legislation coupled with slow implementation means that *kollai*s remain largely unaffected by such reforms (Somanathan 2003: 32). Kallar landlords have used access to *kollai*s as a means to pressure and punish uncooperative lower-caste labourers, especially Dalits, in Western Vaduvur. Non-Dalit labourers (Muttiraiyars) in Northern Vaduvur live on more spacious house sites with small *kollai*s of their own. This has allowed them a measure of independence from the Kallar landlords. Compared to the Dalits in their cement-paved hamlets and small house sites, the Muttiraiyar labourers have more leverage to negotiate with and even repudiate the Kallar landlords. In Vaduvur, the control over a specific form of territory – a *kollai* – is intimately related to the control over a specific labour force.

Kollai Kinship

*Kollai*s should not be understood merely in terms of political interests and economic utility. In predominantly mono-caste Kallar neighbourhoods, they also materialize lineage kinship. Lineage co-residence is defined by the kinsmen's substantial equivalence with the soil on which they live and with each other. However, a semiotic framework – focusing on ecological environments within which there is a constant exchange of substances – tends to over-privilege static notions of autochthony. It elides how substances are also portable. New places and their substances can be *made* compatible to non-native migrants. The Kallars are not native to Vaduvur. However, they have made Vaduvur their native place.

Apart from setting up residence, the most significant way in which to remake a new location into one's native place is to transfer one's lineage deity there. Setting up their lineage deity, delineating this deity's shrine place, resuming worship, and performing sacrifices are all ways in which to fully inhabit a new location. The customary method to transfer deities is through sprinkling a handful of soil that they have brought from their original location onto their new site (Dumont 2000; Mines 2005). Incorporating the handful of soil from their original home into the soil of their new home does not just transfer their deity but also imbues the latter with the substances of their original native place. This ensures the substantial compatibility between the new place and themselves. Autochthony is not a prerequisite. Nor is there a need to travel to any original native place to renew substantial connections. Few Vaduvur Kallars remember or even know[6] their original village, let alone visit it. Their new location has been made into their native place. Indeed, the Upputanni lineage has designated their *kollai* where they first settled down in Vaduvur to live together in a communal house as their 'ancestral' or 'original share'.

Along with the making of substantial connections between a lineage and its soil, the *kollai* is also a political territory. The emphasis on the symbolic aspects of the relationship between people and places tends to underestimate territory, defined as a political entity delimited by jurisdiction. Phenomenological analyses must also consider how rights are exercised within and over *kollai*s, the conflicts that this generates and how this too is lineage kinship. Like the sacrificed goat's carcass, *kollai*s encapsulate the claims, rights, responsibilities, and contestations that define lineage membership. *Kollai*s are not collectively shared, but individually owned plots that neighbour others owned by fellow lineage members. While *kollai*s are generally unfenced, who owns how much of which plot is more or less known. The *kollai*s belonging to a specific lineage are avoided by non-lineage members. *Kollai* ownership is not collective. However, the use of *kollai*s is also not stringently restricted to their individual owners.

The right of way to the lineage shrine may cross each other's *kollai*s. This path is declared common to the lineage and does not feature in any land apportioning to individual lineage-mates. Any assiduous policing of trespassing such that it inhibits access to their common tutelary deity is thus avoided and jurally reinforced. Even if it is an unavoidable part of everyday life, trespassing into other lineage-mates' *kollai*s is not necessarily approved of. Trespass is merely tolerated in the interest of amicable communal living. Lineage-mates with smaller *kollai*s tether their animals in a neighbouring one. Firewood may be gathered from other *kollai*s. One's washing-up area may impinge on or the runoff from one's eaves may drain into another lineage-mate's *kollai*. Unless such forays hinder their own activities or seriously challenge their ownership, owners generally do not contest such incursions. However, they may be brought up in the context of existing quarrels.

Such 'trespassing' by lineage-mates cannot strictly be defined as such or prevented due to the ambiguity of *kollai* boundaries. Like house sites, agricultural land has been minutely surveyed, portioned, and mapped for the purposes of land tenure arrangements and revenue assessments. The boundaries of *kollai*s have been defined externally – vis-à-vis the territories of those not belonging to one's own lineage. Internally – vis-à-vis other members of one's lineage – *kollai* boundaries remain nebulous. Individualized shares are mapped onto the *kollai*s through deliberate practices of denoting ownership and demonstrating boundaries such as manipulating its topography and women's work routines. Along with sinking granite posts, planting hedges or erecting thorn fences, planting trees is a common way with which to establish ownership of a *kollai*. Indeed, older lineage-mates with longer memories will refer to the person who planted the trees and their precise placement to arbitrate boundary disputes.[7] This is not a fool-proof method, dependent as it is on elderly lineage-mates' memories and their impartiality. Govindasamy's mature tree had fallen upon the bamboo grove belonging to the Upputanni lineage's headman, Ayyakannu. Ayyakannu informed Govindasamy who had the tree cut down. However, Mala laid claim to this timber. She started collecting the fallen kindling. Govindasamy and his wife, Samiammal, remonstrated. They reminded the headman that he had asked them to fell the tree, thereby acknowledging their ownership. Their vehement protestations were not only about the loss of valuable timber but also the challenge to their ownership. But it was to no avail. Ayyakannu claimed to know better. He decreed that the tree did indeed belong to Mala. Several Upputhanni lineage-mates imputed that her getting away with this insouciant thievery, aided by their headman's vacillations, was the catalyst to Mala's audacious attempts at further annexation.

Another way to demonstrate ownership is to sweep. Sweeping, a twice-daily duty for village women, involves the transfer of impurities from the interior – the purity of which must be protected – to the exterior where they belong. Sweeping is part of the everyday practices that keep the cosmological balance – preventing the chaos and filth from the exterior from encroaching onto the order and purity ideal to the interior (Mines 1997). While sweeping is framed by the cosmological principles of Tamil culture, it is concurrently a deeply political act.

Given the small sizes of *kollai*s – unlike with house sites and agricultural fields – most owners do not go to the trouble and expense of reinforcing their ownership with official title deeds. Genealogy and their use (*polanku*) of the territory in question serve as title deeds. Mala had married into the Upputanni lineage later than many of her fellow lineage-wives. However, she claimed to know more about the proportions and boundaries of the Upputanni *kollai*s than even elderly lineage-mates and women born into the lineage well versed in its historical permutations. Chinnappa, Govindasamy's older sister and an Upputanni lineage-daughter, raged at Mala's attempts to seize her natal family's *kollai*.

> It is our *kollai*. During the inheritance settlement arbitrated by the street's elders, it was left to my younger brother. My father was the one who planted the tree which Mala had illegally appropriated. My sisters and I were the ones who had to sweep the dead leaves from that *kollai*.

One only sweeps what one owns; ergo wherever one sweeps, one owns.

Sweeping someone else's *kollai* is akin to annexing someone else's territory. It means disputing the current ownership of the property and asserting one's own claim. Often, women initiate intra-lineage quarrels that can persist and threaten to erupt into violence, over who can sweep which parts of a *kollai*. Sweeping is a sensitive issue, precisely because of its political ramifications. After the acrimonious division of their inherited property, Govindasamy and his elder brother, the now deceased Selvaraju, were allocated adjacent *kollai*s with no visible indication of where one ended and the other began. According to Govindasamy's wife, Samiammal, twice daily the wives of the two brothers would sweep their own portions. They kept conscientiously to the allocated boundaries (*poli*). They used the routine mechanism of sweeping not only to demonstrate where the boundary between their *kollai*s was but also as a means to fully claim their respective properties. When the boundaries had become apparent to all and their property need no longer be defended from the other's sly incursions, the assidulty of their housekeeping was relaxed.

These are obviously attempts to define and demarcate into individual plots what is actually an extremely fluid space. There are two specific spatial distinctions in the Tamil grammar of space (Mines 1997: 175). First, there is the distinction between inhabited spaces (village [*ur*], region [*natu*]), and uninhabited wastelands [*katu*]).[8] Second, there is the spatial distinction between the interior (*ulle*, *akam*) and exterior (*veliye*, *puram*) (Selby and Peterson 2008). The *ur* and *natu* are considered interior spaces – coherent, unpolluted, and secure. The *katu*s are deemed exterior spaces – anarchic, places of mixture, threatening and occupied by treacherous elements, including ghosts, demons, and 'fierce gods'. The interior–exterior distinction is not absolute but relative and their delineation is person-centric. The distinction between interior and exterior informs the qualitative difference between the civilized *ur* and *natu* and the wild *katu* and evaluations of the distinctive natures of the specific castes residing in these different landscapes.

Within the *kollai*, such spatial categories collapse. The *kollai* is neither entirely interior nor exactly exterior. It is neither strictly domestic and individual nor public and collective. *Kollai*s are where nuclear households bleed into the lineage. They are also largely dependent on their lineage referent for their definition. *Kollai*s are delineated as discrete when it comes to non-lineage members – as an assertion of localized sovereignty. However, they are elastic when it comes to the lineage-mates themselves. Just as the domestic blurs into the public in the *kollai*, so do individuals bleed into the lineage. Two idioms, oriented towards a now mythic past – 'gestation in the same mother' and 'sharing of blood' – express the sharing and intermingling that underpin lineage kinship. These procreative ties are reinforced through ritual prohibitions (such as post-mortuary taboos), commensality, and everyday practices of sociality: elements that represent and facilitate sharing of substances. This is echoed in the ambiguity of demarcation and the allowance of trespassing that underlies the *kollai*. The *kollai*'s structure – how it expressly excludes non-lineage members and therein objectifies rights, access, and exclusion – produces the lineage. Concurrently, a *kollai*'s fluidity – how it facilitates the intermingling of individualized rights, domestic households, and discrete bodies – also produces lineage. Intra-lineage kinship is framed by the blending of substances and traversals of household boundaries. Lineage-mates have been reluctant to fence in their *kollai*s or enforce the exclusivity of their ownership. The small sizes of their individual plots and the attendant inconveniences posed for everyday living make these actions illogical. Moreover, strict delineation also compromises the very amorphousness that makes the *kollai* a fertile space to assert and cultivate lineage kinship. This became apparent when the Upputhanni lineage's boundary dispute flared up again in 2008.

Before we contend with this, I must reiterate that the *kollai*'s amorphousness does not simply and unproblematically generate lineage kinship but also splinters it. Owners allowing non-owners to use their *kollai*s underpins the flows of lineage kinship and convivial living. However, the seeming exploitation of this fluidity by a recalcitrant few also lies at the root of many disputes. Mala's actions may have exacerbated the territorial tensions within the Upputanni lineage. However, the roots of this dispute originate from two other sources. First, there is Deva, a member of another lineage on K.K.V. Street, who has exploited the resentment of the relatively poverty-stricken and land-poor Mohan family towards their more prosperous Upputanni lineage-mates. Manipulating the pre-existing cleavages among the Upputhanni lineage for his own interests, he has acquired more *kollai* space of his own at the expense of his Upputanni neighbours' property. Second, there is Rani, an Upputanni lineage matriarch. Instead of building the tank to water her cows in her own *kollai*, Mani built it in Selvaraju's *kollai*. Facing no resistance, she allowed the water from this tank to drain onto Selvaraju's *kollai*. Since Selvaraju had not protested, she planted a few flowering shrubs, a banana plant and a lemon tree to take advantage of this moisture. These plants flourished and she fenced them in to protect them from the depredations of lifestock. Mala cited this precedence in her own attempts to annex Selvaraju's *kollai* space. Not policing the boundaries of their property vigorously and letting the *kollai* remain amorphous may ease lineage kinship. Simultaneously, they can also allow exploitative usage and land grabs that can fuel more tensions, violence, and court cases.

Kollai Fences and Fissions

The perceived ubiquity of disputes means that Kallars do not automatically presume peaceful sociality to be the customary state of lineage affairs. Disputes and violent conflicts are not indicative of the failure or absence of sociality. Repudiating any engagement at all is what denying sociality actually entails. Feuding is simply the practice of an alternative, more aggressive kind of sociality (Harrison 1993). In lineage and clan-based societies, feuding has productive social significance.[9] Intense rivalries and protracted feuds may also be traced to socio-structural impetuses. Protracted feuding among the Kallars is produced by the structural tensions inherent to lineages. Like with the Sherpas described by Ortner (1989; also Evan Pritchard [1940] on the Nuer), the tensions between the egalitarian ideal underpinning Kallar lineages, such that no one lineage-mate can be acknowledged as superior to another, and the actualities of socio-economic asymmetries do drive intra-lineage conflicts. However, feuds also arise out of an additional structural tension, one between competing scales.

For Kallars, disputes are ways of defining, experiencing, and expressing lineage. Though they do threaten the corporateness of the lineage, disputes (legal and violent) and aggression (stylized and actual) are integral constituents of the lineage structure. Through conflict, lineage groups separate from each other and constitute themselves as distinct entities. Through conflict, the lineage is challenged and even denied by individuals and households in order to constitute their own viability and assert their often-competing interests. Such feuds also manifest a tension between the discreteness of individuals in terms of their jural rights and their amalgamation into a lineage in terms of their shared substances. This is a conflict between two distinct scales of sovereignty – the individual and household versus the lineage. The assertions of individual and household autonomy vis-à-vis the threat of encompassment by the lineage produce many lineage disputes. Not just sharing the use of the *kollai*s but also feuding over *kollai* territory and asserting individual ownership frame the experience of lineage membership.[10] For Kallars, disputes that may shade into violence are not necessarily anomalous or abhorrent but another – and not entirely negatively valued – means of defining and doing sociality. Feuds result in the rupture (though not obliteration) of some lineage relations. Simultaneously, they reinforce other alliances and even repair previously ruptured ones. Like the use of lineage territory, feuds also materialize the fluid sociality that characterizes intra-lineage relations.

Once morning in 2008, the late Selvaraju's hitherto verdant and fully laden coconut tree was found with drooping and rusty fronds. The Upputanni lineage suspected foul play. After all, large coconuts still hung from the afflicted tree. Moreover, Mala and her husband, Mohan, had asked the *panchayat* president and another landlord from K.K.V. Street to talk to Selvaraju's widow about cutting down the coconut tree. While the tree was in Selvaraju's own *kollai*, Mala argued that the falling coconuts and dead palm frond could potentially damage the newly renovated roof of her nearby house. Felling a coconut tree in the prime of its fruit bearing years due to the possibility of falling debris was considered ludicrous. Furthermore, it was Mala who had actually encroached into Selvaraju's *kollai*. During her house renovations, Mala had extended her roof so that it overhung Selvaraju's portion. Since she had deliberately constructed her house in the path of the tree, she had no cause to complain now. Even so, Selvaraju's widow did promise to have her coconuts harvested and any dead fronds removed before they fell. She even promised to pay for any potential damage to the roof caused by her tree. Two more times Mala insisted the tree be cut and was refused both times. Mala had then roamed over Vaduvur complaining about the tree. To the Upputanni lineage, it was a clear case of arboricide.

Tamils consider it a sin to cut down a bearing mango tree. Not only are the fruits equated with a mother's breasts, both mango and mother are called 'ma' in Tamil (Trawick 1992: 7). If felling a bearing mango tree is equivalent to matricide, destroying a bearing coconut tree is equivalent to filicide and equally sinful as seen in the villagers' aghast responses.

> Killing a coconut tree (*tennam pillai*) is equivalent to killing a child (*pillai*). After all, we also call a coconut tree *pillai*.

> Last month, a child was murdered and drowned in the canal. Killing this tree is the same as that. At least that child had a voice to plead against his murder. This is a voiceless living being, it can't even protest against its own slaughter.

Like a son, protected and cherished for thirty years.... Just as one's efforts were bearing fruit; the tree was lost.

They themselves have two children; how could they murder the tree like this?

The Upputanni lineage-mates consulted a professional coconut harvester. He climbed the tree and brought down the main stalk. He confirmed their suspicions although there was no need to. The stench was unmistakable. Kerosene had been poured onto the inflorescent stalk, at the tree's most delicate and vulnerable spot. The tree was unsalvageable. Enraged, the Upputanni lineage lodged a police report against Mala and her husband.

The Upputanni lineage was well aware that their case against Mohan and Mala was not strong. They had no conclusive evidence. They knew that the police were not going to rigorously pursue an essentially trivial case. However, they persisted because they wanted Mala and her husband to be at least a little cowed by being summoned and interrogated by the police. They were not primarily after Mala's prosecution; that would be a bonus. What they wanted was more tangible and more valuable for their long-term interests. They wanted legal corroboration for their future actions. By lodging a petition that there were imminent threats of damage to their property, future undertakings to address the encroachment problem could be buttressed with legal justifications. Measures to secure their property would therefore be immune from police and legal challenges.

On 7 August 2008, a petition was filed at the Vaduvur police station citing Mohan's culpability in the coconut tree's demise.[11] On 16 August, Mala and her husband were summoned to the police station to be questioned. Mohan denied all the accusations, mirroring the other villagers' appalled reactions, 'I myself have two children. Would I ever commit such a grave sin?' The police warned him about lying. He had had the motive and the opportunity. Mala insisted that it was their enemies who had falsely accused them. Maybe Selvaraju's widow herself had poisoned her tree in order to implicate them? Heeding none of their excuses, the police hinted that they had an iron-clad case. If Mohan admitted culpability, he would not suffer any penalties. If he persisted in denying his involvement, then Mohan would be arrested. An intimidated Mohan signed a statement admitting that he had 'poisoned' the tree, but out of ignorance. He expressed regret for his actions and promised not to disrupt whatever measures the Upputanni lineage took to secure their property. If he flouted the police injunction, Mohan would be detained. This 'confession' was witnessed by members of Mala's natal lineage (Mohan's affines) who had been prevailed upon to post bail.

The other Upputanni lineage-mates agreed that they had to first remove all signs of encroachment. Leaving aside a common path to facilitate unlimited access to their lineage temple, the lineage decided to build wire fences around the contested *kollai*. Eventually, this fencing was extended to several other individual plots by their respective owners. This was despite the minute size of each of their individual plots rendering such acts inane. Trespassing would be prevented but at the expense of massive inconveniences to the lineage's everyday routines. Cattle and goats now had to be led to pasture via the main road instead of just cutting across the *kollai*s. Given the smallness of her own *kollai*, one of the lineage-wives had been using another lineage-mate's *kollai* to tie up her cows to feed and milk them. Though not happy with the situation, the owner had not enforced his ownership, preferring not to remonstrate over such a petty matter. Her incursions were now obviated by the fences partitioning the *kollai*s into individual portions. The plucking of flowers and fruits from trees and shrubs in each other's *kollai*s – which had admittedly resulted in resentment and snide remarks – was no longer possible. Such strict enforcement of individual ownership and exclusive rights to their *kollai*s is quite unusual. Having tolerated Mala's excesses over the years, it was the arboricide that finally provoked the Upputanni lineage to resort to such drastic measures.

Mala and her husband's immoral arboricide violated the *kollai* that materializes lineage sociality. They asserted individual (and illegitimate) rights in a shared, even if not collectively owned, territory. This has had the effect of reducing the characteristic ambiguity of the *kollai* space which underpins lineage sociability. Mala's encroachments and abuses have been detrimental to the shared usage that produced everyday lineage sociality. Ultimately, it was a repudiation of lineage kinship itself. This was confirmed by the verbal encounter at the police station between Mohan and his lineage-mate Govindasamy, who asked,

> How could you do this to us? After all that we did for you and your family ... after your father's death. Your late mother would say that if not for her lineage-mates, she would not have been able to bring you all up. She was only able to keep you fed because of the food she asked for and received from all the Upputanni houses. Whenever my father would sit down for his meal, you would all arrange yourselves around him. Only after he had rolled big balls of rice mixed with curry for you and your siblings would my father himself begin to eat. Do you not even have an inkling of gratitude?

Even Mohan's now married sister later chided her brothers for forgetting how generous their lineage-mates had been when her destitute mother was trying to raise four fatherless children. However, Mohan retorted that he did not owe the Upputanni lineage anything.

> I worked for all the food I have eaten. I worked on your lands, in your households ... I brought your cattle out to pasture.

The Upputanni lineage retaliated by taking Mohan's repudiation of lineage kinship to its logical extreme. They fenced up individual portions of their *kollai*s to the detriment of access and everyday convenience. Putting up the fence was the ultimate symbol of rejecting lineage sociality in favour of the nuclear household's atomism. However, it would be simplistic to argue that this fission resulted in the total breakdown of lineage sociality. What occurred was a reformulation of intra-lineage affinities and a forging of new alliances. What was produced were new fusions as made clear by the rapprochement between kinsmen and long-term foes – Ramanathan and his nephew Govindasamy.

One of Ramanathan's *kollai*s was sandwiched between that of his nephew Govindasamy on one side and, on the other, Surendran and his brothers. In 1996, Ramanathan had claimed the common footpath between these separate plots as his own. Violence had ensued, followed by a protracted and punishing court case. Ramanathan won by paying large bribes to have the title deeds changed in his favour. A few inches of territory had once fractured lineage relations. Not only was the competitive enmity between Ramanathan and his nephew reinforced but there was an altercation with another lineage-mate. Surendran and his family blamed Govindasamy's family for having to lose some of their land. They accused Govindasamy of courting Ramanathan's envy by building an impressive new house and insisting on the plots being surveyed when they were disputed. Therefore, these three households had had a severe falling out.

After the 2008 arboricide, however, Ramanathan as the oldest member of the Upputanni lineage, pronounced that Mohan's strand of the lineage did not have any rights at all in the *kollai* space over which they were bitterly feuding.

> They no longer own any land in this part of the ancestral plot. It's true they did in the past. Their original share of – nine *kuli*[12] of land – lay opposite my elder brother's plot. He owned the same amount in a separate location, near all the other lineage-mate's ancestral plots. So, he asked if they could exchange them. And they did. Furthermore, he gave them an extra nine *kuli* of his own land so that they could set up house in their present location. Half of where they live was actually a gift bequeathed to them by my brother.

Ramanathan was adamant that Mala be punished for killing the tree. What is notable is how all the other lineage-mates managed to set aside their differences and coalesce around dealing with Mala once and for all. She had finally pushed them too far. Fired by their moral outrage at her sin, the Upputhanni lineage-mates came together in solidarity. A rupture in their lineage sociality had been adapted to and reformulated on marginally different terms.

Legal Feuds

During these intra-lineage conflicts, there was a conspicuous and calculated adherence to rules and regulations – both to the formal legal strictures and the informal juridical principles – that govern lineage relations and property division. Physical violence is not as rife as the Kallars' fractious reputation would suggest. Almost the first reaction after the violence of the 2006 fight, with which I began this chapter, was to rush to Vaduvur's police station to lodge a report. The combatants wanted their grievances, alleged victimization, and possible injuries documented by government authorities. This proved very useful for what was often the next step, to launch a legal suit against one's opponents. This case did go to court. Mindful of their rivals' poverty, Surendran's family were initially hesitant. After Mani's unprovoked attack, however, Surendran lodged a counter suit. He did not expect the courts to permanently resolve this dispute. Rather he was hoping for a long running case for which Mani's family would be financially liable. The K.K.V. Street elders advised Surendran to drop the case. He himself would incur substantial financial penalties. Surely this would be akin to cutting off his nose to spite his face.

Surendran replied,

> I can afford any lawsuit, but Mani's family cannot. They will ultimately lose more than I will. I will back down … eventually … but not before dragging their family through at least one hearing and siphoning off part of their savings. Their new-found wealth is responsible for their arrogance and current aggression … causing them to forget the past and all that their lineage-mates have done for them. Once some of this money is extracted, their arrogance will be reduced.

Recourse to the police and the courts is not undertaken primarily to arbitrate or resolve disputes. Rather, it is a continuation of the feud, an extension of it to another and probably even more punishing arena. Murderous litigation and merciless lawsuits are another way of waging feuds. Appealing to the law and the police is a calculated tactic to impose protracted punishment. One may lose some, but the objective is to ensure one's enemy loses even more. Such mutually ruinous tactics are not uncommon either in the Upputanni lineage or in Vaduvur.

The calculated use of the law to wage feuds was made even more apparent in the aftermath to the 2008 arboricide. The Upputanni lineage had to ensure they kept within the law to preclude future legal challenges. However, they also had to be *seen* to be keeping within the norms to ensure that they did not lose their moral edge following Mala's arboricide. No matter how abhorrent the provocation, the Upputanni lineage-mates would lose their leverage if they were seen to be colluding to bully or take advantage of both a fellow and lone lineage-mate, let alone a woman. Therefore, they duly informed members of Mala's natal lineage (the two men who had bailed Mohan out at the police station). They were invited to bear witness to Mala's incendiary antics that the Upputhanni lineage had hitherto borne patiently. These had now become so perverse as to necessitate retaliation, lest the lineage-mates themselves lose face. Members of her natal lineage were invited for the sake of fairness, to ensure that Mala had advocates to oversee her interests. Above all, they were there to ensure that Mala behaved herself and complied with the collective judgement of her husband's lineage-mates.

Having promised to arrive at 10 a.m., none of Mala's supporters turned up.[13] Removing the encroachments on the other side in the meantime, the Upputanni lineage-mates waited until noon, but to no avail. Ideally, the implementation of the collective judgement should not proceed without the presence of Mala's advocates lest justice not be *seen* to be done. The Upputanni lineage-mates considered having the police bear witness instead. Govindasamy went to investigate further. He found Mala's supporters at a tea stall in Vaduvur's commercial district. Asked why they had not turned up as they had promised to, these supporters started demurring. They even urged the Upputanni lineage to just let Mala have the few extra square inches of ground that she wanted. This greatly incensed Govindasamy since it was his deceased brother Selvaraju's land that was at stake. Retorting that the problem that had been festering for thirty years was going to be permanently solved, with or without their presence, he returned. The Upputanni lineage opted to proceed.

The lineage-mates had engaged labourers to handle the entire operation. They were very circumspect about the dismantlement. They ensured that they did not themselves touch anything but merely supervised. The lineage-mates measured the boundaries carefully using a ball of string. The labourers dismantled the illegal erections (Figures 3.1 and 3.2). Mala had an entire outdoor kitchen; complete with a coconut-frond-thatched roof constructed in what is actually Selveraju's *kollai*. So had her sister-in-law. The latter's lean-to was carefully disassembled, and the raw materials were laid carefully by her house. Mala's lean-to, however, was smashed and the components discarded in retaliation for her outrageous machinations. In fact, once the lean-to was removed, the lineage-mates found that Mala had

Figure 3.1   Workers Erecting Fence
Source: Author.

Figure 3.2   Upputanni Lineage-mates Supervising Fence Construction
Source: Author.

illegally constructed a brick wall under cover of tarpaulins hanging from the rafters. They had the workers smash this wall, her earthen stove, and the pillar upon which her granite grindstone rested. They had granite posts sunk into the ground to mark the boundaries (*poli*). Around these posts, they had a fence of steel wire wound. They planted thorn trees next to the artificial fence. In future, these would grow into a living hedge to further reinforce the boundary (Figure 3.3).

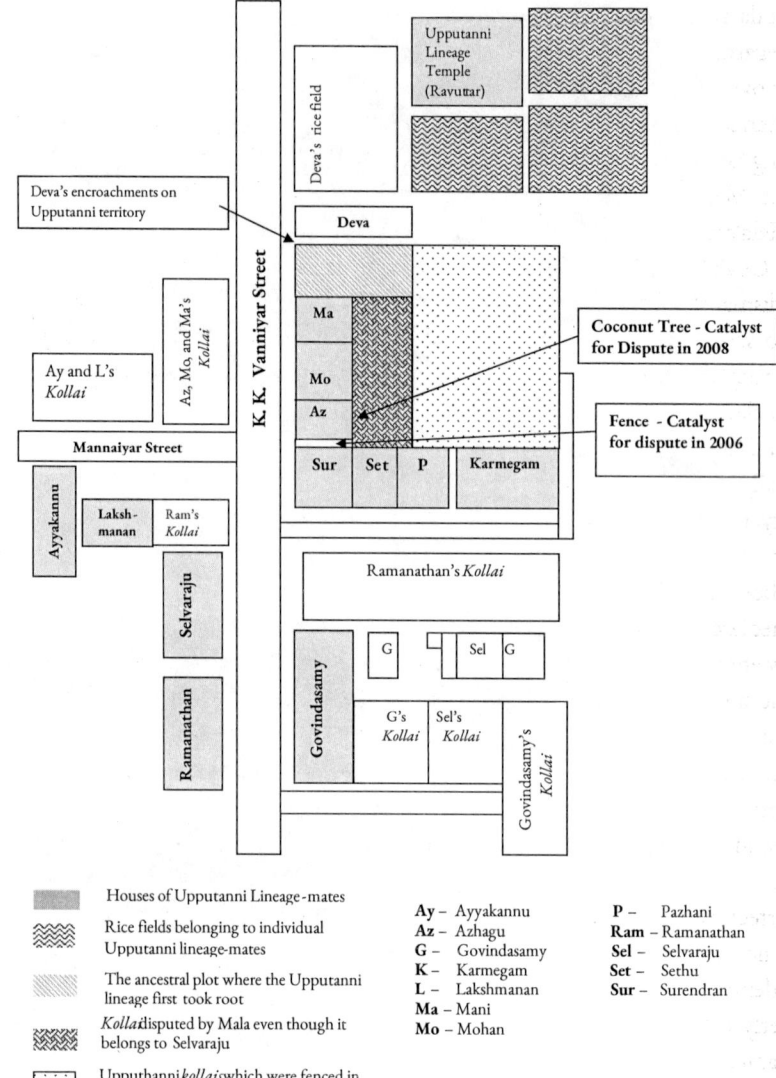

Figure 3.3   The Upputanni Lineage-mates' Residences and *Kollai*s

Source: Author.

Mala rained foulmouthed tirades throughout. Her husband restrained her. Disregarding her crude interruptions, the Upputanni lineage ensured that their own womenfolk stayed well out of the way of any ugly curses, projectiles, or chances of inflaming an already tense situation. Mala even started repeatedly hitting her own sister-in-law blaming her for not stopping the proceedings so that at least Mala's kitchen was spared. Her sister-in-law retaliated by arguing that it was all Mala's fault that her own usage of the *kollai* had also been terminated. She even gave Govindasamy her permission to dismantle her lean-to, another reason why her dismantled kitchen was treated with care.

So scrupulous were the Upputhanni lineage-mates in making the boundary that they actually allowed Mala more space than she was rightfully entitled to. Mala claimed that her share extended much further east beyond the dead coconut palm. However, the other Upputanni lineage-mates were adamant that her portion actually stopped right outside her back door. In fact, she should not have had a backyard at all. She, along with her brother-in-law, had erected a kitchen lean-to when Selvaraju, the owner of the *kollai* and the now-dead coconut tree, had still been alive. Since they were not on speaking terms at that point, Selvaraju had immediately put a stop to their encroachment.[14] After some time, her brother-in-law went to Selvaraju and asked for some space since there was little room to cook inside his own house. Since relations between them had become cordial again, Selvaraju consented. Mala took advantage of this situation to annex Selveraju's *kollai* and erect her own outdoor kitchen. Initially, she had used a circle of stones to form a make-shift stove. She had graduated to a semi-permanent mud stove. Now, she was using bricks to build a permanent kitchen.

After the fence construction, Mala had still been left with enough space to resurrect her outdoor kitchen, albeit on a more compact scale. Why had they had not erected the fence even closer to her house since that was her rightful entitlement? What if she encroached further eastwards in future? First, Mala had cleverly extended her roof such that it jutted over, and the rainwater fell onto Selvaraju's *kollai*. Therefore, the fence could not be physically placed any closer. Second, as Upputanni lineage-mate Govindasamy explained,

We allowed for one and a half feet away from the dead tree. We did not inch closer even though we had a right to. So that we do not have to be embarrassed in future by having to take down an incorrectly placed fence. If at any point, Mala has her land surveyed and mounts a legal challenge, she will find that we have not encroached on any part of her portion. We have kept well within our own land.

Additionally, when asked why they had not left the dead tree standing, as a testament to Mala's atrocities and as a further boundary marker, Govindasamy replied,

> We have fulfilled all and only the measures that we had informed the police we would undertake. If we let the tree stand, then it may be interpreted as us planning to cause further trouble even after our stated aims have been achieved. We demolished the illegal encroachments, erected the fence and felled the dead tree. We left the tree stump. As an additional boundary marker, we planted a living thorn hedge. We meticulously kept to our remit. We made sure our actions had legal justifications. We made certain that we could not be accused, at any point, of overstepping our boundaries to exact revenge.

Twirling one's moustache, wielding one's machetes and bamboo staffs, throwing punches and stones and cursing fluently: these are some ways to wage a feud. Using one's intellect, conferring and cooperating with one's allies (in this case, fellow lineage-mates), and tactically utilizing the police, the law, and the courts: these are equally prevalent and viable ways with which to handle a conflict. At the conclusion of the fencing, Mala was tactically, though perhaps only temporarily, outmanoeuvred. Although she was able to retain, albeit on a smaller scale, the use of her outdoor space, her wider encroachments were severely curtailed. She also lost any support that she had among the villagers who were equally aghast at her resorting to killing a laden coconut tree to assert her claims. Even the representatives that she had sent to request that the tree be felled, the *panchayat* president and one of the landlords on the street that she and her husband often worked for, now repudiated her. Expecting to also benefit from any extra territory Mala may successfully appropriate, both her brothers-in-law (Azhagu and Mani) had supported and added their own claims upon Selvaraju's *kollai*, to the extent of violently attacking their fellow lineage-mates. Azhagu had even publicly renounced all lineage ties. He declared that he no longer needed his lineage-mates. In future, he was going to depend on and defer only to himself; 'I am going to be my own king and minister!' In so doing, he asserted his individual sovereignty in defiance of lineage authority and sociality. Now, however, both her brothers-in-law distanced themselves from Mala. They promised their lineage-mates that they would not intervene in whatever measures were undertaken to secure the property. Mala was literally left spitting (every day at Selvaraju's widow's doorstep as a deliberate and yet indirect insult) and sputtering (about the so-called illicit liaisons between the members of her natal lineage – between her classificatory fathers and brothers – and Selvaraju's widow and daughters). This meant that her natal lineage also withdrew from one of its most important duties – to come to the aid of its daughters in her time of need – and, instead, pledged to abandon her to her fate from then on. An individual (Mohan and his nuclear family) were extracted from his imbrications in sociality (lineage, street, and affinal) and rendered discrete. Premised upon disengagement, this abstracted individuality is not so much freedom as social anathema and therefore a harrowing punishment.

Shared Territory, Individual Rights

The ebbs and flows of a particular feud – its dramatic eruptions, its muted subsidence, and the tense hiatus in between – over territory with one's lineage-mates suggest that the feud is a story that the Kallars tell themselves about themselves: their meta-commentary about their own society and their obsessions. Just like the Balinese and their cockfights (Geertz 1975b), the purpose is interpretive. There is a theatricality not only to the narration of past feuds but the waging of feuds themselves. Among the Piranmalai Kallars, Dumont (2000: 310–311) notes, the 'vehemence of the speech and gestures seemed to convey more than the unbridled violence of the feelings: a certain stylization, with the bystanders looking on ... as if at a spectacle.' Encompassing a specific repertoire of emotional, aesthetic, and cathartic qualities, feuds are definitely a performance of sociality (see also Turner 1996). However, the Kallar preoccupation with feuds also embodies their attempts to grapple with an unsolvable ethical problem.

Lineage territories are framed by the establishment and exercise of a localized sovereignty, at least with regard to non-lineage members. Within the lineage itself, however, matters are not so clear-cut. The tension between their shared lineage kinship and their discrete nuclear households and delineated individual rights lies at the root of lineage kinship. Their narrating of these feuds is part of their struggle to reconcile lineage solidarity and the egalitarian ethic upon which it is premised with intense politico-economic rivalries and the agonistic kinship that this fuels. Their dilemma revolves around a question of intimacy – about where the boundaries should be between the individual and the social.

Mapping the myriad ways in which atomistic individuals and discrete households dissolve and flow into each other in this liminal space, this chapter has demonstrated how the very amorphousness of the *kollai* eases and therefore generates lineage kinship. Measuring, mapping, and fencing represent the isolating, pinioning, and precise division of the lineage into its constituent atoms. The delineation of shared territory into individual shares reduces the ambiguity of *kollai*s and therefore the ease of everyday intra-lineage relations. Lineage sociality thrives within the fluidity of interactions and the nebulousness of territory. Attempts to compromise this ambiguity result in customarily subterranean tensions erupting into violence.

And yet a sense of territory – as a space where rights are asserted and power exercised – also fundamentally constitutes the lineage. Kallar histories have demonstrated how central coercion and violence are to their acquisition of resources, formations of small-scale polities, and exercise of power. Violence has been a vital part of the Kallars' strategy to transform themselves from peripheral subjects to localized but pivotal citizens and sovereigns. For them, violence is productive. Not just of power but also of kinship. Whenever a dispute breaks out between lineage-mates in Vaduvur, someone is sure to remark, 'At five years old, they are siblings; at ten years old, they become lineage-mates (*pankalis*)'. Since their descent is traced to a common ancestor, lineage-mates are classificatory brothers. Since in its etymological and jural sense *pankali* means 'shareholder' with claims on a patrimonial estate, brothers are also lineage-mates. This oblique aphorism simply means that feuding is an inevitable part of fraternal and fraternal-like (lineage) kinship and sociality. Lineage-mates, like brothers, are expected to fight – they have too many things at stake with and in each other. To dwell on its disruptive components would be to underestimate the viability, centrality, and legitimacy of violence as a mode of agency *and* sociality for the Kallars. The ritually and jurally sanctioned division of the collective lineage sacrifice into clearly delineated individual shares articulates one form of lineage sociality. It materializes the values of uniformity (of individual shares) and therefore equality (of the rights of lineage citizenship). When this ethic of individuality meets the messy realities of everyday life amidst the *kollai*, yet another and more disputatious form of lineage sociality emerges. An eruption of a feud into a violent fight may appear to undermine lineage kinship. But this would be to seriously underestimate the generative potential of feuds. Feuds do not dam the fluidity of lineage sociality. They merely redirect the flows, carve out new channels, and therefore produce new tributaries.

Notes

1. Deva, a former president of Vaduvur Vadapathy Panchayat and then current secretary of the Needamangalam Union.

2. Vanitha was referred to a specialist in Thanjavur, where she underwent tests to rule out brain or nerve damage. She remained in hospital for a week. Kavya was discharged after two days. However, the *kaviccu* (fishy) smell from her matted and blood-soaked hair remained even after repeated washing. Sethu had outpatient treatment, although a glass fragment embedded in his leg went

septic and he was in great pain for some time. Azhagu was also admitted for three days to get wounds to his head and arms treated. All of them have since recovered.

3. Hindu persons are composed of substance-codes (blood, cooked food, and knowledge), which are transferred between persons, kin, and castes. These substance-codes may intermingle within bodies but are inseparable from the outside world. Substance-codes continually circulate between persons and their external environment. They are transformed through social interactions, and the exchange of substances changes the internal composition of a person. Therefore, the Hindu person is dividual, relationally constituted, and composite.

4. This was all the more painful given that in 2008 moderately skilled artisans were paid INR 200–250 per day along with two meals, while skilled *acaris* were paid between INR 250 and 350.

5. The father of the then current *panchayat* president.

6. The original village of the Kandiyar lineages of Serrukan Vanniyar Street is Peraiyur, further south from Vaduvur, near the nearby town of Mannargudi. Escaping desperate circumstances in Peraiyur, one of their ancestors had come to Vaduvur in order to eke out a living. In Vaduvur, he married a daughter from one of the three Vanniyar lineages on Serrukan Vanniyar Street and chose to reside uxorilocally. He was the progenitor of the only Kandiyar lineage residing in what had traditionally been a Vanniyar-only street. This is a rare contravention of the correlation between filiation and residence. Members of this Kandiyar lineage say that they know that they still have kin in their original village and that their original lineage deity resides there. However, they have never returned to Peraiyur. Unusually, they have chosen to adopt the lineage deity of their Vanniyar neighbours as their own. Through the cultivation of relations of affinity and uxorilocality, these Kandiyars have made Vaduvur their native place.

7. Such historical information is also referenced when it comes to deciding who has the rights to harvest these valuable sources of timber.

8. Agricultural fields located outside of the *ur* occupy a somewhat nebulous category. They are referred to as *vayal katus* (field-wilderness) and are treacherous places, especially at night. The ghosts that traverse the thorny *katus*, from which the *urs* are relatively protected, also haunt cultivated fields.

9. For examples in Africa, see Turner (1996), Gluckman (1956), Fortes (1970), Evans Pritchard (1940), and Fortes and Evans Pritchard (1940). For the Middle East, see Peters (1990). For South Asia, see Barth (1959).

10. There are also caste and gender dimensions to feuds. Most of the Upputanni lineage-wives intervened so as to prevent their husbands from being hurt

or humiliated. However, one woman, Mala, has been the catalyst to many fights. Her constant encroachments on Surendran's territory and the frequent skirmishes between her and the women in Surendran's household prompted the latter to arrange and pay for a land survey. However, Mala had even disrupted this attempt to permanently resolve the quarrel. Having obviously anticipated the violence, she had stockpiled weapons. Often, new conflicts are initiated or fast fading ones reignited through the involvement of women since this is seen to challenge male honour and masculine aptitude which are premised on the control of women. The association of the Kallar caste with hyper-sensitivity to insults to their honour and resorting to violence to retaliate or coerce also implicates Kallar women. Simultaneously, Kallar women are expected to control such eruptions more than the men are. They are more admired for their fortitude, pragmatism, and self-possession than for outright displays of wrath. At another fight on K.K.V. Street between the then *panchayat* president and several of his lineage-mates and street-mates, his wife did not herself get involved in the fight. Unlike the intervening mother and sister of the main assailant, she did not even come out of her house. She did, however, search the house for machetes, poles, and projectile weapons. She had them lined up behind the door to be handed out to her husband and his kinsmen should they require them. Her insouciant yet practical initiatives that simultaneously did not undermine male prerogatives were greatly admired.

11. Two other members of the Upputanni lineage were also present at this investigation in their capacity as complainants. While I was not personally present at the police station, the account of the inquiry was garnered from interviewing the two complainants.

12. *Kuli* is the local unit of land measurement. A *kuli* is equal to 144 square feet and 13.3776 square metres.

13. It later emerged that Mala had threatened to commit suicide right in front of them if they came. Worried that she might carry out her threats and even more by the prospect of getting embroiled in a potentially even more fraught situation, they opted to stay out of it.

14. When Mala went around the village insisting that Selvaraju had given her the *kollai*, this incident was recalled to repudiate her claims. If Selveraju had given the *kollai* to her when he was alive, why had he then violently dismantled her earlier erections?

4

Juridical Deliberations and Self-Government

Place stories (*sthala puranams*) are a rich genre in Hindu narrative traditions. These narratives evoke and vivify a site through the doings of deities and devout people. The entire Indian subcontinent is a map of myths, legends, and stories layered onto each other (Eck 2012). Bearing the traces of deities and the footprints of epic heroes, remote villages and tiny hamlets are made part of the vast Indian subcontinent and the infinite cosmos. Intensely local stories become part of the great Hindu epics. Vaduvur too is a place where gods may have roamed, kings have tarried, and poets have praised. This rich place history has given Vaduvur many divine sobriquets. Ekadasi Village – because it was on an Ekadasi[1] day that Vaduvur was gifted to the Brahmins. An Abhimana Divyadesam – for a temple dear to Lord Vishnu. Vagularanyam Kshetram or Magizhankadu – for the mesmerizing fragrance wafting from its groves of medlar[2] trees that can charm the gods themselves. Bhaskara Kshetram – the beloved of the sun god. Dhakshina Ayodhya – the southern avatar of Lord Rama's perfect capital, city and court. The current name Vaduvur itself has many meanings. While *ur* refers to village, *vativu* is an adjective meaning beauty. Vaduvur is supposed to have derived its name from its verdant beauty. More prevalent are the notions that the name Vaduvur is derived from imperfection – *vatu* (blemish, scar) and *ur* (village). One explanation is that in 190 CE, a mighty battle was fought between the Chola king Karikalan and his rivals, the Chera and Pandya confederacy and their allies in Venni (now Kovilvenni). Having been victorious, the Chola soldiers rested and recuperated in Vaduvur. The village's name comes from the great battle wounds (*vatu*) that these Chola warriors had suffered. This is echoed in another variant of this etymological exegesis.

Vaduvur's multiple origin myths form the crux of the next chapter. But we will skip ahead to the aftermath of one such myth here, that of the long-lost statue of the god Rama. Somehow Vaduvur acquired the sublime statue of Rama that the god himself had wrought. This, along with a statue of Rama's wife, Sita, was to be established in Vaduvur's main temple. However, they were still missing the icons of Rama's brother Lakshmana and his simian devotee, Hanuman. The sculptor wrought a beautiful Hanuman icon. However, his statue of Lakshmana was flawed – it was too feminine. So, this became the icon of the boundary goddess Pidari in the Pidari Amman temple. They had another statue made. This one had a blemish on its face and had to be discarded. They had a third statue made which turned out perfect and now resides in the main sanctum of Vaduvur's Kothandaramasamy Temple. No one knows what happened to the blemished second statue. But this lost icon is what haunts Vaduvur. Its imperfection resonates through the village's current name. More than epithets praising its serene beauty and divine resonance, these flaws are what capture the ethos of Vaduvur, at least in the Kallar imagination. For Kallars, the collective ambience of Vaduvur is primarily one of trouble.

Vaduvur Vampu, Konur Kompu. Just as the village of Konur is known for its horns (*kompu*) or the quality of its fine cattle, Vaduvur is renowned for its mischief, quarrels, and trouble (*vampu*). This makes those living in neighbouring villages reluctant to contend with Vaduvur residents. Places do not just have stories; they also have a spirit, an ethos. In her evocation of the collective ambience of Sringeri, the pilgrimage town in Karnataka, Prasad (2007: 25) notes that ethics is derived from the term 'ethos'. Ethos, despite being variously glossed over as a characteristic spirit, manners or customs, the prevailing tone of a sentiment, a people, or community, and the quality of an institution or system, is actually also place specific. Ethos brings together 'senses of place, placeness, public, community and moral ambience'. Sensitivity to its locus re-establishes ethos as a 'social act and as a product of a community's character' (Reynolds 1993: 327). Kallars have a reputation for hot-temperedness, sensitivity to insults, and readiness to resort to violence – qualities that have not simply been ascribed to the Kallars but are also unapologetically and actively cultivated by them. These characteristics are also deemed to adhere to their village. Vaduvur has become a metonym for the proclivities, personality, and reputation of its dominant caste.

The substantial equivalence between the Kallars and Vaduvur is a matter not simply of particular qualitative essences but of a specific history of political economy. Their troublesome reputation has been vital to their successes in penetrating into existing agrarian structures, asserting their own control over these productive enterprises, and attaining economic dominance. Being troublesome is a productive mode of agency for the Kallars. It is how they were able to accrue power, exercise political dominance, and thwart resistance. Their troublesome temperament does not just underpin their politico-economic dominance. More fundamentally, their sociality, even among themselves, pivots around this premise. Chapter 3 focused on the Kallars themselves acknowledging that one of the actualities of lineage kinship is a proximate hostility. This hostility is a product of their proximity – as shareholders in a corporate estate and as neighbours sharing space. Precisely because they are equals in terms of status (as caste-mates and agnatic kinsmen) but rivals in terms of politico-economic enterprises is why their antagonism is so intense. The intimacy that underpins their kinship is always an agonistic one. These internecine tensions mean that conflict, while certainly not welcome, is always co-present with cohabitation, so much so that it is an unremarkable feature of village sociality. Given the vitality of disputes to their political hegemony and its ubiquity in their sociality, the Kallars have also devised elaborate mechanisms and erudite protocols with which to process conflicts.

This chapter follows the thread of disputes, this time towards their possible resolution. Having established the polity's territorial foundations in Chapter 3, here I explore its juridical dimensions. How have specific laws been formulated, interpreted, and locally applied to form a jurisdiction? Expanding outwards from the lineage, I turn to yet another kinship-polity – the street and specifically its juridical body, the street tribunal. Rather than the successful settlement of disputes, their chronic failure is what is of concern. Not only did the street tribunal often fail to resolve disputes, but often it could not even convene itself as an adjudicatory body. The defiance of such authorities is indicative of competing assertions of sovereignty – between constituent lineages and the street they constitute – which fuels such kinship-polities. Everyday life on the street appears genial on the surface. However, it is also simmering with hostility, with the potential to escalate into violence. Neighbourly conviviality – even street festivals – are threaded through with competitiveness and pregnant with hostility. Aggression, among the Kallars, is the mode of political relations. Even the very mechanisms set up to temper agonistic drives are themselves often implicated in these political assertions.

Street Life, Street-Civic

The mothers-in-law living on K.K.V. Street pulled at one end of the rope. Meanwhile, their daughters-in-law pulled at the other end. Just when it looked like their perennial battle could be settled once and for all, the rope snapped. Both parties fell onto their rear ends. Their watching neighbours collapsed with laughter. Young men, part of the 'K.K. Vanniyar Street Excellence Development Society', like their fathers before them, had organized this sports day on the third and last day of the Tamil harvest festival, Pongal. They had solicited donations from households on K.K.V. Street to pay for the bunting, music system, and prizes. Bunny, sack, and lemon-spoon races, skipping contests, running races, shot-put, and *kabaddi*[3] competitions are not traditionally part of Pongal celebrations. 'Pongal' means boiling over. As newly harvested rice, rich with ghee, milk, and sugar, bubbles and overflows the rim of its pot, everyone repeatedly shouts, 'Pongalo Pongal!' The ensuing rice pudding is also called *pongal*. Celebrated over four days at the beginning of Tai (mid-January–mid-February) and replete with symbols of abundant harvests and new beginnings, Pongal is the quintessential Tamil festival (Good 1983; Pandian 2009). Along with Panguni Uthiram and the Santhana Kaapu (Sandalwood Protection) for the village boundary goddess Pidari, Pongal is one of the few festivals specifically celebrated as co-residents of K.K.V. Street.

The second day of Pongal is dedicated to cattle, the quintessential pillars of farming life in Tamil Nadu. In the morning, boys and young men herded their household cattle into the pond at the end of their street. They scrubbed the animals clean before steering them home. They wound colourful streamers (often in the colours of the political parties supported by their households) around the cattle's horns and hung flower garlands around their necks. They pampered the animals with sugarcane and leftover rice pudding from the day before. Their mothers and sisters then offered their cattle prayers, waving frankincense smoke and a camphor flame before their heads. They dotted the cattle's heads with vermillion and holy ash. The boys drove the gaily decorated cattle back to the pond. The entire street had gathered on the shores. The men and boys held onto their cattle while the women and girls stood to the side. Lots had been drawn from among the K.K.V. Street residents to determine this worship's sponsors. The sponsors placed raw rice mixed with jaggery syrup, fruits, and flowers onto several banana leaves and offered prayers.

The monstrous blast of firecrackers punctured the relative calm. Released from their restraints, the frightened cattle mooed, kicked, and bolted. The boys and younger men competed to snatch the garlands decorating the cattle while keeping away from their flailing hoofs and sharp horns – a test of manly courage. The women, children, and old folk cheered their family members. This upsetting of innocent beasts induced a carnival atmosphere. Males, terminologically synonymous with bulls in Tamil, proudly held aloft their snatched prizes and compared their 'daring' exploits. The sponsors distributed the consecrated offerings to the milling crowd.

The first day of Pongal is dedicated to the sun, the energy that initiates and flows through all agrarian enterprises. Earlier that day, the households on K.K.V. Street prepared to cook the requisite rice pudding at the auspicious time. Usually, each household digs its own trench (*kotu vettutal*) in the packed earth in front of their porch, into which they pile the firewood casuarina[4] tree kindling to start the fire. Only on K.K.V. Street do the residents wait for a group of senior Kallar men from the street to initiate the digging.

These men walked down the street stopping for a few minutes at each household. They scooped up the top layer of earth at each doorway. Only after they had moved to the next house did the male heads of the households take over the digging, deepening the trenches further. This variation on the Pongal ritual repertoire is unique to their street, the residents claim, and part of their special camaraderie. When I asked Veeran, a K.K.V. resident, why he did not move into his Singaporean sister's more luxurious and then empty house in another street, he was aghast.

> Her house is in East Street! No man would voluntarily want to live on that street! No one would look in on you even if you were lying dead. Even dogs will not look in on you. Those Kandiyar lineages are rich, so they are stuck up and keep to themselves. On our street, we are sociable. We care about each other. We partake of each other's joys and sorrows.[5]

As soon as the fire is lit, a fierce contest developed among the households to see who could make their rice boil over first. The street-mates piled on the firewood and stoked the fire. Triumphant cries of 'Pongalo Pongal' punctuated the smoky air as the winners announced their abundantly cascading rice.

One does not simply reside on a street (*teru*); one belongs to it. The street is an extension of the lineage onto a wider geopolitical terrain. With few exceptions, several lineages from the same clan often live on one street. Residents of the same street are classificatory fathers and brothers. They are termed 'street shareholders' (*teru pankalis*) and 'street-mates' (*teruvan*). On K.K.V. Street,[6] along with three artisan lineages, there are three main Kallar lineages belonging to the Vanniyar clan. The K. K. Vanniyar and Tontini lineages occupy the southern end of K.K.V. Street. They share the same lineage deity (Viranar) and sacrificial cult. This denotes that they are a result of the fission of a large lineage into two now separate but still related segments. Meanwhile, the Upputanni lineage occupies the northern end of the street. They have a separate lineage deity (Ravuttar) and cult. This, along with their street being named after the founding ancestor of another lineage, suggests that the Upputanni lineage are later arrivals to K.K.V. Street.

The fundamental rights that animate the lineage – in kin, deity, cult, and territory – also frame the street. K.K.V. street-mates have rights to the Pillaiyar temple and cult dedicated to the elephant-headed god and his brother Murugan. This temple was financed entirely through levying a compulsory tax (*vari*) on the K.K.V. street-mates. Membership in a street is an automatic right for all males born there. Taxation activates this membership for the male heads of households. Tendering the tax entitles one to full representation in the temple cult and the street council. Every month, each male and married street-mate pays INR 5 into the street fund. Funds accumulated over more than forty years financed the construction of the street temple in 1995. Apart from investing in the temple infrastructure, street-mates also sponsor annual worship ceremonies. During the entire month of Margazhi (mid-December–mid-January), each household on the street, sometimes doubling up with another to give everyone an opportunity, sponsored a forty-eight-day ritual (*mandalabishekam*) at the Pillaiyar temple. Entry for residents of other streets to this Pillaiyar temple is restricted. Since all the street-mates have made equal contribution to the construction of this temple, theoretically everyone has equal rights to it. No one lineage has exclusive rights over this temple.

The street, given that it tends to be constituted mainly by Kallar lineages, is also framed by ideals of equality. Like with the lineage and its individual members and households, there tend to be tensions between the collective interests of the street and that of its constituent lineages. Even amidst the conviviality of K.K.V. Street's Pongal celebrations, the Upputanni lineage stands somewhat aloof. The Upputanni lineage has never waited for their digging to be initiated by the street representatives. They have always dug their own trenches or enlisted the help of only their own lineage-mates.

The Upputanni lineage always maintains some distance from their street. Their comparatively recent arrival to this street and their geographical isolation at its far end foster this diffidence. However, they also actively resist becoming too enmeshed in their street's sociality, so much so that they do not even participate in their street's sacrifice to the village boundary goddess Pidari Amman at her Santhana Kappu festival. The Upputanni lineage does not contribute to the purchase of the live goats. Consequently, they do not have rights to the post-sacrificial meat. They do not even go on the street's procession to tender their worship and tribute to the goddess. According to the Ayyakannu, the Upputanni lineage headman:

> Today the goddess remains in her temple with her worshippers coming to her. Seventy years ago, she went forth, atop a chariot, on an annual procession. She was carried all around her kingdom to receive worship and tributes from her

subjects [see Chapter 8]. During this procession around her realm, her chariot would stop in front of our houses. We offered prayers to the goddess. We sacrificed a goat of our own. Having accepted our worship and sacrifice, the goddess returned to her temple. Until the next year.

Rather than as part of the collective sacrifice on behalf of the entire street, the Upputanni lineage had offered a private sacrifice as a lineage. This singular honour was afforded to few other lineages. Only lineages that had had significant roles in the traditional polity over which the goddess was sovereign were allowed to offer their own sacrifice. That the Upputanni lineage did not have rights to the goats sacrificed by the street denotes their singular superiority. Their relationship with the polity and their divine sovereign had not been mediated by the street. It was direct. The traversals of the goddess may have ceased for over seventy years. However, the distinction accorded to the Upputanni lineage can still be glimpsed amid the palimpsest of irrevocably transformed and/or abandoned rituals in Vaduvur. Together with their digging their own trenches for the Pongal fire, the Upputanni lineage's non-participation in a street festival is an assertion of autonomy – of their own lineage against incorporation into, encompassment, or mediation by the street. Their disavowal of the street's authority and the emphasis on their direct and singular relation to their sovereign goddess manifest competing assertions of sovereignty: between the lineage and the street.

This, as we see, is a fraught milieu. A fiercely egalitarian ethic collides with asymmetrical politico-economic realities. A collective authority's demands of subjection crash against individuals adamant about not compromising their autonomy. Communal imperatives contend with competing interests. This can and does ignite into conflicts and sometimes violence. Notions of customary justice and the processes of local jural bodies are vital to the micromechanics of co-existence in this intensely competitive milieu. To temper these tensions, the Kallars have formulated a number of mechanisms of arbitration and resolution. I turn next to these juridical bodies, specifically the street tribunal.

Street Judiciary and Adjudicatory Failures

Every new moon night (*amavasai*), the male heads of households on K.K.V. Street gather at the bridge over the canal marking their street's boundary. The Street Council President had sent the 'village watchman' (*talaiyari*) around to inform the members. To facilitate everyone's schedules, they convened this regular meeting (*amavasai kuttam*) late at night. They discussed general topics to do with the welfare of their street. Each member tendered their compulsory monthly tax (*vari*) that goes towards the street fund. They use this fund to finance street initiatives – from building and consecrating the street's Pillaiyar temple to staging annual Panguni Uthiram worship there.[7] Only male heads of households tender this tax. Only they form the local government, the street council (*teru kuttam*). One belongs to a street on the basis of residing there. However, only married males have the vote and as such not only represent but also encompass their households. From among their number, they elect a president, vice president, treasurer, and an assistant treasurer. They tried to ensure that these posts are evenly distributed among all the constituent lineages. This is the regular meeting.

Like the lineage, the street is also a sovereign organization, invested in establishing, protecting, and augmenting its independent authority over a localized territory. All Kallar kinship-polities, from the lineage to the regional polity (*natu*), have juridical remits. The street council is charged with arbitrating disputes among the members of its constituent lineages. In the event of an inheritance distribution following the death of a patriarch or a dispute among the members of the street, an extraordinary meeting of the street council is convened. This is a juridical body which is invested with the authority to adjudicate disputes, pronounce judgments, tender punishments, and propose restitutions. Again, only married males form the jurists who hear the testimonies and sit in judgment on the litigants from the street. While attendance to street meetings is technically open to everyone from that street, women and youths tend not to attend unless expressly invited to do so. They are usually asked to attend only if they are litigants, witnesses, or character references. Even so, they do not speak unless expressly invited to proffer their opinions. This is part of these tribunals' protocols.

As a kinship-polity, the street materializes an assertion of self-government and yet another instantiation of a local and parallel sovereignty. More so than pre-colonial states and colonial regimes, the nation state and its agents (the police, law courts, and the attendant bureaucracies) have been able to penetrate much deeper into villages and their local affairs. However, this amplified reach of the Indian nation state and its legal institutions has not entirely dislodged and replaced the Kallar's customary judicial bodies (see also Dumont [2000] in relation to the Piranmalai Kallar in 1950s Madurai). These Kallar villagers continue to appeal to older forms of jurisprudence, not in place of but alongside the nation state's legal institutions. Customary judicial agents and the official functionaries of the state represent different, equally valid and sometimes competing systems of justice. Litigants resort to either or even both systems concurrently depending on their motives for seeking adjudication and where they expect to receive favourable verdicts (see also Kapila 2003). However, it is not just expediency that propels the appeal to plural and parallel juridical authorities. Juridical analogues, namely the kinship-polity and the nation state, are also used to reinforce the authority of each other. The distinctions between customary and state law are collapsed. As evident in the reverberations of the territorial dispute in Chapter 3, their combined weight is used to amplify each other's authority and exact retribution following a feud.

And yet, in nearly two years of fieldwork, I have never been able to witness a property settlement or dispute arbitration. I have never even been able to behold a street council. This is not because there were no disputes during my fieldwork. Nor is it for want of trying on my part. My interest in attending these arbitrations was so acute as to be considered vulgar. Street tribunals are not convened for general entertainment or even for my anthropological edification. They are to resolve real disputes. Time and again, a meeting would be scheduled only for it to be cancelled at the last minute. This was because one or the other of the concerned parties refused to show up or be subject to the street tribunal's directives. I became so frustrated as to threaten (only partly in jest) to throw a rock at someone and start a dispute, even at the risk of hurting an innocent party and inviting my own punishment, just so that I could observe a street tribunal for myself.

This recalls Dirks's (1994) experience with a religious festival, among another group of Kallars in nearby Pudukkottai. He eagerly anticipated attending a ritual dedicated to a village deity, Aiyanar, only to find that this festival had become the casualty of factional disputes. Not only had this festival not occurred for seven years but it was also unlikely to be performed that year. While disappointed, Dirks responded by interrogating the very non-incidence of this festival. Similarly, my own question became not so much why street tribunals are convened or what form they take but why they often do not occur.

Dirks (1994: 494) formulates a theory of ritual based on the non-incidence of said ritual. Defying the dichotomous associations between rituals and order versus everyday practices and resistance, he analyses the ritual, or rather its non-occurrence itself, as a site of contention. A ritual is an arena of contestation not only among elite groups or between elite and non-elite groups; it is also 'a struggle between discourse and event, between what could be said and what could be done'. Similarly, arbitration tribunals are also sites where power is asserted, and authority disputed or defied. The non-incidence of street tribunals and the negotiations for their occurrence, which often do not bear fruit, are a 'core arena for resistance' – for subversion of norms of authority. Such tribunals are not only sites for struggle between rival individuals and competing lineages; they are also arenas for the contesting of the very power of these tribunals. Their non-incidence is in itself a commentary on the mandate that street tribunals wield. What is at stake is the very constitution of the authority of these juridical bodies.

Next, I contend with the obdurate impediments to the street council's adjudicatory processes, to the very convening of this juridical body. Delving into the details of two disputes – (*a*) a territorial dispute among the Upputanni lineage-mates and (*b*) a dispute over an insult to honour among the lineages on K.K.V. Street – that came under the K.K.V. Street council's jurisdiction, I grapple with why these tribunals repeatedly fail to occur. What are the and why are there persistent challenges to their legitimacy? What constitutes the authority of such bodies?

Boundary Disputes and Contravened Protocols

The previous chapter was concerned with territorial disputes among the Upputhanni lineage. Before Mohan and his wife, Mala, resorted to arboricide, they had pressed Western Vaduvur's *panchayat* president, from K.K.V. Street, and two other prominent street-mates to convene a street tribunal. The couple wanted the tribunal to consider their claims to more land in the Upputanni *kollai*. They also wanted their lineage-mate Selvaraju's coconut tree, which they claimed was intruding upon their land, to be felled. Upon receiving the complaint, the street tribunal sent the village watchman to inform the Upputanni lineage-mates that a meeting was to be convened that night. The Upputanni lineage-mates were incensed. They categorically refused to attend.

Convening a street tribunal is not a mundane matter. Specific protocols must be followed. In this agonistic milieu, where the absolute equality of agnatic kinsmen is vociferously asserted, these protocols constitute the authority of these juridical bodies. Given that no superior capacity or status is accorded to these judiciaries, adhering to these protocols is what legitimizes these informal bodies. The Upputanni lineage-mates cited two specific violations of juridical precedence to substantiate their non-compliance to the street tribunal's summons. Govindasamy explained:

> As the defendants in the suit, we should have been consulted first; before the proposed meeting. About whether a tribunal should be convened at all. And if we agreed, we should have been conferred with about mutual arrangements for the meeting. Not simply informed of its prearranged time and location.

That the entreaties of such an odious member of their lineage had been privileged before the rights of reputable landlords like themselves added insult to injury.

Second, it was not the prerogative of the *panchayat* president to call for a street council meeting. Even if he did live on their street. The *panchayat* president is a democratically elected functionary of the Indian nation state. He is responsible only for implementing national and state initiatives at the village level. Rather, the remit belonged to the head of the street council. It was he who had been chosen by his fellow street-mates to govern street matters. Only he had the authority to convene street council meetings and call for his fellow street-mates to attend. Citing these procedural discrepancies, the other Upputanni lineage-mates ignored the summons. While refusing to attend this improperly convened meeting, they conveyed their willingness to attend future meetings over this dispute, provided they were convened according to the correct procedures – with the consent of both parties and by the street council's actual president.

The Upputanni lineage's defiance angered the other street council members who had waited for them for several hours. They sent the watchman to find out why the Upputanni lineage-mates had not arrived. When apprised of the reasons for the Upputanni lineage's non-compliance, a street council member thundered:

> They spurned our offer to arbitrate. They do not respect our efforts. Upputanni men clearly do not respect their street. So, we will not convene a meeting to arbitrate their matters again.

My hopes of finally being able to witness a street council meeting in action were extinguished.

Insulted Honour and Postponed Tribunals

Every year, the teenage boys of K.K.V. Street organized a *kabaddi* competition. They solicited donations from the street's households, especially the wealthier ones, to finance this sporting event. Only if these funds proved insufficient would the organizers approach merchants in Vaduvur's commercial district. The street-mates do contribute. Since the more generous donors' names are printed on the programme and also read aloud during the prize-giving ceremony, prominent landlords sponsored the larger cash prizes to flaunt their status. In 2007, Tontani lineage-mate and current *panchayat* president, Masilamani, pledged INR 1,000 and Upputanni lineage-mate Surendran promised INR 500. Their names were duly publicized during the event. The next day, when the boys approached Masilamani and Surendran for their pledged donations, they were told to return later. The boys came by again and again only to be repeatedly rebuffed. They were

also shouted at and even threatened. K.K.V. Street residents criticized these two
men in private.

> Why did they pledge the money and allow their names to be announced on stage
> if they did not intend to fulfil their commitments? They could have donated a
> small sum and forgone the publicity. They wanted to show off that they are 'big
> men'. However, the did not behave like big men. They are cheating young boys.

In 2008, remembering the previous year's rebuff, the boys approached everybody
on the street and even merchants in the markets. However, they deliberately
ignored Masilamani and Surendran. When Masilamani heard of this, he offered
to make good on his pledge this year. He emphasized that he had the money ready
and waiting. However, the boys refused to budge.

With the backing of Masilamani's defeated opponent in the elections for
panchayat president, fellow lineage-mate and brother-in-law Velayutham, as well
as K.K.V. lineage-mates with whom Masilamani had recently fought, the boys
persisted with the competition. The rented radio and speakers blared Tamil film
songs. Bunting and streamers gaily flapped in the wind. Groups of young boys
started congregating on the field. The opening moves of the first game were in
progress. However, the competition never reached its conclusion. A humiliated
Masilamani called the police. They came and confiscated the audio equipment and
took the adult overseer of the competition into custody. Following the murder of
a Muttiraiyar boy by a Kallar man from K.K.V. Street in 2008, the police had to
give permission for all large gatherings. The boys were caught unawares. As the
panchayat president, Masilamani had known:

> The advertisements state that the *kabaddi* competition is organised by the
> 'K.K. Vanniyar Street Excellence Development Society', consisting of all the
> street's residents. Then, I should also be included. How can you say that this
> event is brought to you by everyone on the street, and then exclude certain
> residents? Then say it is organised by a particular person not the entire street.
> Otherwise, I will not allow this competition to take place.

Enraged, the boys vowed:

> We will hold the competition next week. This time, we will make sure we inform
> the police. We will even have a policeman standing at the venue to oversee the event.

His perceived humiliation, especially at the hands of young boys, no doubt
motivated Masilamani to stop this event. However, the support that the boys

received from and the machinations of Masilamani's politico-economic rivals from K.K.V. Street exacerbated an already tense situation.

Yet other street-mates felt that such a stalemate did not reflect well on their street, especially in the aftermath of the gory 2008 murder. They counselled the two opposing parties to settle their differences. They planned to convene a council meeting to discuss subsequent proceedings. These plans were also abandoned at the last minute. One of their street-mates was getting married the next morning. The residents did not want any fallout from the meeting to disrupt the wedding. Instead, they offered to reschedule the meeting for the next night. By this time Masilamani had been pacified and he rescinded his threat. Although he still felt it was wrong to exclude a street-mate from an occasion bringing honour to the whole street, he would not disrupt the competition again. This tribunal was abandoned because the main litigant withdrew his complaint. A sort of peace returned to the street. And once again, my hopes were dashed.

Juridical 'Non-Events', Precarious Authority

How can a people so independent, so quarrelsome and so reckless in their disputes and their claims as the Kallars obey an authority chosen from their own rank, without any other guarantee than its technical competence – an authority represented by a more or less fluctuating group of villagers?

Dumont (2000: 324) himself wondered about the efficacy of these local tribunals. After all, among certain similarly socially located castes such as the Uthumalai Maravar, there is no 'indigenous justice, for nobody would obey it – each family head is as independent as a king' (Dumont 2000: 324). Refusing to recognize, let alone subject oneself to, a higher authority is an assertion of sovereignty. Dumont (2000: 315) concludes that the singular dispositional equanimity and the technical competence of the headmen jurists imbue the tribunal with authority. These exert a moral pressure onto the relatively more volatile and aggressive litigants to conform. The Vaduvur Kallars, on the other hand, often contest the jural competency of the judges at their tribunals. They cite their incompetence in casting doubt on the veracity and impartiality of their judgments. Moreover, the repeated failure to convene street council meetings allude to the precarity of the street tribunal's authority and the limits to its remit. More importantly, they also allude to the tensions between individual rights and collective government – contestations about the definitions and limitations of political authority.

The long-drawn-out discussions whether to even convene the tribunals, the recurrent adjournments, last-minute abandonments, and protracted appeals are a function of these customary tribunals' differential purpose. Customary judicial bodies and procedures are reparatory rather than punitive – a distinction that has long preoccupied legal anthropology (Gluckman 1956; Cohn 1959). Rather than punishment, the aims of such local juridical institutions are compromise and conciliation. Even the K.K.V. Street tribunal, notwithstanding its rivalrous milieu, was more oriented towards restitution than revenge, at least most of the time. In the matter of the thwarted *kabaddi* competition, the disputants did not approach the street council. Rather the council itself volunteered to convene a meeting to settle the differences which were seriously undermining street sociality and K.K.V. Street's reputation. Their genuine concern with not adversely affecting their street-mate's future prospects prompted the street council to postpone the tribunal. The street council's president, Kanthan, explained:

> If the street tribunal opened up bigger wounds or resulted in violence, the issue could escalate. Aggrieved parties may refuse to attend our street-mate's wedding. A sparse turnout could affect the bridegroom and his family's prestige before their affines. This is why we postponed the meeting.

They also quietly persuaded the boys not to hold their *kabaddi* contest, deferring it to the next year, to safeguard Masilamani's honour, especially since he also represented the street as the *panchayat* president. Injury to honour is as much a consideration in the tribunal's deliberations as the future welfare of the litigants, certainly more so than punishing the guilty.

These juridical bodies try to avoid judgments based on deficient facts or verdicts that are too clinical or rigid. They try to promote measured and moderate outcomes that are perhaps more demanding of the jurists. Additionally, the tribunal's authority is plural. Although more mature and experienced jurists are deferred to, there is no hierarchy among the constituents of the tribunal and therefore no ultimate authority. The verdict has to be unanimous. Therefore, deliberations can drag on without being resolved. Unexpected twists in the case or the bringing up of new evidence can mean further delays as the jurists are given more time to consult with each other. Determined obstruction by the opposing parties can also prolong these deliberations. Like the tutelary rituals in Chapter 2, the judicial process is also eminently permeable to politics. Their familiarity with the litigants means jurists are aware of the character of the parties involved and the historical permutations of the case. Embedded within the local social structure, the jurists are invested in their neighbourhood's everyday life. Therefore, the jurists are especially sensitive about not harming the petitioners' future prospects. They are also careful about not risking their village's everyday sociality by making a tense situation worse. Efficiency is often sacrificed to concerted attempts at arriving at equitable verdicts.

Jurists of street tribunals tend to live close to potential litigants. Their familiarity with the litigants' demeanours and the given case does contribute to more compassionate verdicts. However, this also entails the jurists themselves often being in direct politico-economic competition with the litigants whom they must judge. They may have a vested interest in a specific legal suit which then provokes doubts about their impartiality and the objectivity of their verdicts. Their being insufficiently removed from their street relations has the potential to compromise the moral authority that should underpin their adjudicatory undertakings and the detachment upon which perceived justice hinges. However, the interpenetration of social and spatial structure and the ubiquity of politico-economic rivalries make it impossible to entirely exclude interested parties as jurists. Apart from the Upputanni lineage itself, the other two Kallar lineages on K.K.V. Street are segments of what was once a single lineage. Could the K.K.V. Street tribunal's verdict, numerically dominated by an interested party's lineage-mates and/or by one's fierce competitors, be trusted?

More significantly, the street council's own incompetence was largely responsible for undermining its authority. Their profligacy with the funds for the Pillaiyar temple's construction and consecration cast doubts on the K.K.V. Street tribunal's prudence. Members of the K. K. Vanniyar and Tontani lineages had formed the main organization committee. As bitterly related by an artisan resident:

> These organizers spent thousands of rupees ... just stringing electric lights and speakers all the way to Vaduvur's main thoroughfare. They hired expensive musicians and lavishly spent on food and alcohol for themselves. They depleted the taxes collected from us. To generate more funds, they sold a plot of land belonging to the Pillaiyar Temple. When this proved insufficient, they borrowed from moneylenders to fund an extravagant consecration ceremony. They could not keep up with the rapidly accumulating interest payments, let alone repay the principal sum. Now, they want us to pay more tax to settle these debts. But why should we have to pay more. They are the ones who frittered the money away on frivolous things.

The Pillaiyar temple was completed in 1995. Even after two decades, however, the debts have not been settled. The newly elected street council president continues to trudge up and down K.K.V. Street persuading residents to pay additional taxes.

This exasperated the other street-mates and contributed to their persistent doubts about the council's judiciousness. Their avarice and intensive competition for localized power has undermined the moral authority of the street's 'big men'. In contrast to the objectivity that Dumont's (2000: 321) interlocutors attribute to their jurists, the K.K.V. Street residents mistrust their compromised jurists' motives, doubt their impartiality, and suspect the justice they mete out. As a result, they are unwilling to subject themselves to the street tribunal's arbitration. Given that the street tribunal's claims to influence is premised almost entirely on the voluntary (and temporary) subjection of the individual's or households' autonomy to its collective authority, this has deleterious effects on its powers.

The jurists' uneven competence and inconsistent neutrality are reasons why there is such stress on adhering to the established protocols when convening and managing street tribunals. The watchmen do formally inform all the street-mates about the monthly street meetings beforehand. However, this is more for practicality's sake. The meetings themselves are rather informal. The men leisurely saunter in, wait on the bridge, settle any outstanding matters and leave promptly after having tendered their tax. The extraordinary meetings – to resolve matters relevant to the street temple or among contending street-mates – however, are explicitly formal. There are correct procedures regarding: who should staff a street council, when and by whom a meeting should be convened, whose and how consent should be sought beforehand, when and how the respective parties must be informed, and where the council can be held. The parity between the constituent lineages and the moral authority of the judicial body itself hinge on adhering to these established protocols. Convening the street tribunal – to have a dispute subject to the scrutiny of the entire street and the judgment of the council – is a serious matter. The form it takes and its protocols are as important as the final judgment in reinforcing the tribunal's authority The Piranmalai Kallars' village or regional-level tribunals documented by Dumont (2000: 319–324) have more formal procedures. The street tribunals I describe are much smaller and more private. They are restricted to the street-mates themselves and staffed with less experienced jurists primarily constituted by the street's middle-aged male residents. Nevertheless, they retain some of the same protocols and a significant measure of the authority of the larger village tribunals. The formality of these judicial proceedings and their adherence to precedence are fundamental to the constitution of their – albeit contested – authority.

The street tribunal jurists' investment in, rather than abstraction from, their judgments contributes to perceptions of their compromised impartiality. Consequently, potential litigants attribute more neutrality to the police and the courts. After territorial and particularly violent disputes, there tends to be an automatic recourse to the law. An unfavourable verdict from a street tribunal may lead to appeals to the police and the courts and (albeit much less so) vice versa. State and non-state judicial bodies represent competing alternatives to each other. Buttressed by the law, the state, and scriptural authority, the police and judges are still deemed the ultimate arbitrators. Their legibly governmental authority supersedes that of the street tribunal's primarily moral and oral powers. Potential litigants choose between judicial bodies tactically, according to their assessment of their given options and especially chances for a favourable verdict. The result, however, is a further hollowing out of the authority of these street tribunals and their constituent jurists. This manifests a tension between but also the eventual reconciliation of two forms of citizenships – in the nation state and in a local kinship-polity.

These judicial inefficacies ultimately reveal the helplessness of a tribunal whose authority is constituted by the parties themselves rather than contingent on any external or ultimate authority. The cancellations, adjournments, and rejection of the street tribunal's attempts to arbitrate, let alone its verdicts, are testimonies to the frequent and obdurate challenges to its authority. Its authority can never simply be assumed. It is not durable but is constantly subject to contestations. Claims to authority must be repeatedly constituted, asserted, demonstrated, and defended in the teeth of competing claims for individual rights and household autonomy. Whatever influence this street tribunal has is accorded to it by the street-mates themselves. It is viable and legitimate only as an edifice of local self-government.

This is borne out through two constitutive premises: (*a*) caste isonomy and (*b*) consent. Rather than being subsumed under considerations of kinship, kingship, or divine sanctions, these principles must be analysed on their own terms. The protocols for convening street tribunals or the dispositions of the jurists materialize and elaborate upon these two principles. In the absence of coercive reinforcements, these are the only grounds upon which Kallars are willing to surrender their own autonomy and subject themselves to another authority, however reluctantly or temporarily.

First, the Kallar tribunals are never staffed by the litigant's caste inferiors or superiors. When it comes to the local judiciary, these Kallars insist on being judged only by their own and therefore their caste equals. Vaduvur's lower-caste Muttiraiyars or Dalits do take their private disputes to their caste superiors, the dominant Kallar landlords. Kallars, however, deem this an indication of the lower castes deferring to others' authority and being unable to govern themselves. Such actions on the part of the lower castes are seen as willingly conceding that final authority does not rest either in their own hands or among their own caste. K.K.V. Street's artisan castes submitting to the judgments of Kallar jurists is similarly interpreted as indicative of their subjection to a dominant caste. One of the blacksmiths was discovered to be having an affair with a lower-caste Muttiraiyar girl. This is deemed detrimental to the discipline (*kattu-patu*) and therefore co-existence of a village community premised on caste endogamy. The blacksmith's aghast parents asked the street tribunal to intervene, especially since the girl was intent on marriage. There were rumours of a plan by her kinsmen to ambush the couple's clandestine meetings, catch them red-handed, and force a marriage. This plan was relayed to some of the Kallar landlords on K.K.V. Street by their Muttiraiyar agricultural workers. Convening a meeting, the landlords prevented the artisan man from meeting his Muttiraiyar lover. They found a bride of his own caste and quickly got him married. Apparently, the street tribunal's prompt response prevented not only the artisan caste but the entire street from being humiliated. However, this also materializes the artisans' dependence on and subjection not only to an external authority but a superior one. However, such an acknowledgement is anathema to the Kallars in Vaduvur. They are adamant about being judged, *if at all*, by a jury only of their peers. This is the apotheosis of their assertions of sovereignty.

Second, their acknowledgement of the jurists' authority and the voluntariness of their subjection to it are fundamental to the constitution of the street tribunal's authority. Especially given the tribunal's waning ability to coercively enforce its judgments, the compliance of the subjects is critical.

Even then, as evident in the numerous adjournments and even non-incidence, the sovereignty of the street as articulated through these tribunals is fragile, fragmented, and subject to challenge. Litigants seek the tribunal possibly to avoid costly police and legal hearings, and pledge to be bound by its eventual rulings. However, the street tribunal's mandate comes from the *voluntary* subjection of the litigants to its authority. This was why the tribunal convened on behalf of Mohan and his wife, Mala, about the allegedly intrusive coconut tree did not have legitimacy for the Upputanni lineage-mates. Not having been properly consulted on or having given their consent to convening the hearing, they did not feel obliged to be subject to its judgments. Given that the force of such tribunals is largely moral, the defiance of the Upputanni lineage not only debilitated its mechanisms but also undermined its authority. And there was nothing that the street council could actually do to make the Upputanni lineage comply – except threaten to withdraw their adjudicatory interventions for future disputes. This impotence has not always been the case. The most serious sanction in the street tribunal's arsenal had been social ostracism. Used for especially heinous offences or in serious cases of juridical insubordination, this entailed the entire street being prohibited from 'giving them [the guilty] water if they were thirsty or fire if their hearth went out'. Lest they themselves be subject to the same sanctions, all street residents must disengage from the guilty party. The withdrawal of street sociality and the consequent atomization of the household or individual was the ultimate punishment. However, such excommunication is no longer a punishment that the street tribunal can enforce. The consensus is that the tribunal's authority is no longer as conclusive as it had been. People are no longer afraid of defying the street tribunal precisely because there are no serious consequences to their transgressions. The tribunal cannot punish, even as a last resort, but merely persuade.[8] Therefore, subjection to the authority of the tribunal involves the willingness of litigants to sublimate their autonomy and to defer to an authority that they accept, at least temporarily, as being higher than their own.

Conclusion

While there are other competing etymologies, Vaduvur is also named after a flaw – on a statue of a god who is the epitome of fraternal devotion and selfless love. To ensure that his father fulfilled his vow to an ambitious stepmother, Rama – the heir apparent, filial son, god-incarnate, and perfect man – willingly agreed to be banished for fourteen long years. Not being able to bear the separation from his brother, Lakshmana abandoned his wife, sons, royal prerogatives, and palace luxuries to follow Rama and his wife, Sita, into exile. For fourteen years, he too endured the rigours of forest life, demon attacks, and finally a long and bloody war with Ravana, the ruler of Lanka. Only when Rama and Sita's exile was over did Lakshmana also return to Ayodhya. This perfectly selfless brother's statue was the one that refused to embody the perfection a religious icon accepting worship must. Its successive 'imperfections' – femininity and then a blemish – meant that it had to be wrought three times. Despite the perfection of the third and final statue, the imperfect one is what continues to haunt Vaduvur not just through its name but also in the chronic struggle between fraternal solidarity and individual freedom, between what should be and what actually is.

Given that aggression is a medium of socio-political relations among the Kallars, feuds as much as temples, rituals cults, festivals, and plain fun constitute the street as a geopolitical entity. Yet another facet of this medium are the judicial bodies set up to temper the consequences of this aggression. Fights and the councils to arbitrate them manifest the tensions between collective investments (whether in the lineage or the street) and the atomistic thrust of competition between rivalrous kinsmen. And yet these agonistic struggles are not only a departure from but a materialization of lineage ideals – of equality and consent. This is evident from the principles that imbue these local bodies of justice with authority but also make this authority precarious. Legitimate power here is neither derived from one's superior position and the coercion it makes possible, nor the compliance forced into being by the acceptance of one's subject position in a hierarchy. The Kallars are free to challenge, refuse, and boycott if they disagree with those who are in essence their peers sitting in judgment of them. Contestations are especially vociferous given that their peers on the street tribunals are not abstracted from the everyday entanglements of kinship co-residence on the same street. Unlike jurists on bigger tribunals for the village or the region, they are not and can never be entirely disinterested. This, along with these indigenous bodies' dominant concern with preserving consensus rather than meting out punitive justice, explains their frequent defiance, adjournments, and cancellations with respect to conflict resolution and justice. This reflects their contested and precarious authority. They are also an intrinsic part of the tribunal's constitution of an authority premised upon equality among peers and compliance only through consent. Coupled with the intense competition that typifies relations between equals, this makes subjection to or even acceptance of a higher authority problematic. Competing assertions of sovereignty – individual, household, and especially separate lineages versus wider political configurations such as the street – frame Kallar kinship-polities. A mark on the face may be a blemish that mars perfection. But perfection also petrifies. The final perfect icon was fixed to the temple, to receive worship, in a pose of eternal fraternal devotion. Imperfection have produced icons that became other goddesses in other temples, gave their name to a village, and eventually led to another perfect icon. Their 'warts' – the dilemmas, contestations, defiance, failures – give life to Kallar polities. The struggle to reconcile ideals (multiple and contradictory ones at that) with everyday life makes their politics come alive and remain energetic.

Notes

1. This is the eleventh lunar day (*titi*) of each of the two lunar (the waxing and the waning) phases in a Hindu calendar month.
2. *Mimusops elengi.*
3. *Kabaddi* is a popular Indian sport that involves two teams occupying opposite ends of the field and sending a raider into their opponents' end. The raider must try to score points by tagging or wrestling members of the opposing team and returning to his own half, all the while holding his breath and chanting 'kabaddi kabaddi' repeatedly.
4. *Casuarina Equisetifolia.*

5. This comment was made also with a view to teasing me since East Street is my natal street. My father is a member of the Mela Kandiyar lineage that resides there.

6. There are two other segmentary offshoots of the larger Vanniyar lineages – which are small, each consisting only of the households of a pair of brothers.

7. The K.K.V. Street fund was even used to finance the legal defence for several street-mates following their dispute with the neighbouring Mannaiyar Street. The residents of K.K.V. Street and Mannaiyar Street have shared rights to the pond located between both their streets. This is the pond to which both parties lead their cows on Cattle Pongal to wash them and stage the necessary festivities. There is a rota of use, which the Manniyars were seen to have breached. The dispute was over precedence in access to the shared pond and the breach of customary protocol (*mamul*). A fight broke out, and police and courts were involved. Street funds were expended negotiating the court case.

8. It must be noted that the authority of local tribunals has always been based more on moral force and moderation than on punitive measures. The use of ostracism has always been exceptional (Dumont 2000: 324–327).

Part II

Parallel Citizenships, Intersecting Sovereignties

5

Vernacular Polities, Intersecting Sovereignties

The Kothandaramaswamy temple's month-long annual festival began. The elaborate eagle chariot bearing the icons of Rama, Sita, Lakshmana, and Hanuman wound its way around the streets surrounding the temple. This Garuda Sevai is held on the festival's fourth day. As I joined the deities' procession, I noticed a mechanical crane doggedly following the palanquin. The chariot, for all its grandeur, was made of wood. Fuelling its movement was human labour. There was little chance of the chariot developing mechanical failure. Even if something were to happen to the chariot, there were plenty of eager volunteers to render assistance. To bear god on his way around his realm is considered a blessing, not something to be taken lightly. So why was the crane there?

Before this annual festival itself, during the celebrations of Rama Navami (Rama's birthday), there is a flag-raising ceremony. The standard of Hanuman, Rama's most ardent devotee, is raised to signify the onset of the annual festival in a month's time. This flag, denoting the imminence of this temple's grandest ritual complex, continues to be raised before the Kallar headmen and under the Vaduvur inter-village regional polity's (*natu*) aegis. In the south Indian context, the extension of ritual honours, and the order of their distribution, is a medium for establishing and publicly displaying rank (Appadurai and Breckenridge 1976; Appadurai 1981: 73; Dirks 1993: 120–126, 289–292; Fuller 2004: 80–81; Dumont 2000: 156, 337). Here, these ritual honours publicly signal the sacerdotal authorities' (Brahmin caste's) acknowledgement of the Kallar *natu*'s authority. The Brahmins have staked prior and primary claim to the Kothandaramaswamy temple. They also increasingly appeal to a far-flung Tamil Brahmin diaspora to fund its rituals and subsistence. Kallar villagers mutter darkly about the Brahmin clergy behaving as though the temple is a diasporic project, unmoored from its situation in Vaduvur. Nevertheless, the temple's annual festival cannot commence without the oversight of Kallar headmen. Whatever the actualities of political authority, this is a symbolic admission of Kallar political dominance in Vaduvur. It ritually demonstrates the assumption by Kallar headmen of the royal role of patrons of this ritual and temple.

The right to pull the massive chariot along its processional path during the annual festival's Garuda Sevai is a singular honour. This honour is the exclusive right of the Vaduvur *natu*. Again, this is a public reiteration that this Sanskritic temple, to which the Brahmins claim priority, is firmly embedded within an overtly Kallar polity. In making visible the *natu*'s rights to this temple, this ritual makes apparent the Brahmins' admission of their deference (however loosely, temporarily and symbolically) to the political authority of the Vaduvur *natu* and its Kallar headmen – that, whatever administrative, financial, and sacerdotal regimes may be in place, the Kothandaramaswamy temple is essentially a *natu* temple.

Rama's massive chariot was dragged through the streets with the two massive ropes attached. One rope was given to a team of men from Vadapathy and the other to Thenpathy. If the heavy chariot is to move, both teams must cooperate. More often than not, however, the chariot barely moves. The intense rivalry between Vadapathy and Thenpathy breaks out into competitive flaunting, shouting matches, and skirmishes. A procession over a mere kilometre takes an entire night. One year, the dispute became so intense that the Thenpathy team simply abandoned their posts. Rama in his chariot was stranded. If more Vadapathy men had stepped in – essentially to take over Thenpathy rights to pull the chariot even if the latter had been derelict in their duties – the skirmish could have escalated into violence. This is why the mechanical crane trails behind the procession these days. It is ready to step in and move the chariot in case another clash renders it immobile. This ritual, more than anything, encapsulates the essence of just what the *natu* is: a self- (and status-) conscious and insistently egalitarian alliance of Kallar men from separate villages for the purposes of steering the sacred chariot of the polity. Rendering graphic, the current constituent villages of the Vaduvur regional polity – Vadapathy (West) and Thenpathy (South) – it also captures the competitive infighting endemic to the enterprise of self-governance. Once again, politics relentlessly stalks and often routs a ritual struggling to transcend them.

In this chapter, I delve deeper into the micro-mechanics of self-governance and sovereignty cast onto the larger canvas of the *natu*. Formed around a confederacy of neighbouring villages, the *natu* is a regional polity. Cemented by kinship ties (of agnation and affinity) and delimited by territory, *natu*s are political institutions responsible for the collective management of its citizens' economic, political, and juridical affairs.[1] The *natu* is premised upon the same constitutive principles as the lineage and the street but applied onto a wider territory and a larger population. Embedded in particular territories, *natu* refers both to (*a*) the governing assembly of headmen from the constituent villages and (*b*) the geographical region over which this assembly has jurisdiction. Etymologically, *natu* refers to inhabited or agricultural land, in contrast to *katu*, which means wilderness or non-agricultural land. In Tamil classical poetry, the act of civilizing and establishing political overlordship is framed as 'killing' or clearing the wilderness (*katu konru*) to make the polity (*natu akki*) (Stein 1999: 91; see also Selby and Peterson 2008). How do the acts of making and maintaining *natu*s themselves embody exercises of statesmanship and political manoeuvering?

The *natu* is a south Indian politico-economic formation that predates the rise of the Chola empire (849–1279 CE). Laying the foundation for this first pan-south-Indian empire were various *natu*s jostling for power and position by leveraging their military prowess to offer protection to the peasant villagers and extracting tributes and land in return.[2] While the Chola emperor did enjoy comprehensive ritual sovereignty, he had only limited political authority away from his courtly core, among the semi-autonomous peripheries. The actual control of village affairs remained with the local *natu* and its assemblies of headmen. Within this model, which Stein (1999) terms the 'segmentary state', the centralized monarchical state's sovereignty was often less tangible than that exercised by the localized polities, where much of the 'actual taxation and adjudication over life and death took place' (Hansen 2005: 172). The sovereignty claimed by the centralized state was certainly more than simply ritual in nature (Inden 1981). However, historians do concur that the king did not have absolute territorial hegemony over his entire realm (Subbrayalu 1973; Dirks 1979, 1993; Ludden 1985, 1999; Heitzman, 1991; Champakalakshmi 1996; Habib 1999; Karashima 2000; Champakalakshmi et al. 2002). This meant that there were rival, if hierarchically organized, networks of power and authority which sought to control violence, rights, and reprisals (Dirks 1993; Stein 1999; Champakalakshmi 2011).

Pre-colonial India had enduring traditions of 'segmented, overlapping and stratified forms of sovereignty' (Hansen 2005: 172–173). Arguments about the remit and capacity of historical segmentary states are also attempts to grapple with Indian conceptions of sovereignty (Shastri 1975; Stein 1999). Assertion of local sovereignty in the face of attempts at centralized state control is a recurrent political phenomenon in Tamil Nadu (Mosse 2003a, 2001; Fuller and

Benei 2001). So much so that challenges to state power are apparent under the aegis of the Indian nation state as well (Brass 1997: 275–279; Fuller and Benei 2001; Mosse, 2001). Sovereignty is a 'fundamental, if often unacknowledged, dimension of different forms of power and authority'. And yet, Hansen (2005: 170) notes, 'the conceptual history of sovereignty in India has not yet been fully written'.

This chapter addresses this lacuna not so much from a historical standpoint but from an ethnographic perspective. Against this landscape of political devolution (Stein 1980; Hansen 2005), I argue that the Vaduvur *natu* is an iteration of sovereignty. Sovereign power is understood as sharing some characteristics and having some continuities with divine kingship (Graeber and Sahlins 2017; Dirks 1993; Geertz 1980; Heesterman 1985; Hocart 1969). Kingship serves as a means to bring and keep together a people and rule over them. The king is simultaneously profane and sacred, encapsulating as he does two bodies: his organic one and the 'body politic' which outlasts his material body (Heesterman 1985). Kings employ ethical violence to protect their subjects and the potential for excessive violence to respond when they feel threatened (Gilmartin 2015; Hansen and Stepputat 2006). Contemporary sovereignty, even within avowedly secular regimes of power, also evidences this mediation – between the profane and sacred and premodern and modern forms of power (Spencer 2007; Hansen and Stepputat 2006, 2005).

Hobbes (1981) argues that subjects facing a 'state of nature' saturated with violence were forced to, for their protection, enter into a social contract with an absolute sovereign power. Departing from this concentration on a singular supreme being, Foucault (1979) proposed a more dispersed notion of sovereignty. Sovereignty emerges from plural and disparate actors and institutions engaged in disciplining and regulating bodies and populations through governmentality and biopower. Following Schmitt (2005), Agamben (2005) argues that sovereign power emerges through the production of a 'state of exception' and the enacting of violence, showcasing the power to strip a person of political subjectivity to reduce them to simply 'bare life'. This allowed Hansen and Stepputat (2006: 297) to understand sovereignty as emerging through violence and concentrate on the body as a site for the performance of its power to 'generate loyalty, fear, and legitimacy'. More recent scholarship has tried to rethink the notion of sovereignty beyond its overwhelming dependence on enactments of violence, privileging of biopower and the body, and perspectives of claimants to sovereignty (see Folch 2016 on the control of natural resources and markets and Rutherford 2012: 15 on multiple audiences to and their 'processes of recognition' of sovereignty). Complicating the underlying monotheist Christian political theology, other scholars offer alternative conceptions of sovereignty not contingent on a singular, absolute, and totalizing sovereign power. Using the concept of 'varying thresholds of life' to understand the relationship between humans and spirits in central India, Singh (2012) proposes a 'bipolar sovereignty' consisting of an unresolvable tension between Vedic deities Mithra (force) and Varuna (contract). Premised on a polytheistic Hindu theology, Maunaguru's (2019) work among Sri Lankan Tamils proposes a distinctive idiom of sovereignty, emerging through recognition of, interdependence, and coexistence with multiple powers, which also renders it particularly vulnerable to doubts, non-recognition, and dissolution.

Assertions of sovereignty like that of the *natu* polity in Vaduvur are similarly plural, contested, and susceptible. While engaged in making claims about the past, the *natu* is actually in and of the present and parallel to that of the contemporary Indian nation state. Drawing on the perennial tensions between different scales of authority (such as centralized authorities and local assertions of power) that manifest themselves in Vaduvur, I explore the *natu* not simply as a historical relic or a juridico-political concept but especially as a working polity. From the operations of the *natu*, what conceptions of sovereignty emerge? On what basis does the *natu* claim sovereignty? Autonomy – not countenancing any interference from other competing and even higher-level authorities, in governmental but especially in its juridical affairs – lies at the heart of the Vaduvur *natu*'s assertions of sovereignty.

Natu Histories, Competing Claims

Vaduvur offers a palimpsest of histories. In Chapter 4, I described how place stories evoke an ethos, not untethered and free-floating but rooted in a place and shaped by the qualities of its people. Place stories are an evocation of a past. They are assemblages, mixing together the mythical, allegorical, and moral. They are also a patent narrating of a past, of a history. In *Textures of Time: Writing History in South India, 1600–1800*, Rao, Shulman, and Subrahmanyam (2003) argue that not all textual traditions should be judged entirely and exclusively on the basis of the verifiability of the facts contained within. The presence of the non-verifiable within such accounts does not necessarily detract from their historical sensibility. Instead, they suggest that a historical narrative is constituted not in its writing but in the act of reading itself. Readers must read for texture – the openness of the text, the fusing of genres – and resist the temptation to draw absolute distinctions between the fictive and the factual, in order to access the subtle historical possibilities of pre-colonial narratives. Sifting through, for example, place stories, it is possible to discern historical referents in terms of a specific location, time period, proper names, and 'eventful anchorage' (Pollock 2007: 369).

Accordingly, I sift through the claims about Vaduvur's past made in the present, not so much to verify what actually happened but to show the multiple and competing claims that different communities make upon this village. Each history, myth, and story narrated is an assertion of the right to be in Vaduvur – not just to be a part of it but also to be the first to, or indeed the only ones who should, have rights over it.

As different castes claim the rights to reside in and preside over Vaduvur, different origin myths, place stories, and folk narratives collide and compete with, become effaced by, and are superimposed over each other. There is the story recited by the Brahmins. Articulating with the pan-Indian epic, the Ramayana, their story has become institutionalized as the Kothandaramaswamy temple's official place story. Rama's fourteen-year exile was finally over. In a brutally bloody conflict, he had defeated the ten-headed king of Lanka, Ravana. His wife, Sita, Ravana's erstwhile hostage, was restored to him. Rama was ready to return to his kingdom, Ayodhya. Rama bid farewell to the sages with whom he had spent most of his sylvan exile. However, they begged him not to leave. They could not bear being separated from his divine presence. Moved, Rama consented to tarry a little longer. However, every time Rama tried to leave, the sages fervently prayed for him to remain with them forever. But, as per his vow to his brother and regent Bharatha, Rama had to return and begin ruling Ayodhya. Crafting his own form as a charming idol, Rama left it at the hermitage's threshold. The next morning, the sages came to greet Rama as usual. They were immediately struck by the statue's exquisite beauty. Its enigmatic smile captivated them. When the sages made their usual entreaties for him not to leave, Rama asked if they wanted him or his statue. Enamoured of its beauty, the sages opted for the idol. If Rama were to leave his statue behind, they would let him leave. With an enigmatic smile, Rama departed for Ayodhya, leaving his image behind. Years passed and the statue became lost.[3] Buried in legend, the enigmatic idol soon passed into myth.

Many years later, in the nearby royal city of Thanjavur, a scion of the Maratha kingdom, King Serfoji II (1777–1832),[4] was visited by a dream. Rama appeared to the king and related that his idol, presumed long lost, was buried under an auspicious Arasa tree[5] in Thalai Gnayiru village (present-day Thalanayar in the adjoining Nagapattinam district). Rama asked the king to unearth these statues, build a temple for them, and establish regular worship. Shaken awake, King Serfoji immediately went to Thalai Gnayiru and had these idols unearthed. Concluding his divine-inspired mission, the king prepared to leave the village. The Thalai Gnayiru villagers protested vociferously. They entreated the king not to take the idols found in their village away from them. Managing to convince them, the king left the statues of Rama's brothers, Lakshmana and Bharatha, behind in Thalai

Gnayiru[6] as a consolation. Taking possession of the statues of Rama, his wife Sita, and their simian devotee, Hanuman, the royal entourage proceeded to his court in Thanjavur. When night fell, King Serfoji tarried in a village along the way. He had the icons temporarily lodged in its main temple. This village is Vaduvur.

In Vaduvur's main temple, the blue-hued Krishna as Rajagopalaswamy (along with his consorts Satyabhama and Rukmani) presided as the reigning deity. Apparently renowned for their solidarity, the people – meaning only the Brahmins – of Vaduvur came to know of the king's precious cargo. Awe-struck by their beauty, particularly Rama's enchanting smile, they pleaded with the king to leave the statues behind. They begged him to install the icons in their Rajagopalaswamy temple's main sanctum. King Serfoji categorically refused – until, that is, the villagers threatened to collectively leap from their temple's main tower and commit mass suicide. Forced to relent, King Serfoji allowed them to keep the statues of Rama and Sita, only taking the statue of Hanuman back with him to Thanjavur. Since then, Rama has been the presiding deity of the main (and erstwhile Krishna) temple – now renamed the Kothandaramaswamy temple – and of Vaduvur itself.

At least according to the Brahmins. The priestly interlocutors I consulted at the outset of my fieldwork said that establishing the icons of Rama, Sita, and Hanuman in a temple hitherto dedicated to Krishna represents the earliest known history of Vaduvur. This and that Vaduvur had been gifted to the *vitwan*s (sacerdotal specialists, the Brahmins) by the Thanjavur kings on an Ekadasi[7] day which gave rise to Vaduvur being known also as Ekadasi village. When I enquired about Vaduvur's past, Brahmin interlocutors inevitably and repeatedly evoked the main temple's place story (*sthala puranam*) and the royal gift. What is significant is how the narrative of the Kothandaramaswamy temple conflates the re-configuration of a hitherto Krishna temple as a Rama temple with the origins of Vaduvur and privileges the centrality of (only) the Brahmins to Vaduvur's genesis. Their threatened suicide elicited a royal concession. The Brahmin's prospective collective sacrifice was – why a Krishna temple became the Rama temple – the impetus for Vaduvur becoming renowned for the singular beauty of its Rama icon. More importantly, their actions were responsible for why and how Vaduvur became legible in historical narratives. Excluding other peoples and perspectives, the Brahmins became the dynamic core of and the vital catalyst for the commencement of Vaduvur's history. No details about a pre-Brahmin history were offered. In their narratives, Vaduvur existed merely to be presented as a royal gift to the Brahmins and as a site for the proposed collective Brahmin self-sacrifice, which was powerful enough to thwart even the royal will. However, to be viable as a gift, Vaduvur must have already been a prosperous village. This suggests that Vaduvur predates Brahmin prominence. In addition, when we consider the other temples and their own distinctive origin myths, we discern different claims about Vaduvur's past and a more intricate history. Other villagers, of other castes, had other stories – of older temples and other more hot-blooded gods who had prior claims on/to Vaduvur. Gods who had a deeper affinity with Vaduvur's soil and its people.

While most renowned, the Kothandaramaswamy temple is not the oldest in Vaduvur. It is predated by the temple dedicated to the pan–Tamil Nadu rural deity Aiyanar. The Azhagiya Sundari Amman temple for the boundary goddess Pidari Amman precedes it. Even the Kailasanathar temple dedicated to the ascetic avatar of Shiva is older than the temple dedicated to Rama. So insisted the traditional headmen of Vaduvur, whose claims were also corroborated by the Brahmin priest administering to these other temples during their annual festivals. In Vaduvur's southern periphery, there is a large lake which has now been transformed into a bird sanctuary. On the banks of this lake is situated the Aiyanar temple. On thorny grounds, open to the scorching sun and the driving rains, armed with a massive sword stands Aiyanar. Flanked by his guard Munnadiyan holding his horse, the deity is surrounded by votive offerings of giant terracotta horses and elephants. Aiyanar is the guardian deity for the entire village. On his horse, and followed by Munnadiyan, he rides around the village, policing its borders and defending it against chaos and evil. He also forewarns about the threat of floods. If the lake's waters ever rise to reach his statue's nose, then the banks will be broken and Vaduvur will be entirely submerged.

In what was once Vaduvur's western boundary lies Pidari Amman's temple. Once nestled within dense forests at the village's periphery, this temple now stands in the midst of the commercial centre, crowded with houses, shops, and a busy road. This temple is connected with the Rama temple, this village goddess's icon being the first imperfect statue (see Chapter 4). In Thalai Gnayiru, where he unearthed them, King Serfoji was forced to forsake the statues of Bharatha and, most importantly, Lakshmana. In Vaduvur, where he rested before returning to his kingdom, Serfoji was forced to leave behind the statues of Rama and Sita. Rama and Sita became the new presiding deities in Vaduvur's main temple. However, Vaduvur was bereft of the icons of Rama's most devoted brother, Lakshmana, and most ardent devotee, Hanuman. The holy nuptial tableau (*tirukalyana kolam*) could not be complete without Lakshmana and Hanuman. Hanuman was easily wrought. However, the statue of Lakshmana emerged looking too feminine. After one more failure, they eventually had a perfect statue of Lakshmana to install in the Rama temple. The original feminine statue, the failed Lakshmana, was reclassified as the icon of Pidari Amman, installed in her own temple and equipped with a Brahmin priest to perform ritual services. She was renamed Azhagiya Sundari (Beautiful) Amman.

This is obviously part of Sanskritizing an autochthonous Tamil goddess and an already existing local village cult (Fuller 2004: 41–44). An indigenous goddess was rendered an aspect of Shakti, the pan-Indian female potency. She who roamed free all over Vaduvur was fixed to an icon, rooted to a new temple, and pacified into a beauteous but bland serenity. But Pidari Amman preceded her re-inscription into Azhagiya Sundari Amman. She is not a Sanskritic deity that receives only vegetarian offerings. Animal sacrifice continues to be at the heart of her ritual cult. Pidaris, all over Tamil Nadu, are worshipped as guardians of villages, specifically of their boundaries. That Pidari Amman worship precedes her Sanskritic iconography is not surprising. Pidari Amman has been particularly pivotal for constituting the Vaduvur *natu*. As a boundary goddess, she guards the integrity of the *natu*'s borders. As a rain goddess, she is responsible for the *natu*'s fertility.

The placement of both Pidari's and Aiyanar temples at its peripheries marks the boundaries of Vaduvur. Their defensive patrols not only thwart demons and evil spirits but also map Vaduvur's geographic contours. Pidari Amman's and Aiyanar's capacities as fertility deities and portents of catastrophes ensure that rain falls so that the crops can flourish but not so much as to inundate Vaduvur respectively. These deities define Vaduvur as a religio-political territory and as a prosperous socio-economic entity. More significantly, they actualize competing genesis narratives which challenge the Brahmin monopoly over and exclusively Sanskritic cast to Vaduvur's past. Narratives of their roaming and their undertakings offer frustratingly elusive but also tantalizing glimpses of an older, richer, and more complex history of Vaduvur.

Natu Geographies, Festival Cartographies

Just as its history is composed of competing claims about its past, Vaduvur is also constituted by manifold cartographies. In the maps serving as the basis for revenue assessments, village administration, electoral register, and population census, the contours of Vaduvur do coincide but are not entirely consistent. Adding to these multiple geographical representations is the religio-political *natu*. Currently, the Vaduvur *natu* comprises two major villages (*gramam*): West Vaduvur (Vadapathy) and South Vaduvur (Thenpathy).[8] I conducted fieldwork primarily in Vadapathy. It includes the settlements of North Vaduvur (Melpathy), the Vaduvur Agraharam (the former Brahmin colony), Kondaiyur, Vadakkithoppu, Erikarei (where the Muttiraiyars reside), and Gandhi Nagar (with primarily Dalit residents). Thenpathy includes the neighbouring but separate hamlets of Pudukkottai, Adicheri, Akkarei, and the southern part of the Agraharam (Map 5.1).

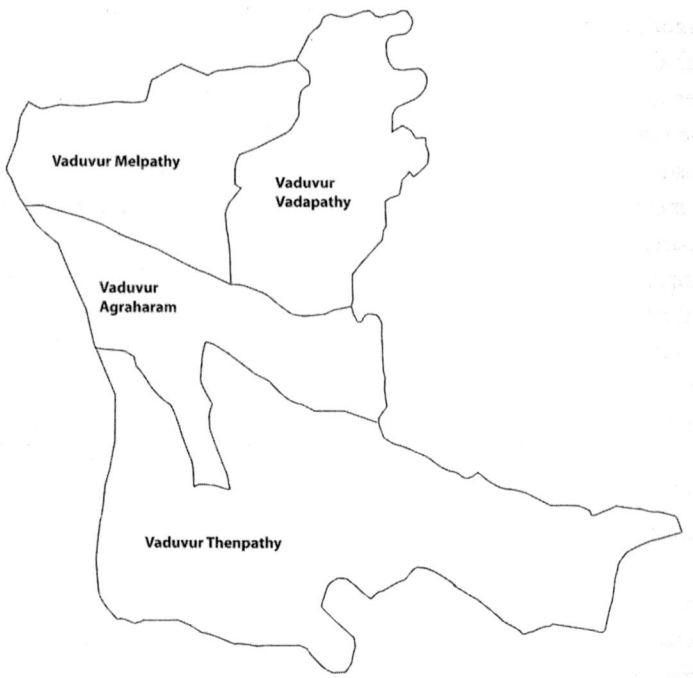

Map 5.1   Constituent Villages of Vaduvur

Source: Author.

Despite its present dichotomous structure, Sevu Vanniyar, advisor to Vaduvur's headmen assembly, insisted that Vadapathy was the original basis for the Vaduvur *natu*. To substantiate his claims for Vadapathy's precedence, he declared:

> All the *natu* temples are located only in Vadapathy. There are none whatsoever in Thenpathy. Temples were the nucleus around which the *natu* formed. So, Vadapathy, where all the *natu* temples are located, was obviously the basis for the Vaduvur *natu*. At a later date, Thenpathy seceded from neighbouring Orathanadu to join the Vaduvur *natu*.

Rituals, specifically deity processions, also delineate the Vaduvur *natu*'s geographical contours. At least they used to when they were still enacted, in a spectacular fashion. Now, all that remain are memories of how these festivals used to be observed and whatever ritual vestiges persist.

Pidari Amman's annual festival has not been celebrated for nearly seventy years. This ritual complex made manifest the Vaduvur *natu*'s realm and reach. It was the *natu*'s apotheosis. In the procession concluding her festival, Pidari Amman's movable icon was carried out of her shrine and into her realm. Her festival procession around her dominion, specifically its peripheries, traced the boundaries of the *natu* and illustrated its extent. However, this ritual too has succumbed to agonistic politics. Intense competition among the constituent components of the *natu* meant that they were unable to come together to celebrate the festival. Pidari Amman's procession is no longer performed.

Approximately forty years ago, however, Vaduvur initiated another type of sacred procession – the Santhana Kappu (Sandlewood Protection). In the past, the goddess was the one to venture out of her temple. She set forth to survey her kingdom, inspect her subjects, and receive their worship and offerings. Today, however, her subjects – metonymically representing her kingdom – come to her, on a street-by-street basis. The goddess herself never leaves her temple. Preceded by four Dalit men playing brass horns and cowhide drums and letting off firecrackers, her subjects undertake a procession to the Pidari Amman temple bearing offerings of fruit, flowers, and the ingredients to make flour lamps. The Dalits also led two live goats. The sacrificial animals were bought with the tax tendered by the participating residents of the street that had been allotted the right to offer worship. They are her subjects' tribute to their regnant goddess. Stood at the temple's threshold, the live animals were presented to the goddess. This is an acknowledgement of her demand for animal sacrifice, an allusion to the unbound and unruly local goddess of old. Today, however, no blood sacrifice can be enacted before her now Sankritized form and in her orthodox temple. The goats were taken away to the shores of Vaduvur lake, to be slaughtered near the Aiyanar temple. The next morning, the sacrificial meat was distributed to the street-mates entitled to a share. In Chapter 2, I described how a share of sacrificial meat materializes membership within a lineage, exclusive rights to their lineage deity and ritual cult as well as the equality that should characterize lineage relations. Concurrently, this goat meat is a consecrated offering imbued with the goddess's grace. The sacred meat objectifies the hierarchical engagement between a deity and her congregation as well as a sovereign and her subjects.

On Tuesdays and Fridays throughout the month of Tai (mid-January–mid-February), different streets in Vadapathy and Thenpathy alternate among themselves to sponsor and undertake this procession. Many other villages once constituted a much larger Vaduvur *natu* under Pidari Amman's aegis. Intense disputes lead to most of them seceding from this religio-political union. Consequently, the goddess's kingdom and subjects have shrunk considerably. Now only Vadapathy and Thenpathy remain subject to her reign.

Political Office: *Natu* Headmen

The notorious source of many long-standing disputes, also at play in the gradual fracturing of the Vaduvur *natu*, is the distribution of sanctified offerings after worship (*pracatam*), especially the system of 'honours' (*mariyatai*) (Appadurai and Breckenridge 1976; Dirks 1993: 120–126, 289–292). After the worship, all devotees receive *pracatam* – food, ash, flowers, coconut halves, bananas, betel leaves, and areca nut shavings that have been blessed by the deities. However, they are normally offered first to the highest ranked devotee, usually a patron or the sponsor of the ritual, which is why they are called 'first or foremost' (*mutalmai*). *Mariyatai* – a garland and/or a shawl from around the shoulders of the deity then draped like a turban around the recipient's forehead – however, are exclusive. Their presentation always singles out dignitaries. A recipient of *mariyatai* is normally also the first recipient of the *pracatam* so that his superiority is doubly signified (Fuller 2004: 79–80). Both these practices publicly confirm rank and can be hotly disputed. Sevu Vanniyar, the *natu* headmen's councillor, claimed:

> By rights of precedence and given their larger population, the Vadapathy headmen should have the foremost honours. Moreover, four of the *natu* temples are either in or on the border of Vadapathy itself ... far north from Thenpathy. Vadapathy is the foundational core of the Vaduvur *natu*. By right, it is Vadapathy's representatives that should receive any and all honours due the *natu*.

Despite their joining the Vaduvur *natu* at a later date, the Thenpathy headmen insist on receiving the foremost honours.

> Vadapathy has conceded its rights. So, we can preserve the peace at the assembly. So, we can ensure that the temple festivals continue. Vadapathy has conceded to Thenpathy as an elder brother does to a recalcitrant younger brother.

Embedded in Sevu Vanniyar's claims is the insinuation of the Vadapathy headmen's magnanimity and the superiority their altruism entails. Relinquishing the precedential honours rightfully due to them demonstrated the Vadapathy headmen's superior statesmanship. They were willing to sacrifice their own honours in the interest of *natu* solidarity. Obviously the Thenpathy headmen would disagree with this interpretation; Sevu Vanniyar also conceded. With a mischievous smile, he asked me not to write this point down. It would definitely annoy the Thenpathy headmen. Then he watched as I carefully noted his recounting of Vaduvur's political history. He even repeated some of the details I had missed the first time around so as to ensure that I had a complete account.

Only Kallar men can be *natu* headmen. There is one headman to every two Kallar streets.[9] Eight headmen come from Vaduvur Thenpathy, including three from the hamlet of Pudukkottai and one from Adicheri. Kudikadu contributes six headmen. Given its bigger population, Vaduvur Vadapathy contributes ten headmen, including one from Kondaiyur hamlet. Sevu Vanniyar, the consultant to the *natu*, is also from Vadapathy (Table 5.1). As he is not a headman, he has no vote within the *natu* assembly. He advises the headmen on matters of Kallar jurisprudence, judicial precedence, and Vaduvur *natu* history to aid them in their deliberations over temple and ritual issues and when adjudicating disputes. Within this coterie of headmen, there is a ranked hierarchy which dictates protocols regarding the distribution of honours. The chief headman (*mutal nattamai*) has precedence in receiving the honours at the end of a ceremony (*mutal mariyatai*). There are two chief headmen, one each from Vadapathy[10] and Thenpathy.

The office of headman is a hereditary one. It has tended to be concentrated among a few families, the 'headmen families' (*nattamai kutumpam*). Primogeniture is the primary criteria for succession to headmanship. Other considerations include age (middle-aged, preferably older), experience, property ownership (residence in

Table 5.1 Components of the Vaduvur *Natu*

Constituent Regions	Constituent Villages/Hamlets	Residents' Caste Profile	Headmen Contributed	Total Number of Headmen
Vaduvur Vadapathy	Vaduvur Vadapathy	Kallars		
	Vaduvur Melpathy	Kallars		
	Vaduvur Agraharam	Formerly Brahmin, now mixed caste		10
	Kondaiyur	Predominantly Muttiraiyars, also significant Kallar population	1	
	Vadakkithoppu	Muttiraiyars		
	Erikarei	Muttiraiyars		
	Gandhi Nagar	Dalits		

(Contd)

Table 5.1 (*Contd*)

Constituent Regions	Constituent Villages/Hamlets	Residents' Caste Profile	Headmen Contributed	Total Number of Headmen
Vaduvur Thenpathy	Vaduvur Thenpathy	Kallars		8
	Pudukkottai	Kallars	3	
	Adicheri	Kallars	1	
	Akkarei	Kallars		
	Southern part of the Agraharam	Formerly Brahmin, now mixed caste		
Kudikadu		Kallars		6

and familiarity with *natu* affairs), and marital status. Single men are thought not to have borne the full responsibilities of adulthood yet. They cannot even enjoy the full complement of rights and obligations of lineage-membership, let alone aspire to *natu* leadership. Headmen officiate at many temple functions and ritual occasions. As such, the auspiciousness that their married status bestows is also an important criterion. Widowers, unless they remarry, are persuaded to relinquish their headman position. Along with denoting maturity, these indicators also demonstrate investment – personal, familial, property-wise – in the Vaduvur *natu*. Moral character, disposition, and personal merit are also important considerations for headmanship. They should ideally be articulate, just, wise, calm, and judicious (see also Dumont 2000: 154–155 on criteria for *natu* jurists). Their authority is partly contingent on their character, as attested to by their past interactions with other villagers. Outside of the *natu* assemblies and their official capacities, headmen are also regularly consulted in their personal capacity and asked to arbitrate domestic quarrels. When I was interviewing Sevu Vanniyar, we were interrupted by a woman seeking his advice. Her elder brother, contrary to custom and fraternal duty, had married before her. Worse still, he was not at all concerned about getting her married. Admonishing her elder brother, Sevu Vanniyar consoled the woman by promising to advise her brother to immediately find a husband for her.

Just like with the street tribunals in Chapter 4, the protocols governing *natu* assemblies are also integral to constituting their authority. Since they help forestall disputes among the assemblies' constitutive villages and their respective headmen, these proprieties are vital for successfully convening *natu* assemblies. Elaborate and precise, they are designed to avert slights to honour and the attendant quarrels – mechanisms of pre-emptive diplomacy. The headmen have recourse to custom and jural precedence as embodied in the person of the advisor. To settle disputes over protocols, Vaduvur *natu*'s headmen frequently consult Sevu Vanniyar. Among the varying scales of tribunals, the most formal is the *natu* assembly. As with street tribunals, contravening the *natu* assembly's elaborate protocols can undermine the legitimacy of its proceedings.

Yet again, I never had the chance to personally observe a *natu* assembly. Due to the Thenpathy headmen's remonstrance, *natu* meetings were few and far between. The one meeting convened during my fieldwork, of which I was informed and had permission to attend, was adjourned at the very last minute. Nevertheless, through extensive interviews with Sevu Vanniyar, several *natu* headman, and the Muttiraiyar watchman (*talaiyari*) in the *natu*'s employ, I was able to piece together an account of the protocols governing *natu* assemblies and their deliberative processes.

Where are *natu* assemblies convened? Primarily in *natu* temples. Lineage or street temples are private edifices over which only their respective lineages and streets have claims. *Natu* temples are public institutions over which the *natu* collectively has rights. Their political neutrality – venues to which no one individual, household, lineage, street, or village can claim more rights than any other – makes them ideal for assemblies. *Natu* temples are also where the *natu*'s tutelary deities are. As already described, the consonance between ritual and politics underpins kinship-polities like the *natu*. That *natu* assemblies are convened where the deities that sanction them and the rituals that animate them are also enacted is therefore apt.

Who can convene a *natu* assembly? Only a headman can do so. And even then, only with the cooperation of the other headmen. How must the meeting be convened? A Dalit crier, employed by the *natu*, must first formally inform all the headmen. This same messenger then walks through the streets of the *natu*. Beating his cowhide drum, crying out his message, he informs the ordinary *natu* residents of the meeting. Who may attend the assembly? Anyone who lives in the *natu* can do so. Women and children are not expressly forbidden from attending. However, they tend not to unless specifically asked to. Neither the higher-caste Brahmins nor the lower-caste Muttiraiyars and Dalits are allowed to attend the *natu* assemblies, unless expressly bidden to do so, as I will elaborate later. Mostly, only the headmen and other interested male Kallar elders attend these meetings.

What are the protocols during the meeting? For fear of initiating conflicts, the headmen do not directly speak to each other during the meeting. They convey their opinions to a go-between, a Muttiraiyar employee of the *natu*, who then conveys it to the other headmen, and vice versa. All matters are communicated only via this intermediary. This intercessory protocol breaking down – such that the headmen directly address each other – denotes a heated conflict. Despite these precautionary protocols, disputes and impasses are fairly common. Again, this is due to the egalitarian ideals upon which these assemblies are founded. Parity is due to *all* the headmen. There may be a chief headman, but this is largely a ceremonial position. The chief headman is the designated representative who receives the offerings distributed and the honours conferred after worship at *natu* temples. These honours are due to the *natu*. The chief headman receives them on behalf of all the headmen and residents of a *natu* polity. Each headman has an equal vote. Moreover, when it comes to temple functions or judicial negotiations, *all* headmen have to agree before they can proceed further. There should not be any overt power disparities or differential inputs in the decision-making process. The absence of an overt hierarchy – the egalitarian imperative itself – gives rise to the competition over status and therefore impasses in *natu* governance.

Worship Rites and Political Rights: Ritual Sovereignty

The nucleus of the *natu* is the temples. The *natu* emerged from the temples. First, the *natu* assembly is here to care for the temples. The headmen are the ones who know the customs and traditions (*palakka-valakkam*) and can solve disputes through their counsel. They deal with problems arising from the temples. They also mediate the fisticuffs (*ati-piti*), land disputes and contested transactions (*kututtal-vankal*) through the village *panchayat*. Headmen are respected because they know the truth, they have seen it all.

Sevu Vanniyar explained that there are two main and interrelated pivots to the political conception of the *natu*: (*a*) temples and (*b*) arbitration, the ritual, and the judicial. Here, I consider the ritual formulations of political power. The *raison d'être* for the Vaduvur *natu* is the administration of the temples within its jurisdiction. Headmen themselves are aware of the religious foundations of their polity and the political implications of their rituals. It was explicitly and unequivocally stated by the headmen themselves.

In Vaduvur, the *natu* and its headmen have assumed the royal function in the absence of the monarch and the distance of the nation state. Establishing and administrating religious institutions and sponsoring rituals such as sacrifices, they ensure a cosmic order that encompasses the socio-political order. First advanced by Appadurai and Breckenridge (1976), the religious underpinnings or at least the temple-centred nature of south Indian politics has become a broadly accepted thesis (see Madan 1987; Heitzman 1991; Fuller 2004: 106–108; Dirks 1993; Sax 2000). As monarchs are divine, deities are royal and sovereign (for example, Singh 2012; Maunaguru 2020). Socio-political order in the earthly kingdom both mirrors and is a function of the universe's cosmic and moral order. The maintenance of this order is a dual responsibility shared between the monarch and the deity. Statecraft is not only political but inherently cosmological. The transactions between the deity and its worshippers are homologous to that between the king and his subjects. The king is styled as both the foremost worshipper and the chief subject of the deity. He is the first, if not the only one, to receive the sanctified offerings and honours after worship. Constituted as a holistic assemblage of ritual enactments and material power, the state is an intrinsically religio-political institution.

The Vaduvur *natu* is defined by the administration (*nirvakam*) of corporate bodies (*niruvanam*) – its temples. The very locations of these temples – either at the centre or at the boundaries of the *natu* – serve to map this polity's geographic contours. Their situation is a matter of both political and sacred geography. Indeed, the initial centripetal force that brought various neighbouring villages together into an alliance was custody over the *natu* deities' icons. The smaller villages constituting the Vaduvur *natu* did not have permanent temples to house their deities' idols. Only 'in use' during their respective annual festivals, these idols and their valuable accoutrements were vulnerable to theft. So, they were securely housed in a central location, a *natu* temple in Vaduvur. According to Sevu Vanniyar:

> Neivasal's Sinna Ayyan, Pudukkottai's Periya Ayyan and Kondaiyur's Selli Amman – all these icons from neighbouring villages were kept securely locked at Vaduvur's Azhagiya Sundari Amman Temple.

> Before their festivals, the headmen from these neighbouring villages would come to Vaduvur to fetch their respective idols. Both the chief headmen from Vadapathy and Thenpathy must be present at this ceremony to sanction this transfer of custody. Since they controlled the access to their deities' statues, the Vaduvur *natu* headmen were treated with tremendous respect. They were ceremonially invited to the temple festivals at these neighbouring villages. At the end of the worship, the headmen were given their due honours.

Today, all the icons have been taken back by their respective villages.

Even the smaller villagers have constructed their own temples. The idols have been permanently installed in their own newly built or refurbished temples.

Securing and holding the icons of Vaduvur *natu*'s constituent villages 'hostage' were critical for consolidating affiliation with the *natu*. They were vital for the centralization of the *natu*'s authority structure. Today, competitive temple building has become a means of asserting status. Additionally, individuating themselves from collective membership in public temples to assert autonomous rights to separate private temples has led to the proliferation of smaller temples. Eroding a constitutive basis of the *natu* collectivity, these actions have led to its fragmentation and the dilution of *natu* authority.

Currently, five temples fall within the purview of Vaduvur *natu*, with three belonging entirely to the *natu* (Table 5.2).

Table 5.2 Temples Belonging to Vaduvur *Natu*

Temple	Main Deity	Location
Kailasanathar	Shiva	Vaduvur Vadapathy
Azhagiya Sundari Amman	Pidari Amman	Vaduvur Agraharam
Aiyanar	Aiyanar	by Vaduvur Lake

Vaduvur's Brahmins and the Kondaiyur hamlet's residents claim primary ownership of the remaining two (Table 5.3).

Table 5.3 Temples That the Vaduvur *Natu* Has Rights Over

Temple	Main Deity	Location
Kothandaramaswamy	Rama	Vaduvur Agraharam
Selli Amman	Selli Amman	Kondaiyur

However, the *natu* still retains its rights to these temples. The *natu* assembly must be consulted on major decisions regarding these temples. The *natu*'s cooperation is vital to any of their major undertakings. Rights to the remaining *natu* temples and participating in their rituals remain central to the corporate governance of the Vaduvur *natu*.

Sovereign Polity: Ritual

Emblazoned above Pidari Amman's main sanctum in the Azhagiya Sundari Amman temple is the declaration of Vaduvur's status as a self-governing polity (Figure 5.1). Vaduvur is not simply a *natu*. It is a sovereign polity (*tannaracu natu*).

This sovereignty in itself is a historical development. Vaduvur was initially part of a larger regional assembly that stretched 14 kilometres away to the nearest town, Mannargudi. A dispute broke out within this polity. No one remembers exactly what it was about now. What they do know was that this conflict was decided by a contest. Competing against each other were Dalit (historically referred to as Paraiyars) representatives, each nominated by one of the constituent villages of this regional polity. According to Sevu Vanniyar, and corroborated by a *natu* headman, the contest was a test of strength and multitasking dexterity called *virutu putunkutal*:

> *Puntu pul* is a type of grass that clings stubbornly to the soil and is tough to uproot. The Paraiyar had to wrench a blade of this recalcitrant grass out of the ground, turn it upside down and plant it back in the ground this time with the leaves in the soil and the roots in the air. He had to do all this with only one hand. His other hand had to be on his brass horn instrument. Placing his mouth on the mouthpiece, he had to continuously blow on the instrument throughout the contest's duration. If he failed to uproot the grass or if the sound from his horn faltered at any point, then the village he represented was deemed to

Figure 5.1   Proclamation of Vaduvur's Sovereign Status

Source: Author.

have lost. All those from the other seventeen competing villages failed. Only the Paraiyar from Vaduvur succeeded. This is why Vaduvur is a sovereign *natu*.

Ideologically, rhetorically, and politically, Kallars align themselves with martial values. They profess, above all, to value independence and abhor loss of honour. Any insult to honour may invite retaliation, sometimes with violence. Even these particular Kallars who have been settled agriculturalists for some time cultivate an image of being sensitive to insults, quick to anger, and possessing an unpredictable violent streak. Violence, as we have seen, is considered a mode of agency. Their willingness to resort to coercion has been instrumental to their accruing politico-economic power. These Kallars are not ashamed of their penchant for violence, their quarrelsome dispositions, or their histories of feuding. Indeed, they cherish their reputation for anger and aggression even if they do not engage in violent pursuits as often as they may have in the past or are presumed to do in the present. This carefully cultivated reputation – among their tenants, labourers, the upper-caste Brahmins, and the neighbouring villages – means that very often they do not actually have to engage in actual violence to further their interests. Their fearsome reputation itself is sufficient. Given the valour they associate with their own caste, it seems ironic that the independence of their caste polity was achieved not through their own efforts. Rather, it was a product of the skill and strength of that most despised of social inferiors, the 'untouchable' Dalit. What this contest also illustrates are certain principles of sovereign power that the Kallars were able to exercise and to which they could subject presumed caste inferiors.

Virutu, Dirks (1993: 672) explains in his ethno-history of the Kallar-ruled Pudukkottai kingdom, means 'both title and emblem as well as banner, trophy, badge of victory, pedigree, genealogy'. He argues that the 'king's emblems not only signify his own sovereignty, but their presentation to lesser kings and nobles marks and establishes a special relationship, a substantial bond'. It is highly suggestive that the test that had established the Vaduvur *natu*'s sovereignty is termed *virutu putunkutal*, or 'grabbing the emblem [of sovereignty]'. Furthermore, this emblem was grabbed – meaning that independence was competed for, achieved, and asserted among caste-equals – rather than gifted by an external and superior authority to which they were then beholden in relations of patronage. The latter forms the basis of legitimate but hierarchical political relationships between superior kings and inferior subjects.

What this test of 'grabbing sovereignty' alludes to is the political authority of the Kallars. An authority through which the Kallars could command other castes to align themselves with Kallar interests and coerce them to act for their cause. In Vaduvur, the Kallar *natu* involves, even though it does not fully incorporate, other non-Kallar castes. The Kallar *natu*s described by Dumont (2000) and Karuppaiyan (1990) are constituted entirely of Kallars and therefore primarily subject to the morality of, albeit a politicized, kinship. Vaduvur's situation is more reminiscent of Dirks's (1993) Pudukkottai Kallar kingdom, although on a significantly more limited scale. Compared to the royal Tondaiman Kallars, the Vaduvur Kallars' dominance is markedly less regal, less comprehensive, and more precarious. In Vaduvur's multi-caste milieu, the Brahmins, the Muttiraiyar labourers, the Acari artisans, and the Dalits seem to have been integrated into and largely cooperated with an essentially Kallar polity. These non-Kallar castes are not extended the full complement of rights and obligations of *natu* citizenship enjoyed by Kallar males. All the decisions to do with the *natu* may still be made by a coterie of Kallar headmen. Nevertheless, the Vaduvur *natu* does involve other castes.

The *natu* employs representatives from a number of castes, drawing upon their services as and when needed. These *natu* employees include the Brahmin priest who performs periodic ritual services at several, but not all, *natu* temples. Two Muttiraiyar workers (one each from Thenpathy and Vadapathy) are to perform certain sundry services. Two artisans (one blacksmith and one carpenter) contribute smithing (*kollu*) and carpentry (*taccu*) services. A washerman is responsible for providing clean *dhoti*s that serve both as floor-mats and roof canopies for all auspicious occasions. A watchman (*talaiyari*) from the Muttiraiyar caste serves as the intermediary among the headmen, who in the interest of diplomacy, are not supposed to directly address each other during *natu* meetings. Also included are some Dalits who inform headmen of and gather them together for scheduled *natu* meetings and relate decisions made at the assembly to the *natu* residents. Besides helping to convene meetings and clean the meeting venue, they also precede any procession (be it of humans or of deities) playing their drums and horns. All these employees are paid from *natu* funds. These are generated mainly from income from *natu*-owned properties and donations from devotees to the *natu* temples. Apart from the priest, the workers are paid roughly INR 10 each for their work. Only if their service is to the Kothandaramaswamy temple are they also given honours (*mariyatai*) to recognize their service in addition to their salary.[11]

Even if not for the temples' everyday operations, the cooperation of the *natu* headmen is still necessary when important decisions must be made. Furthermore, major ceremonies such as the temples' annual festivals or consecration ceremonies can only occur in the presence of the *natu* representatives. Ideally, headmen must take the lead in the proceedings at *natu* temples. Even at the Kothandaramaswamy temple, to which the Brahmins stake primary claim, the *natu* has certain fundamental rights. It must always be honoured first. The Kothandaramaswamy temple is now overseen by the Tamil Nadu government's

Hindu Religious and Charitable Endowments Department. Under this authority, the day-to-day administration of the temple is in Kallar hands. Tensions exist between the Kallar-dominated temple administration committee and the Brahmin sacerdotal body. The Brahmins accuse the Kallar administrative body of corruption and ineptitude. The Kallars accuse the Brahmins of disrespecting the *natu*'s primary rights to this temple and acting as though it belonged to a Brahmin diaspora. Despite these tensions, the Kothandaramaswamy temple's consecration ceremony in 2007 was nevertheless inaugurated under the auspices of the chief headmen of Thenpathy and Vadapathy. Welcomed with special prayers, the headmen led the procession of the main deity's movable icon around the temple compound. They climbed up the makeshift stairs to watch the proceedings from an honoured spot on the roof of the temple. At the conclusion of the consecration, they were given the offerings first. In addition, the presiding priest tied a shawl dedicated to the deity around the foreheads of the chief headmen (*parivattam*). Such honours are usually only given to the sponsors of temples and rituals. In the pre-colonial era, these were primarily the kings. Patronage of Brahmins, temples, and rituals was a fundamental component of kingship. This is a schema which continues to be employed by those wishing to claim power and legitimate their authority (Raheja 1998, 1988; Michelutti 2014 on dominant castes in villages assuming royal function following the demise of kings). Here, the conferring of honours to the chief headmen acknowledges that the Kothandaramaswamy temple is a *natu* temple even if most of its patrons and devotees are Brahmins. Recognizing the temple's physical location within the *natu*, it also concedes to being within its political ambit. Additionally, it is a symbolic concession, of their own subjection, to the *natu*'s authority.

To underscore their preeminent rights to this temple, the *natu* headmen ensured that they presided over the temple's consecration ceremony. To demonstrate the political authority that temple patronage represents, the *natu* assembly contributed INR 100,000 towards the Kothandaramaswamy temple's renovations and subsequent consecration ceremony. What is significant is not the size of the donation but the act of sponsorship itself and the insouciant presumptuousness with which it was extended. As representatives of the village's dominant caste and therefore the inheritors of the royal function, the *natu* headmen had the duty to sponsor temples and rituals. As the *natu* headmen, whose assembly customarily has had authority over this temple, they simply assumed they had the right to give – a right which they 'must and will never give up', at least without a fight. In other Vaduvur *natu* temples, uncomplicated by competing Brahmin claims, this interpenetration of religious rites and political rights is even more readily apparent.

Politically Sovereign: Juridical Artistry

The 'grabbing of sovereignty' contest did not only allude to Kallar authority over other castes. More fundamentally, it was the catalyst for Vaduvur's becoming a sovereign polity. After Vaduvur's Dalit nominee won the contest, and been the only one to do so, Vaduvur was free to secede from the larger regional polity to which it had once owed allegiance. From then on, Vaduvur was no longer subject to the administration or laws of the surrounding polities. It would be governed only according to those laws devised and enforced by its own *natu* assembly. Concurrently, Vaduvur's laws would also not apply to those not belonging to the Vaduvur *natu*. Sevu Vanniyar described the Vaduvur *natu* headmen's juridical talents.

> They were renowned for their skill as jurists. They were in great demand throughout the region. Neighbouring villages would approach them to adjudicate particularly complex disputes beyond their own headmen's capacities. Vaduvur's headmen would go and propose solutions which were acceptable to all parties. They have managed to resolve conflicts that had baffled even the police.

Other villagers' disputes may be arbitrated by Vaduvur's headmen. However, Vaduvur itself would be governed only by its own headmen. While ritual forms the first axis of the Vaduvur *natu*'s assertion of sovereignty, the other axis is the judicial. The *natu* may be defined by principles of kinship and caste. Temples and ritual cults may delineate the *natu*'s boundaries and functions. However, its claims to sovereignty are contingent on a jural definition. Vaduvur *natu* is sovereign precisely because of its legislative powers, delimited by territory as they are. Ultimately, sovereignty is centred on jurisdiction.

Vaduvur functioned with little interference from a centralized state before the advent of the colonial and the nation state. During the pre-colonial period, the *natu* assembly was constituted by three offices (Table 5.4).

Table 5.4 Local Government

	Office	Function
1.	*Aracu*	local representative of the king
2.	*Ampalam*	advisor to the headmen
3.	*Nattamai*	headmen

Serukkan Vanniyar – the representative of the Maratha kings of Thanjavur – was the last *aracu* at the Vaduvur *natu* assembly. According to Sevu Vanniyar, to acknowledge this prestigious position,

> during Pidari Amman's annul procession, her chariot make its first stop at the street where the *aracu* lived. This street is now named after him – Serukkan Vanniyar Street. Only after accepting the sacrifice from the residents there will the procession continue around the rest of the *natu* and accept other sacrifices.

This had been a singular honour denoting the power and prestige attached to this political office. Pidari Amman no longer leaves her temple to survey her kingdom. Royal rule itself ended in 1855. The office of the king's local representative no longer exists. Only the positions of advisor and headman remain operational. Nevertheless, a measure of the deference accorded to the *aracu* resonates even today. According to Chinnappa, an elderly resident of Serukkan Vanniyar Street, to this day, presumed ritually polluting elements do not enter their street.

> Paraiyars [Dalits] cannot enter but must go around. Funeral processions also do not enter. They must stop at the street junction.

Sevu Vanniyar is the *ampalam*. He is the advisor who has the role of convening and closing the *natu* assembly. He does not intervene in the proceedings, only speaking at the end. After summing up the views of all the headmen, he then gives his own opinion. The *ampalam* is a living repository of Vaduvur's history, *natu* customs, and juridical precedence. The *aracu* is the representative of the monarch's authority at the *natu* assembly. The headmen represent the authority of the Kallar *natu*.

The *aracu* is the living embodiment of the link between the centralized monarchical state and the peripheral *natu* segment. Amid vociferous arguments over the possibility, inception, remit, reach, and durability of the segmentary state, in Vaduvur, the office of the *aracu* is what articulates how the segmentary state model manifested itself in everyday political practice. The *aracu* is key to the political devolution characterizing the segmentary state that allowed the *natu* structure to flourish. Through the *aracu*, the centralized state's largely moral and ritual authority over the periphery was represented at *natu* assemblies. The *natu*'s admittedly limited association with the centralized state served to further legitimize its authority and its headmen. What is significant is that the *aracu* was not a representative sent from the centre but was actually a local resident. The *aracu* was also not superior to the headmen. He could not veto their decisions, but merely advice as to the king's and court's interests. The final decision ultimately rested with the headmen.

Parallel Citizenships, Alternative Sovereignties

Kallars in Vaduvur are not just citizens of the Indian nation state. Simultaneously, they are also citizens of their localized kinship-polities – the lineages, streets, and inter-village regions. Citizenship in a *natu* incorporates an indigenous jural status which invests its citizens with specific rights and responsibilities. *Natu* citizens have the right to access *natu* temples and participate in the *natu* ritual cult. They have the right to approach the headmen individually or ask for a tribunal to be convened to arbitrate their disputes. These rights come with several attendant responsibilities. Having asked for a tribunal to be convened, in return, citizens have the responsibility to abide by its judgments. They are also obliged to contribute their labour and other services when called upon to do so. Most of all, their tax contributions are vital to financing certain *natu* initiatives – largely concerning the *natu* temples. Representation, for most citizens, is dependent primarily on taxation.

Having said that, only the headmen tend to be actively engaged in *natu* politics. Their office, rather than their persons, is vested with legislative, judicial, and executive powers. However, headmen exercise them on behalf of *natu* citizens. Their headmanship does not make them superior to ordinary citizens. Headmen are *primes inter pares,* or first among equals – simply representatives of the citizens. Given the assertively independent nature of most Kallars, the headmen's authority is based on the consent of the governed. Nonetheless, not all citizens enjoy the same rights, nor are they enjoined to undertake the same responsibilities. Citizenship is differential. It is largely a Kallar *and* male privilege. Just as they do with the lineage and the street, only male and married Kallars are recognized as full citizens and directly vested with the full complement of rights and obligations. Kallar women's citizenship is mediated through or subsumed under that of their male kinsmen.

Non-Kallars are not citizens of the *natu*. They do not have any rights in and responsibilities to the *natu*. They do not attend the *natu* assembly's deliberations. Brahmins have an ambivalent relationship with the *natu*. They do acknowledge that the Kothandaramaswamy temple that they lay claim to is part of a *natu*. At least one of them is employed by the *natu* for their sacerdotal services at other *natu* temples. However, Brahmins tend to avoid all other interactions with the *natu*, especially with respect to its judicial functions. They neither recognize *natu* law when it comes to their own affairs nor do they resort to publicly airing their disputes to, let alone have them be arbitrated by, the *natu* council. They are simultaneously part of and not part of the *natu*. They themselves are not subject to its authority but neither do they contest the *natu*'s authority over Vaduvur. Indeed, they publicly acknowledge Kallar authority through temple rituals.

In keeping with their caste ethos, Brahmins are supposed to restrict interactions and transactions to limit their susceptibility to ritual pollution and maintain their symbolically pure status (Marriott 1959; Beck 1972; Moffat 1979). Their ritual status is critically dependent on them being seen as independent of and detached from entangling relationships, especially with caste inferiors (Fuller 2004). With their own separate and parallel institutions of self-government, Brahmins neither partake in nor challenge *natu* authority. By contrast, intermediate land-owning castes like the Kallars derive their influence from mobilizing kin ties, managing labour, and their willingness to resort to violence. Kallar power is directly premised upon not just actively participating but actually taking the leading role in local transactions and interactions (Raheja 1998; Beck 1972).

The lower castes, on the other hand, are unequivocally subject to *natu* authority and must adhere to the *natu* assembly's pronouncements. They are not allowed to attend the assembly unless expressly bidden to do so. They have no rights to the *natu* temples unless expressly given them by the *natu* assembly. They do not hold political offices like the *natu* headmanship. Their serious disputes, with Kallars and among themselves, are adjudicated by Kallar headmen, who also have the authority to mete out relevant punishments. Kallars, as we saw in Chapter 4, will not allow any other castes to arbitrate their disputes, which means acknowledging some other caste's authority over themselves (Gough 1981 on justice in Kumbapettai, Thanjavur). This is the fundamental premise upon which Kallar assertions of sovereignty are built. Non-Brahmin and non-Kallar *natu* residents do not enjoy the rights of citizenship although they continue to be made to fulfil their responsibilities to the *natu*. They serve as employees of the *natu*. They must tender their labour when called. They are subject to the *natu* tribunal's arbitration and punishment. Underpinning the *natu*'s authority over its Kallar citizens may be the consent of the governed. Framing its authority over Vaduvur's lower-caste residents is the coercion premised upon the numerical, economic, and political power of the Kallars and their implied and explicit threats of violence. Unlike the Brahmins, their subsistence being dependent on employment with Kallar landlords (more so in the past than today) rendered the obedience of lower-caste residents to *natu* authority necessary if not mandatory. Rather than citizens enjoying political rights, lower-caste residents are largely subjects ruled by Kallar authority.

Conclusion

A clump of grass clinging stubbornly to the grasping earth. A struggle to wrench this grass from the packed soil's clutches, then push it back in, this time with the roots up. All with just one hand. A horn's plaintive wail, and the player's breath, not flagging throughout the contest. A now forgotten conflict that led to a public tournament. Fellow Kallars from neighbouring villages competing to achieve this coup. A Dalit labourer compelled to perform this feat on behalf of higher-caste Kallar villagers. The Kallar headmen hailing the Dalit man's victory as their own village's independence from a larger regional polity. These are the unlikely beginnings of the Vaduvur *natu*'s claims to sovereignty. From these modest beginnings was wrought a byzantine edifice of power, privilege, citizenship, egalitarian rights, subjection, exclusion, and coercion. Banding together, Kallars had established rights to Vaduvur's major temples in order to establish the *natu* polity. Forging relations between gods and humans, the *natu* is founded upon the endowment and administration of temples and animated by the sponsorship and supervision of religious rituals.

The bones of the *natu* polity may be constituted by kinship and caste relations. Its flesh may be formed by temples and rituals. However, its breath – its sovereignty – emanates from and condenses around the juridical. While inhering to the kinship-polity and constituted by its ritual practices, sovereignty is primarily expressed in terms of the Vaduvur *natu*'s juridical powers. The Vaduvur *natu* is sovereign because it is autonomous from and not accountable to other and especially higher authorities – a *tannaracu natu*, or self-governing polity. Vaduvur had been the exception – it could author its own laws and apply them within its own jurisdiction. This legislative independence was buttressed by its headmen's judicial talents and authority in arbitrating disputes and rendering judgments. Vaduvur's residents were subject only to Vaduvur's own laws. Its laws applied only to its own residents. The *natu* assumes for itself the de facto authority to discipline, punish, and even kill with impunity – but only those within its delimited jurisdiction.

At the heart of this juridical apparatus is the power to define – those within the polity and those without, those fully part of the polity and those only partially part of it, those vested with full and equal rights and those who have only limited or no rights at all. Vaduvur's sovereignty is a product of it assuming the authority to declare the exception – define citizenship for or within itself (Agamben 1998). Only Kallar men are citizens. Kallar women are subsumed by their men and made marginal to the polity. Non-Kallars may participate in the polity, but they do not have political rights. Excluded from political sovereignty, they are rendered into mere subjects of Kallar authority. Like the goats sacrificed to the tutelaries, they are embodiments, to varying degrees, of the bare life, the governance of which defines social power and sovereignty. More significantly, male Kallars build their own political subjectivity and sovereign power by appropriating women's and non-Kallar lower-caste bodies, lives, labour, capacities, and rights (see Kapila 2022 on predation as a rubric of sovereign power). Kallar claims to political agency, equal rights, and exercises of citizenship are exclusively male and intermediate-caste based. Their assertions of sovereignty are premised upon the subjection of women and the subjugation of non-Kallars, especially Dalits. Brutal as their impositions may be, marginalizations, exclusions, rampant discriminations, coercion, and violence are the very lifeblood running through and animating the Kallar polity.

Notes

1. Paddy cultivation, contingent on the management of irrigation facilities and mobilization of scarce agrarian labour, meant that the economies of neighbouring villages were inevitably enmeshed. The exigencies of this regime of production demanded some form of extra-village organization to enforce responsibilities and adjudicate disputes. Therefore, the headmen from surrounding villages organized themselves into collective political bodies, the *natus*.

2. Historians such as Shastri (1975) and Stein (1999) have surmised that the Chola emperors themselves were a lineage or clan of petty lords or chiefs that had been able to attain a superordinate position within the *natu* configurations.

3. Some accounts relate how some villagers brought the Ramar statue and those of Sita, Lakshmana, Bharatha, and Hanuman and established them in their village of Thirukannapuram. After many years, they had supposedly transported the icons to Thalai Gnayiru, a village in present-day Nagapattinam District, and buried them under a tree.

4. The Marathas ruled the last pre-colonial kingdom in Thanjavur (1674–1799).

5. *Ficus Religiosa*.

6. Apparently the statues of Lakshmana and Bharatha were installed in a temple in Thalai Gnayiru but worshiped as Rama and Lakshmana instead.

7. This is the eleventh lunar day (*titi*) of each of the two lunar phases (the waxing and waning) in a Hindu month.

8. The neighbouring village of Kudikadu used to be part of Vadapathy. However, nearly eighty years ago, it became part of a different revenue division (*taluk*). Even before this administrative decision in 1947, the six headmen of Kudikadu opted to secede from Vaduvur Vadapathy over a dispute at a consecration ceremony. They chose to attend the *natu* meetings as an autonomous village, not subject to Vaduvur *natu*'s authority.

9. Given Vaduvur's comparatively large size, the headmen attending the Vaduvur *natu* assemblies represent streets housing multiple Kallar lineages.

10. The descendants of the Nondi Kandiyar lineage, of Raman Kandiyar Street, serve as the chief headmen of Vadapathy.

11. In the past, each Kallar family had had their own Dalit servant family (*kuti-paraiyar*) who performed ceremonial tasks for life-course rituals and practical labour in exchange for monetary and other remunerations. Similarly, some Dalits were traditionally engaged to perform certain services for *natu* temples. Responsibilities towards the *natu* took precedence over services owed to individual households. Today, the Dalits have refused to undertake their customary occupations so that this exchange system has been all but abandoned, except perhaps in the nominal sense (Deliege 1999; Clark-Decès 2005). Some Dalits do still turn up for the more prestigious temple services. However, during my fieldwork, the Dalits went on strike. Due to a dispute over the distribution of honours, they refused to perform their customary duties during the Kothandaramaswamy temple's annual festival.

6

Articulations with Electoral Democracy

The procession that usually concludes the goddess Selli Amman's festival was nearly abandoned. In 2007, her newly refurbished temple was ritually consecrated. Meanwhile, the Kallars and the lower-caste Muttiraiyars were disagreeing about the goddess's procession route. At stake was the question of who has the right to offer their sacrifice to the goddess first. The Selli Amman temple is another *natu* temple. A Kallar, of the Vandaiyar clan, was the first to initiate a festival for Selli Amman. However, the temple itself is located in the Kondaiyur hamlet, which is numerically dominated by the Muttiraiyars. The Kallars reside only on two streets. Customarily, the goddess's procession had stopped thrice. First, it stopped at Vandaiyar Street so that the exclusively Kallar congregation could offer sacrificial worship. Next, it stopped at two Muttiraiyar streets – Vemban and Mela – where the Muttiraiyars sacrificed to the goddess. Several years ago, three Kallar families had moved into the hitherto exclusively Muttiraiyar Vemban Street. According to Kamban, the Muttiraiyar watchman (*talaiyari*) of the Vaduvur *natu*:

> These newly arrived Kallars insisted on offering sacrifice near where they lived. They were adamant that the procession should stop for them *before* it went to the Muttiraiyar houses. They said Kallars could not be expected to worship after the lower castes....

The Muttiraiyars pointed out that the Kallars already offered a sacrifice on their own street. Theirs was the first sacrifice to the goddess. The newly arrived Kallars should not expect further privileges. Kamban elaborated:

The Kallars were adamant. Even if they could not sacrifice a goat, they wanted to at least break a coconut and worship first.... Before the goddess went to the Muttiraiyar houses.

Fearing this to be the thin end of the wedge, the Muttiraiyars refused. Kamban retorted, 'We too pay the temple tax. So, we are also entitled to rights in the temple.'

Sevu Vanniyar, advisor to the *natu* headmen, disagreed. Ever since they moved to the street, these Kallars had been worshipping before the Muttiraiyars. But the Muttiraiyars were only protesting that year. This agitation was about the Muttiraiyars wanting more than the rights they had already been allotted to the temple.

The Muttiraiyars want a more advantageous spot for their own sacrifice. They think that if you sacrifice your goat in front of the Selli Amman temple itself, it means that you have equal rights to this temple and its cult. Obviously, the Muttiraiyars cannot be allowed to receive full and equal shares to what is a Kallar *natu* temple.

Neither side was prepared to budge. Selli Amman's icon remained within her temple. The sacrifices were in imminent danger of abandonment. If the procession went ahead, there was a very real threat of inter-caste violence. Since the *natu* had rights over this temple, the headmen intervened. As Sevu Vanniyar put it:

We could not stand idly by and allow the possibility of Muttiraiyars raising their hands against Kallars. We decreed that no one, neither Muttiraiyars nor Kallars, had the right to sacrifice their goats in front of the temple. Custom (*mamul*) did not allow this. The Muttiraiyars could perform their sacrifice at their usual spot, on the road, to the side of the temple.

The headmen also threatened anyone flouting the *natu*'s decree with a punishment (*avataram*).[1] In this way, they ensured that the goddess's procession could proceed.

What Kallars define as their right is, from the perspective of the Muttiraiyars, a privilege. Given their increasing population, education, and prosperity, the Muttiraiyars are now more willing to challenge Kallar privileges. They are no longer satisfied with an inferior form of *natu* membership and restricted access to its ritual cult. On the basis that they paid the same amount of taxes to sponsor the temple and the rituals, they are agitating for equal rights with Kallar citizens. The Kallar headmen, however, argue that Vaduvur is a Kallar *natu* and the *natu* temples are therefore Kallar temples. Non-Kallars (including the Brahmins but especially the lower castes) can have access but should not expect equal rights. They want to retain citizenship and equal rights as a privilege of the Kallars. The headmen's machinations to prevent their greatest threat and fear – the usurpation of equal rights to the *natu* cult by their caste inferiors – were ultimately successful. They may have sacrificed some new and exceptional privileges accorded to some Kallars in order to do so. However, they had achieved their ultimate aim: to maintain their superior rights to the *natu* temple and to retain the Vaduvur *natu*'s definition and government as a singularly Kallar concern. But for how long more?

I began this book with a crisis in the kinship-polity. The primordial deities were no longer roaming their realms. Their devotees could no longer sense their deities' presence. The deities' prowess to intervene in mortal affairs was also waning. From those worshipped by a group of agnatically related kinsmen (lineages and clans) to the sovereign ones of much larger inter-village polities (*natu*): the old gods were deemed to be losing their power (Arumugam 2015). Most vociferously questioning the contemporary potency and relevance of the traditional gods are the headmen of the traditional polities themselves. Their laments are an elegy to the loss of their own authority. Headmen were at the apex of village politics, wielding significant powers with little oversight given Vaduvur's sovereign status and the relative non-intervention of the pre-colonial and colonial authorities. Their decrees applied – albeit with differential severity – to all *natu* residents and especially the lower castes. Given its history of frequent territorial reformulations, headmen were the fulcrum around which the *natu*'s configuration and its sovereignty were premised. However, a more interventionist state and more instrumentalist political actors have emerged to erode the *natu*'s political dominance and evacuate the headmen's authority. The attenuation of its headmen's authority has undermined the *natu*'s continued political viability. So much so that, as we saw in the introduction, a headman questioned why I was even interested in finding out about a dying authority.

Against the headmen's sombre judgements, however, this book concludes on a more ambivalent note. First, the headmen have not been standing idly by as their political power becomes excavated from under them. Instead, they are shoring up their traditional authority using new tactics. As their political capital dissipates, they are leveraging their symbolic and ritual resources onto more secular, specifically philanthropic platforms. The flesh of the kinship-polity may have begun decaying and will probably die soon. However, its bones are still more or less intact. More significantly, its spirit is not only resilient but also infecting and inhabiting new political bodies (Arumugam 2019b). As they are utilized to fight electoral campaigns and mobilize popular votes, the mediums and idioms of the traditional polity are coming to shape democratic politics as well. The polity itself may no longer dominate. However, its politics continue to resonate.

Political Resilience, Developmental Projects

Despite the very real corrosion of their political power, rumours of the headmen's absolute demise have been exaggerated. Their powers may have become more ceremonial than bureaucratic (see also Dirks 1987 on the hollowing out of the kings' crowns in the 'little kingdom' of Pudukkottai). However, the headmen have not passively watched their authority slowly dissipate. Striving to consolidate their traditional bases of authority, their patronage of the *natu* temples continues unabated. Kattaiyar Mannaiyar, a headman elaborated:

> We contributed INR 50,000 towards the extension and refurbishment of Pidari Amman's temple. We had a road built through the agricultural fields to [the hitherto relatively inaccessible] Kailasanathar temple.

To supplement the donations from Panchayat Union funds, the headmen decreed that each Kallar household must contribute INR 1 and the labour of one of their members. The severely dilapidated Kailasanathar temple was refurbished, and the consecration ceremony staged under the headmen's aegis.

> We also financed the renovation works of the Kothandaramaswamy temple. The *natu* contributed INR 100,000 to replace the chariot's wooden struts with metal ones. Having not been used for twenty-eight years, the wooden struts had rotted away. This temple had its consecration in 2007. We also contributed to the refurbishment and consecration of Selli Amman's temple in Kondaiyur.

Patronage of religious establishments – through taxing citizens and decreeing *corvee* labour to serve temple ends – has always been part of the *natu*'s remit and even formed its raison d'être (see Chapter 5). Their continued patronage of temples and rituals is illustrative of how the headmen themselves have not completely withdrawn from the political arena. However, their current sponsorship is framed not so much as a proclamation of their power but an assertion of their rights. As headman Kattaiyar Mannaiyar insisted:

> We cannot give up our rights. These are *natu* temples. The *natu* must have the primary claim over them. We must make this clear.

Their giving is an assertion of the *natu*'s foremost rights to these temples. These are rights which they are unwilling to concede and which they endeavour to claim through their continued and public patronage. The *natu*'s patronage of its temples and rituals may now be fragmented and shared with other parties such as the state government, wealthy individuals, and diasporic villagers.

Nevertheless, it continues to be asserted. The *natu*'s rights are reaffirmed through the politics of gifting. The headmen give to demonstrate that they have not given up – on the power and politics that they are adamant are the *natu*'s right and their own responsibility.

In addition to persisting with these enduring moral idioms of or for doing politics, the headmen have also adopted new strategies to remain relevant to contemporary Vaduvur. Their patronage has even been extended onto less traditional platforms. Cooperating with political parties and state initiatives to construct non-temple-oriented infrastructure and fund non-ritual initiatives, the headmen are striving to demonstrate their continuing relevance. Since the 1970s, the headmen have been involved in lobbying, fund-raising for, and partially financing public infrastructural projects. When the All India Anna Dravida Munnetra Kazhagam (AIADMK) political party first come to power in Tamil Nadu in 1977, the headmen claimed to have personally and tirelessly lobbied the authorities. Upon receiving the necessary permits, Kattaiyar Mannaiyar said:

> The *natu* assembly paid for the purchase of the land and the erection of the buildings for a regulatory market (INR 200,000), a veterinary hospital (INR 320,000), electricity substation (INR 550,000) and a primary health care centre (INR 1.9 million).

On separate occasions, I asked both the headman and the advisor to the *natu* assembly how they were able to generate such considerable funds. Both of them looked sheepish, demurred, and avoided answering. I pressed them further. They both conceded:

> We bought a cheaply priced liquor shop. Then we sold it on for INR 3.3 million. We used the money from selling the liquor shop to help finance the public projects.

Headmen have not themselves contested elections. They have not translated their traditional power into popular power. Not because they cannot but because they claim that they do not want to. Headmen express a marked disdain for democratic politics, considering it 'dirty' and for politicians whom they dismiss as venal. For them, popular politics is oriented towards accruing personal power and amassing economic resources for the politician and his adherents. It is not about exercising power with the mandate of tutelary deities, maintaining the social order and sacred 'purity' of the polity (also Shah 2007 on the Mundas of Jharkand juxtaposing the self-interested and divisive politics of the nation state with their own sacral polity). Democratic politics does not have the cosmological and moral dimensions that their own traditional power did. But just because they have not carved a prominent place for themselves in electoral politics does not mean that they have retreated from active governance into purely ceremonial roles. The politics of patronage have been adapted to contemporary political dynamics (see Piliavsky 2014 for further permutations of patronage in contemporary South Asia). To fortify their waning political capital, the headmen are forging new political alliances and leveraging their remaining economic and symbolic resources. Headmen give because it is their right to do so. But they give also to assert their rights – to constitute the polity and affirm their own place at its governmental apex. Next, I turn to how the logics and ethics framing the *natu* not only persist but also flourish within electoral politics.

Political Idioms and Popular Democracy

Gathering penetration by the nation state and momentum of electoral politics have rendered the Vaduvur *natu* progressively dysfunctional and its headmen increasingly irrelevant. However, the cultural and political logics behind the *natu* still appear to resonate. These logics have not only been made compatible with but have, in fact, facilitated acclimatization to the demands of and indeed are thriving within popular democracy (see Spencer 1997; Michelutti 2004; Witsoe 2011b; Piliavsky 2020). Myths of the transcendental nation state and an ideal democracy may still persevere (Fuller & Benei 2001). However, they have been interpreted and operationalized through established idioms and recognizable mediums such as (sacred) kingship (Price 1996), (divine) kinship (Price 2004; Michelutti 2022, 2008), religious rituals (De Neve 2000; Chibber 2014), gifts (Price 1989; Clark-Decès 2018), caste (Jaffrelot 2010; Michelutti 2019; Kumar 2024), and patronage (Piliavsky 2014; Michelutti et al. 2018). So much so that what were once thought transcendent – politics, the nation state, democracy – have been rendered also routine, even intimate.

Contemporary statecraft for the Kallars – claiming the nation state, utilizing its resources in the interests of one's kin, caste-mates, and clients, and managing the resistance to these efforts – now hinges more upon persuasion rather than coercion. Their customary political ideas, lexicon, and techniques have proven adaptable to the amplified populist imperatives of electoral democracy. They have helped the Kallars to translate and extend their traditional power onto electorally oriented political platforms as evident in the heated electoral campaign for the post of *panchayat* president in 2006.

Vaduvur Vadapathy Panchayat is constituted by two revenue villages – Vadapathy and Melpathy. At the 2006 local bodies elections (LBE), the contest for the president of this *panchayat* was particularly heated. Four compelling candidates in serious competition with each other and the kinship connections between two of them made this a particularly diverting contest (Table 6.1).

Masilamani, the eventual winner was the dark horse. His limited profile in the village meant that his win was unexpected. For the legislative assembly elections (LAE), which determine the government of Tamil Nadu, the votes tend to be determined primarily by political party affiliation. The political party is critical at the LBE as well. Candidates, especially for the top posts, are selected by the main political parties, financed by party funds and supported by their electoral machinery. At the LBE, however, especially in villages, party affiliation is not the only or perhaps even the primary motivation. Given that that the candidates tend to be more proximate to the voters – their kinsman, neighbour, business associates, or employer – local elections tend to be fought also on more intimate grounds. The voting calculus also revolves around the candidates' perceived personality and demeanour, their status in the local socio-economic hierarchy, and their ability to mobilize their kin, clients, and employees. Masilamani and his activities

Table 6.1 Candidates for *Panchayat* President: 2006 Local Bodies Elections, Vadavur Vadapathy

Candidates	Political Party	Village	Street	Kinship
Senthil Kandiyar	Dravida Munnetra Kazhagam (DMK)	Vadapathy	Raman Kandiyar Street	
Kanthan Vanniyar	Independent	Melpathy	Serrukan Vanniyar Street	
Velayutham Vanniyar	Independent	Melpathy	K.K. Vanniyar Street	**Brothers-in-law** (married to a pair of sisters)
Masilamani Vanniyar **(Winner)**	All India Anna Dravida Munnetra Kazhagam (AIADMK)	Melpathy	K.K. Vanniyar Street	**Lineage-mates** (not immediate) **Street-mates**

were not as rooted in the village as his rivals Kanthan and Velayutham. When he announced his candidature, his chances were immediately dismissed. However, Masilamani ran a smart campaign, tactically consonant with Vaduvur's voter profile.

Even as they remain the dominant caste, Kallars are not the key to winning elections in Vadapathy. Not only are they less numerous, Kallar votes tend to be fragmented along party affiliations and kinship lines. Most Kallars were related to one or another of the candidates in some capacity and so their votes tend to be split accordingly. Critical to electoral victory in Vaduvur are actually the bloc of votes from the Dalits and especially the Muttiraiyars. No one from Vadapathy village itself has ever managed to be the Vadapathy *panchayat* president precisely because of the years of rancour between the Dalit and Kallar residents.

The Kallars still consider the Dalits to be their caste inferiors, as ritually polluting 'untouchables'. They have subjected the Dalits to considerable exploitation, discrimination, exclusion, abuses, and violence. Governmental legislation, administrative scrutiny, and legal penalties (primarily the 1989 Scheduled Caste and Scheduled Tribe Prevention of Atrocities Act) have managed to deter some of the more egregious cruelties. Expanding access to education and employment through affirmative action (reservations) and welfare schemes has allowed more Dalits the option to gradually extricate themselves from prevailing caste and class hierarchies in the village. This prompted a Kallar landlord to mutter about the Dalits' more emboldened stance:

> They are now so arrogant. They even refuse to come to work. They talk back. All because of the government. They get all the state benefits – schooling, jobs, etc. The police, the courts all only listen to them. All this support has filled them with temerity. It is not like before.

According to Govindasamy, an Upputhanni lineage-mate and prominent landlord:

> The Dalit settlement of Gandhi Nagar is in Vadapathy. The friction with the Kallars is also particularly acute there. The Dalits will not vote for a Kallar from Vadapathy. Therefore, from the outset, Senthil never had a chance.

This was strictly a contest among the three candidates from Melpathy.

Velayutham and Kanthan were the early front-runners. Both had a strong presence in Vadakkithoppu and Kondaiyur where the Muttiraiyars predominate. With its significantly higher population, Kondaiyur was especially critical to this contest. Both candidates had invested time and effort in cultivating good relations with the agricultural labourers that predominate in Kondaiyur. Since the last elections, Velayutham had been preparing the ground in anticipation of his next campaign. He knew everybody in Kondaiyur, More importantly, he was known by everybody in Kondaiyur. According to his street-mate Govindasamy:

> Since Velayutham has agricultural fields in Kodaiyur, he is very familiar with the area. He also treats his Muttiraiyar workforce well. He attends their weddings and especially their funerals. He is known for being helpful, someone to depend on when in trouble.

Having once been imprisoned for manslaughter, Velayutham was also rumoured to have contacts with criminals. These illicit connections and his street-smarts were deemed to add to his value as a canny and efficacious patron (see Michelutti et al. 2018 on how crimes help establish patrons' reputation and authority). Since deciding to stand for elections, Velayutham began spending even more time in Kondaiyur. Another candidate, Kanthan, used to live nearby and also had fields in Kondaiyur. He spends a lot of time there and knows the Muttiraiyar labour force well. Therefore, Kanthan also has a high profile in Kondaiyur.

Against these competitors, Masilamani, the eventual winner, was severely handicapped. He was practically unknown outside his own street. All his agricultural fields are near where he lives. Most of his labourers are fellow Kallars. He was not conversant with the whole *panchayat*, especially the non-Kallar areas. In a local election where victory hinges also on the electorate's prior knowledge of the candidates as well as their own, their kin's, neighbours', and friends' interactions with them, Masilamani's low profile in the village was an almost insurmountable shortcoming. However, Masilamani had two mitigating advantages. First, he was the AIADMK political party's chosen candidate. Second, he appealed to, rather than repudiated, the familiar protocols of kinship.

Masilamani was backed by the AIADMK. Having lost the LAE elections in May 2006, they did not form the government of Tamil Nadu. However, they had won in Vaduvur. Therefore, Masilamani had access both to considerable party funds and the party machinery. The Tamil Nadu State Elections Commission demands that accounts of election expenditure be lodged with the District Election Officer within thirty days of the election. It has also instituted spending caps on election expenditure for both the rural and urban local bodies. For election as president of the village *panchayat*, the candidate could spend no more than INR 15,000.[2] However, village speculation was that Masilamani had spent somewhere between INR 200,000 and INR 400,000. Since this spending is illegal and therefore clandestine, these figures cannot be unequivocally confirmed. I am providing the range of estimates ventured by a party worker and several voters.

When campaigning began, posters with the candidate's photographs and party colours were pasted around the village. Notices printed with the candidates' photographs and their symbols were distributed to each household. As the elections neared, cars and auto-rickshaws with attached loudhailers circulated the streets ever more frequently, exhorting voters to elect their candidate (Figures 6.1–6.3). Touting their candidate's master's in history, Masilamani's party proclaimed, 'He's an educated man!' His much less educated opponent's supporters countered with, 'He is a cultured man!' Masilamani's side retorted back, 'He will rush right over to answer your calls of distress!' This was merely the beginning.

Coercive Gifting, Electoral Transactions

Most of the party's funds went towards 'gifts' to voters in exchange for their votes. INR 100 was presented to each household in the non-Kallar labourers' areas of Gandhi Nagar, Kondaiyur, Erikarai, and Vadakkithoppu – an amount that was almost double of that offered by the AIADMK's winning candidate for the LAE just five months earlier. Every adult male was offered a 'quarter' (250 millilitres) of local brandy, each costing INR 80.[3] Each woman received a *sari* worth INR 100. Masilamani's supporters went out late at night when most of the voters were sleeping. To avoid discovery by his opponents and especially the authorities, they

Figure 6.1 AIADMK Flags and Procession
Source: Author.

Figure 6.2   Supporters and Firecrackers

Source: Author.

Figure 6.3   DMK Supporters

Source: Author.

simply dropped the gifts on their voter's doorsteps. Velayutham and Kanthan similarly tried to court the voters with gifts. Kanthan reportedly distributed INR 50 to each household in Kondaiyur. Velayutham had *sari*s to give away as well. Receiving a warning that his votes would not count if he were caught, he became alarmed. The night before the elections, Velayutham's supporters had still gone to distribute the *sari*s. Frightened by the prospect of a fight with Masilamani's entourage, however, they had refrained from dispensing them.

The villagers widely believed that Masilamani won largely because of the women's votes. Women outnumber men in this *panchayat*. However, this was the first time that women had been singled out for electoral gifts. After the elections, several male Muttiraiyar respondents from Vadakkithoppu and Kondaiyur blamed their female counterparts' greed for the election results.

> The women fell for the *sari*.
> They took the *sari* and voted for Masilamani.
> Because of their desire for the *sari*, they played Kanthan out.

Gifting the *sari* tipped the balance in Masilamani's favour. Blaming the women allowed the Kondaiyur men to absolve themselves of their own contribution to the result. Simultaneously, it reiterates Masilamani's political acumen. Having canvassed the labourers over a longer duration and much more assiduously, his opponents had much more traction in the Muttiraiyar areas. However, they neglected to woo the women. Masilamani actively focused on women voters as part of his election strategy. After the elections, Ravanan – a member of the defeated Kanthan's retinue – was reported to have remonstrated with Ammakannu, the overseer (*kankani*) of the female Muttiraiyar agricultural workforce. The sight of her in her new *sari*, ostensibly Masilamani's gift, incensed Ravanan. He swore at her for 'betraying' Kanthan's trust and 'selling' her vote for a *sari*. In a feat of strength attributed to his inebriation, Ravanan lifted the hefty woman up by the neck with one hand. His friends had to force him to let her go and drag him away. Afterwards, Ammakannu lamented:

> What can I do? Four Kallar landlords insisted on contesting the elections. But I can only vote for one of them. There is no use blaming me. Someone had to lose.

More than any other gift the *sari* was deemed decisive to the outcome of these elections.

The gift of titles, emblems, and land was, according to Dirks (1993, 1986), the fundamental symbolic means for establishing political relations. This gifting in turn represents and reaffirms hierarchical relations. Superior kings reallocated resources accumulated from their revenue collection to little kings and conferred legitimacy. In return, little kings rendered military assistance, tendered loyalty, and confirmed their overlord's suzerainty. Redistribution more than administration was the mode of statecraft and was the foundation of the pre-colonial south Indian state (Shulman 1985; Price 1996; Mosse 2003b, 2000). These political gifts 'linked individuals and also corporations, symbolically, morally and politically with the sovereignty of the king and created both a moral unity and a political hierarchy' (Dirks 1986: 312). The king ruled and derived his sovereignty through granting endowments. Departing from Dumont's hierarchical and relational configuration of the caste structure, Raheja (1998) proposes a centre–peripheral dynamic. She argues that granting and receiving both ritual and ordinary prestations form the bases of inter-caste and also political relations. With the demise of kings, the dominant caste assumes the prerogatives and responsibilities of gifting and kingship in their village.

The logic of the gift is similarly persuasive when analysing both *natu* and electoral politics in Vaduvur. *Natu* headmen, in their capacity as the administrators of *natu* temples, had once remunerated the artisan castes with parcels of land in K.K.V. Street for their services during the refurbishment of the Kothandaramaswamy temple. Those who have historically contributed (artisans) and continue to contribute (Dalits) their services are still presented with honours following the annual festivals of *natu* temples. Receiving these honours – in recognition of their services to *natu* operations – also represents their subjection and loyalty to *natu* authority. The granting of these honours is yet another representation of the *natu* and its headmen's authority. The right to give is part of their sovereignty. Apart from the initial endowment of land upon the artisans, most of the subsequent *natu* gifting involves the distribution of honours. More than the redistribution of resources, the Vaduvur *natu*'s sovereignty, as explained in Chapter 5, revolves primarily around the right to legislate, arbitrate, and punish.

Within Vaduvur's electoral politics, gifting as a medium of political relations is even more salient. The alcohol, *saris*, and money presented to the electors was explicitly termed 'gifting,' in English. This 'gifting' was in exchange for votes and with the overt aim of establishing a political relationship. Obviously, gifting within the context of electoral politics is not exactly the same as that under kingship. Electoral 'gifting' is a short-term and furtive transaction. Unlike monarchical gifting, it does not form the public foundation of a long-term political union. In the monarchical state, cycles of repeated giving and receiving were the basis of both the state's political operations and the king's legitimacy. In electoral politics, however, the gift initiates the political relationship, tempts the voters to vote for a specific candidate, but plays little part in sustaining that relationship. Legitimacy is gained through popular votes, not continued redistribution. Nevertheless, along with the sponsorship of religious institutions and rituals, gifting continues to reverberate with political meanings. It remains a viable medium through which to initiate short-term political transactions.

Political 'gifting' in Vaduvur is framed by clearly understood but unstated protocols about who can be given as gifts in exchange for votes. It is not an exchange between acknowledged equals, but a hierarchical transaction between caste and class superiors and inferiors. Kallar candidates would never presume to offer such inducements to fellow Kallars. This would ricochet badly on the candidate who would be judged insolent. With her husband active in the Vaduvur branch of the DMK party, Kavya herself follows local politics closely. She explains:

> Kallars offering electoral gifts to other Kallars is not done. People will get offended. They will retort – who do you think you are? You think you are such a big man, you can give *me* money?

Many Kallars, especially the less well-off or younger ones, are not averse to accepting drinks or food when accompanying the candidate on his rounds. They may also expect some recompense after their candidate wins the elections such as winning a tender for a government contract which they then subcontract and recoup their initial outlay. If they have assisted with canvassing, particularly as party workers, they will accept payment for their services or expect their expenses to be defrayed. What they would not accept is the naked equivalence of being given gifts and money with expected votes for the gift-giver. Given the structural and moral emphasis on equality among the Kallars, this would be considered an insult to a caste and class equal. Protocols of electoral gifting re-inscribe key differences in the political relations – (*a*) between fellow citizens of a polity and (*b*) between a sovereign and their subjects – that define *natu* politics.

Such political gifting can only be transacted with those of lower castes like the Muttiraiyars and the Dalits. This may not be a permanent or even a long-term relationship, but a short-term transaction that lasts only over the election cycle. Nevertheless, it is a form of hierarchical gifting like that between patrons and clients (Graeber 2009: 114–116). The logic behind this gift does involve a form of reciprocal exchange – gifts and cash for votes. Having accepted the gift, the receivers do consider themselves to be under an obligation. There is a morality, and a gendered one, inherent to this exchange. This is why the *sari* was a particularly tactical gift, as Kavya elaborated.

You can just spend the money, drink the alcohol, and then forget about the vote. Men often do. But if a woman accepts a *sari*, then every time she wears it, she will be reminded of her promise. If she does not fulfil her obligation, her conscience will be pricked. She will feel guilty.

Despite this expectation of reciprocity, that one would not presume to conduct the same exchange with one's caste-equals but confine it only to one's acknowledged inferiors, affirms that this is not an equal transaction.

The hierarchical logic behind this transaction is further compounded by this political gift being an unwanted and therefore coercive one (Arumugam 2019b). This is a category that Graeber does not consider in his delineation of the typology of transactional logics behind various gift relationships. Most non-Kallar workers had no real choice in deciding whether to accept the gifts. Some may have refused when first offered. However, their refusal may not have been heeded. Either such gifts were pushed into their hands or simply left at their doorsteps while they were sleeping. Govindasamy, Masilamani's street-mate and clan-mate (both are Vanniyars), had accompanied Masilamani on a gifting mission to the Dalit settlement, Gandhi Nagar. He explained:

We went around at about 6 pm. Only the women were home. They all said that they did not want any money. They would still vote for Masilamani. But I assured them that this money was just for their expenses. We would not ask for its return. We would not retaliate. Even if Masilamani lost. The women then acquiesced. They took the money.

Actually, these non-Kallar agricultural labourers can ill afford to refuse the inducements for a number of reasons, only one of which is their inferior status. A wealthy and powerful landowner specifically coming to one's house (*vitu teti vantu*) and politely asking for a favour from a poor labourer is a reversal of the status quo. Workers may want to refuse but still find it difficult to do so. This ethical dilemma cannot be divorced from the consideration of politics.

These Dalit workers also do not have the real choice to refuse the landowner because they depend on him for work. He may need their favour this one time, but they will need it throughout the year. They cannot afford to spite him. The Kallars resent the Dalits' improved socio-economic conditions since this frees the latter from depending almost totally on the landlords for their livelihoods.[4] As a result of government initiatives, legal protections, and policy shifts, Dalit prospects have certainly improved. Nevertheless, the agrarian milieu continues to be structured by the economic interdependence between labourers and landowners, lower and higher castes, clients and patrons. This also feeds into electoral politics.

Accepting bribes for votes is considered shameful. It indicates one's lower status and powerlessness in the village dynamic. This is why the artisans, who are acknowledged as superior to the Kallars caste-wise but not class-wise, publicly declare that they would never accept bribes. However, the poorest of them are known not to be above doing so, but again only surreptitiously. A Kallar who would not dare insult his caste-mates, even the poorest among them, with a direct bribe to buy their votes would not hesitate to do so to Muttiraiyars and Dalits. It is not about saying yes to the gift but the fact that they do not have the real choice to say no. Or rather, they can refuse but may then face a potential backlash. Retaliatory tactics may include landlords not hiring them for agricultural work, withholding the use of their yard space (see Chapter 3), and perhaps – but more so in the past when police and legal protections for the Dalits were laxer – even violence. This unwanted gift to the receiver and a forced gift from the donor is evidence of a coercive transactional logic. Despite the *natu* polity's decline, the Kallars' political dominance still reverberates and has even been adapted to the differing demands of popular politics.

Such an interpretation was corroborated by another of Masilamani's tactics. The gifts may have been the carrot. However, Masilamani was not above, although not personally so, using the stick. Raman is actually a lineage-mate of Masilamani's rival, Kanthan. As an AIADMK supporter and dismissive of Kanthan's chances, Raman had instead elected to join Masilamani's campaign. When he won an infrastructural contract, Raman had overseen the laying of a road through the Muttiraiyar-dominated Vadakithoppu. He now threatened to rip up that road if the Muttiraiyars did not vote for Masilamani. This was simply an implied threat and most likely an empty one. However, it resonated among the susceptible Muttiraiyars. Raman also threatened to beat up the Muttiraiyars in Vadakithoppu and Kondaiyur if Masilamani lost. How effective these intimidatory tactics were is debatable. What is noteworthy is that Masilamani neither reined Raman in nor distanced himself from Raman's threats. However, he did promise to intervene and protect the Muttiraiyars if any of his defeated opponents threatened them or sought to revenge themselves for their loss. When such an occasion did arise – when Kanthan's supporter Ravanan threatened the overseer Ammakannu – the Muttiraiyars did call on Masilamani. He and his supporters did rush to their aid, fulfilling at least one of his election promises.

Kinship Protocols, Political Mobilizations

Gifting may provide the means to build political support among one's caste and class inferiors. The protocols to do with gifting – knowing who to approach, how to approach, and most importantly through whom to approach – is supplied by the relations and rules of kinship. Given Masilamani's low profile in the village and his relative lack of rapport with the Muttiraiyar and Dalit labourers, approaching them on his own with blatant material inducements to vote for him would have proved tactically disastrous. This was especially so in Vadapathy with its long history of friction between Kallar landlords and Dalit labourers. A more subtle approach was necessary. Masilamani had to mediate the political prerogative of gifting through the diplomatic protocols of kinship.

When approaching Vadapathy's Dalit labourers, to whom he was almost completely unknown, Masilamani cannily enlisted the help of his street-mate and clan-mate Govindasamy. Govindasamy lives in Melpathy. However, he is well known to the Dalits in Vadapathy. His mother was born in Vadapathy. Two of his elder sisters are married to Vadapathy men. He also cultivates the Vadapathy lands of the sister living in Singapore[5] and had periodically employed these Dalits. Govindasamy's still renowned winning of a long-running legal battle over this sister's lands had earned him the notice and respect of those in Vadapathy, including the Dalits.[6] Govindasamy was also renowned throughout Vaduvur as a popular comedian in amateur dramas. Govindasamy is one of the rare Kallar landlords who has any profile at all, let alone a good reputation, among the Dalits. This prompted Masilamani to recruit Govindasamy to assist him in the efforts to secure the three hundred Dalit votes available. The fact that Govindasamy usually kept out of politics and was not one of the serial vote canvassers also meant that his rare request would be considered. Govindasamy was clearly successful. As Govindasamy said:

> On his way to a funeral, Senthil [the Vadapathy candidate] stopped me. He shook his head ruefully. He said his entire campaign had come undone in a two-hour stint. When I went with Masilamani around the Dalit settlement.

Unlike in the traditional *natu* polity, contemporary electoral politics in Vaduvur is not founded upon and framed entirely by kinship. Nevertheless, it does draw from and feed into kinship – specifically lineage, street, clan, and affines. The key to electoral victory may lay with the non-Kallar blocs. However, the support of one's own kin remains the first step in one's campaign to attain political office and a vital means to access votes (even non-Kallar ones). It serves as a certificate of electability. If a candidate cannot even muster the support of his own kin, how can he hope to win over other voters?

There are two reasons for why kin support demonstrates electability – (*a*) the electoral format and (*b*) kinship ethics. For the LAE, all one can realistically base one's vote on is the party, its manifesto, and the candidate's promises. At the LBE, however, one is electing a fellow villager, and the means available to evaluate a candidate are both wider and more intimate. Face-to-face interactions, personal history, observation of their everyday conduct, the kinds of people they associate with, their work, how they treat their employees, character studies cobbled together from a variety of sources including rumours, and the demands of kinship: all these figure in the villagers' decisions as to who to vote for. Embeddedness in the village and its activities – which in turn generate a local profile – is a primary determinant of a candidate's electability. Support from those who know them best, their kin, serves both as the candidates' résumé and their character reference.

This requires an appreciation of the morality implicit to kinship relations. Bloch's (1971: 75–77) definition of kinship morality is premised upon reciprocity. He clarified that it is a 'special kind of reciprocity whose characteristics derive from the categorical moral nature of the dogma' (also De Neve 2008). Kin are expected to help each other. More importantly, kin are also expected to tolerate delays in reciprocation or remuneration. The moral dynamics framing and fuelling kinship forces actors to accept imbalances in relationships, at least in the short term (Clark-Decès 2014: 76–97). Kinship's moral imperatives allow one to assume the reliability of kin over time. All kinship relations, Bloch (1971) surmises, have both a moral meaning and a tactical utility. The task is to unravel the moral meanings behind different kin relationships and the differential expectations they imply. Members of a lineage and/or street should safeguard their fellow members' interests, especially when their own kin's interests are threatened by other lineages, streets, villages, or even affines. At the heart of lineage morality lies the duty to defend one's own, as if oneself, against not just non-kin (strangers) but also not-so-close kin. Govindasamy was initially reluctant to assist Masilamani and refused his appeals. He did not particularly like or trust Masilamani. Govindasamy explained:

> In 1998, my father's younger brother and I had a dispute over the boundaries between our adjoining lands. My uncle bribed the officials and had the land documents changed. He now claimed part of my land as his. I appealed to Masilamani for help. He knew I was in the right. But he refused to get involved.

Govindasamy has never forgiven Masilamani for this betrayal. However, Masilamani finally wore his resistance down.

Most persuasive was Masilamani's appeal to the many kinship ties that mutually entwined them.[7] The appeal to kin morality has its limits – people are discerning about its exploitative potential (De Neve 2008). Overemphasizing kinship morality reveals very little of itself or people's motivations. Kinship's implicit morality does not preclude but actively includes self-interest. Masilamani had to motivate Govindasamy to act in his individual interest by appealing to the morality of kinship and therein their common interests. More than not letting his kinsman down, Govindasamy was motivated by contributing to his clan and street's prestige.

> If Masilamani won, then it brings glory to the entire Vanniyar clan and especially to K.K.V. Street. I finally relented not for Masilamani's sake.... My wife still does not like that I helped him. But I wanted my clan-mate and street-mate to win.

Govindasamy wanted Masilamani to win not so much because it would be good for Masilamani himself but because it would reflect well on their common clan and street. Masilamani exploited this combination of obligations – kinship's moral imperative, the collective prestige of one's kin group, and self-interest – to further his own interests. Masilamani is a successful politician largely because he was sensitive to these intersections of moral obligations and egotism – loss of face and gaining prestige as well as competing self-interests and collaborative mutual interests – effectively leveraging them to convince others to act on his behalf.

Framing any relationship – let alone a political one – in terms of kinship obligations means that the framers themselves become obligated to their kin. By extracting obligations from his kin – through asserting the morality underpinning kinship – Masilamani had to in turn reciprocate by acknowledging his own obligations to them. What candidates owe their kin is the acknowledgement of that kin, the candidates' own genesis. From where and from whom they come defines a villager. Despite my reservations about the totalizing impetus of autochthony (see Chapter 3), Daniel's (1982) overall thesis – the significance of a native village and its substances to constituting personhood, especially once the persons have left – remains indisputable. One can even take this further. Who a person is, is constituted by not only the substances of their natal village (*conta ur*) but also its inhabitants or their kin (*contakkarar*). Masilamani is never just Masilamani but simultaneously an assemblage of his household, lineage, street, and affines. To express who they are, they must acknowledge who their kin are. More significantly, they must signify how integral their kin are to their endeavours by according to them the honour of precedence. Masilamani was politically successful because he understood these protocols of reciprocity and precedence and discharged them accordingly.

Upon deciding to stand, Masilamani ensured that he not only had the support of his lineage-mates, clan-mates, and street-mates but also his affines, Vadapathy's

Sakkarei Kandiyar lineage. This contrasted sharply with the actions of his brother-in-law and rival, Velayutham. Having severed ties with them, Velayutham did not even bother informing his affines of his political intentions. Kanthan too had handicapped his own campaign by flouting the kinship protocols. He not only failed to secure his own lineage-mates' support but also did not even consult them before deciding to stand for office. This incensed his lineage-mates. They felt that Kanthan was not worldly wise enough to handle Vaduvur politics. Consequently, they refused to vote for him. He could not secure the votes of his street-mates who had similar doubts about his suitability for the job. Conversely, despite there being a competing candidate from his own street, Masilamani managed to secure the majority of his street-mates' votes. Even as the sole candidate from his street, Kanthan failed to secure the majority of the votes available. According to Govindasamy, who once again accompanied Masilamani to rival candidate Kanthan's own Serrukkan Vanniyar Street:

> When we went to Murugesu Kandiyar's (Kanthan's street-mate) house to ask for his support, he made an extraordinary move. Though half of his household's six available votes would go to their own kinsman Kanthan, he promised that the rest would go to Masilamani. Masilamani is not kin. He is also from the neighbouring street.

Masilamani was sufficiently overcome as to tightly hug the old man.

Kanthan's neglect of his base (his own kin) was a grave mistake. This cast severe doubts on his electability and aptitude. According to Paapa, one of Kanthan's neighbours, his lineage-mates and senior, more experienced street-mates accused Kanthan of not respecting them. Becoming swayed by the blandishments of some younger street-mates had laid the foundation for his eventual downfall.[8] The village consensus was that Kanthan had spent so much time in Kondaiyur, he became unused to political protocols in Vaduvur. So immersed was he in Kondaiyur that he was not conversant with other labourers' or even other Kallar areas. Worse, he had trusted the Kondaiyur Muttiraiyar labourers too much when they assured him that they would vote for no one but him. All their promises came to nothing. Both Kallar and Muttiraiyar men patronisingly surmised, 'The Vadakkithoppu and Kondaiyur women were seduced by Masilamani's free *saris*'. They even framed Kanthan's reputation for honesty as a reflection of his naïveté rather than an unequivocal virtue. Perhaps he was not corrupt because he did not know how to be crooked without getting caught. A successful politician must not only be able to swim in the 'sewer that is politics' but must also emerge unscathed. More than virtuous incorruptibility, Vaduvur villagers appreciate street-smarts, shrewdness, and adaptability in a politician (see Witsoe 2011a on Yadavs in Bihar framing corruption as a resource for accruing power).

The interpenetrations of politics, kinship, and patronage within rural electoral politics especially mean that politics has to be conducted according to specific diplomatic proprieties. These protocols dictate not only who to approach and, more importantly, in what order – since precedence must always be given to kin – but also how best to approach them. Masilamani is a successful politician because he understands these protocols and approached each type of voter in the manner appropriate to them. As further evidence of his political savvy, he was not above canvassing votes from anyone with a valid vote. He approached everyone from low-caste labourers to even the wives of his rival's lineage-mates. He would engage everyone for a few minutes even if he had been introduced to them only recently. I watched him go from door to door to each and every house to ask for votes. Several women from his own street joked:

> If we had said we are too busy grazing our life-stock to vote on Election Day, he would have offered to take over the grazing so we could go and vote instead.

He arranged cars to ferry the elderly to the voting venue. He also did this for a recently widowed voter (who should not be seen venturing away from her house until her husband's first death anniversary) so she could vote at her convenience. Admittedly, these are elementary tactics. Nevertheless, they were somehow beyond Masilamani's rivals.

Kanthan is painfully shy. Even at the head of his own motor-cavalcade going around canvassing for votes, he faced straight ahead, arms held stiffly up, and palms cupped together in the traditional gesture of greeting. He only ventured hesitant smiles. His demeanour telegraphed his discomfort. Velayutham, however, was deemed arrogant in stark contrast to his friendly wife, Selvi, who herself had been a *panchayat* president in the past. Velayutham did not go from door to door to canvass votes. Although his wife did so on his behalf, this merely reinforced the widely held opinion of him as dismissive. He often just casually waved while riding past on his motorcycle, not even bothering to stop and greet people along the way. His lineage-mates advised that one could not assume one already had the votes or disrespect or coerce the voters. In a democracy, to garner votes, one must persuade voters, even subordinate oneself (*ati paninccu*) to them if necessary. However, they were dismissed with Velayutham retorting that he did not need the votes that could only be acquired by bowing and scraping to the electorate. His glib aloofness invited counter-retorts, especially from fellow Kallars, 'Who the hell does he think he is?'

Despite, Masilamani's AIADMK support, political acumen, and respecting of kinship protocols, until four days before the elections, the race still hung in the balance. Velayutham and Kanthan were quietly confident. Post-election village opinion was that without Masilamani's party backing and resulting access to monetary resources, Kanthan would be the *panchayat* president. We must not understate how decisive Masilamani's massive expenditure – which far outstripped that of his rivals – was. Gift and monetary incentives may have been the deciding factor for the non-Kallar voters. However, the Kallar voters' choices were shaped significantly by the considerations and moralities of kinship.

The Kallar voters did consider each candidate's demeanour when deciding whom to elect. However, they could only do this because of their intimate awareness of the candidates' character due to their long associations with them as fellow kin. Chinnappa, from the Serrukkan Vanniyar Street's Kandiyar lineage, announced:

> I was born on K.K.V. Street. So, Masilamani and Velayutham are also my classificatory brothers. But Kanthan is from my [marital] street. He is also my classificatory son-in-law.[9] I cannot think about voting for anyone else but Kanthan.

Serrukkan Vanniyar Street's male residents, however, were more wary. They did not allow the moral imperatives of belonging to the same lineage, clan, or street to push them to unequivocally vote for their kinsman. They considered other similarly compelling ethical motives – precedence and reciprocity. Kanthan did not come to them first before electing to stand, as he should have. Indeed, he had never consulted them at all. If Kanthan himself defied kinship protocols, why should they be bound by their kinship obligations? On K.K.V. Street, kinship proved resonant; the majority opted for Masilamani because he was their kinsman – their lineage-mate and/or clan-mate and/or street-mate. Velayutham too was kin to them. However, his arrogance mitigated the advantages of kinship, at least for his street-mates who responded more equivocally. Distaste for Velayutham's personality triumphed over their obligations to him, especially since there was another more attractive candidate also from their street. Nevertheless, all of Velayutham's lineage-mates, with more proximate ties and therefore a keener sense of moral imperative, felt obliged to vote for him. However, Masilamani and Velayutham's affines, the Sakkarei Kandiyar lineage, faced a real quandary. Two of their daughters' lives were involved.[10] Velayutham disregarded them while Masilamani was more respectful. Nevertheless, they could not antagonize one of their sons-in-law by favouring Masilamani to Velayutham. It would humiliate their daughter on the losing side and also jeopardize their future relationship with her. Balancing their considerations for both daughters required careful calculations and a scrupulous rationing of their votes. Like the Serukkan Vanniyar Street patriarch mentioned earlier, they too split their households' available votes equally between their rival sons-in law.

Conclusion

Politics is vitally premised on killing (and dying). Ruling depends on a cycle of killing and giving. The sin accrued through killing is alleviated through gifting – donation to sacred and sacerdotal causes. To have the resources to give necessitates more conquering and therefore more killing, giving rise to an impossible dilemma (Clark-Decès 2018; Shulman 1980a: 306). Shulman (1980a: 90–91) elaborates: 'The Hindu universe is a closed circuit, nothing new can be produced except by destroying or transforming something else.' Shulman was referring to how the sacrificial act is understood to generate new life. This also applies to politics in the Tamil universe. As already mentioned in Chapter 5, in the classical poetic text the *Pattinappalai*, the Chola king Karikalan is extolled for killing the forest (*katu kontru*) to create the polity (*natu akki*) (Venkatachalapathy 2006: 59). A new political body cannot be built out of nothing. What precedes it must be killed (and incorporated) into the new political body.

*Natu*s and other such kinship-polities themselves are premised upon tempestuous histories of destruction, decomposition, and re-creation.[11] The current Vaduvur *natu* itself, according to several headmen and their advisor Sevu Vanniyar's accounts, used to be part of a much larger configuration of eighteen villages that stretched 14 kilometres to the nearest town of Mannargudi. This polity's headquarters was the Paruthiappar temple near Kumbakonam. Due to a dispute over the rights to this temple, this polity broke apart. The current Vaduvur *natu* was established upon the remains of this much larger entity.[12] Vadapathy together with three other villages, namely Thenpathy (which had itself separated from nearby Orathanadu), Pudukkottai, and Neivasal, then formed a greater polity (*peru-natu*) called the Kulantaivala Natu. Pudukkottai and Neivasal seceded from this Kulantaivala Nadu over temple disputes. Today, only Vadapathy, Thenpathy, and Kudikadu (historically part of Vadapathy but now a separate village) form the Vaduvur *natu*. Cartographic precision has never been the basis of the *natu*'s definition. *Natu*s are rooted in territory as far as their sovereignty is dependent on delimited jurisdiction. A specific *natu*'s constituents and its frontiers, however, have waxed and waned according to prevailing religio-political disputes.

Once again, *natu*s are changing, but this time not so much in size but in terms of significance.

The *natu* – as a political formation – is unravelling. Tutelary deities are no longer policing and protecting as assiduously as they had in the past – at least fewer people are encountering them doing so (Arumugam 2015). The sharing of icons, temples, and rituals around which the *natu* had revolved is fragmenting as agonistic politics threaten and engulf them. Headmen complain of being unheeded. Political parties and politicians are now ascendant. More than any other previous authority, the Indian nation state and its institutions have penetrated deeply into rural Tamil Nadu. The old *natu* polity, if not actually dead, is dying. The newer electoral politics is becoming ever stronger. However, democratic politics has been able to thrive in part by feeding upon kinship-polities and their political organs. By imbibing older, more familiar, and more localized political idioms and mediums – kinship, rituals, and the gift – electoral politics, far from having to struggle to be born and to grow, has burgeoned in Vaduvur. As this newer politics thrives, however, *natu* polities continue to fade. *Natu* polities are slowly becoming a frailer, paler shadow of their once glorious pomp and real power. And yet they are still fighting for relevance in a crowded and competitive political landscape. However feebly, *natu* polities do cling on to life.

Notes

1. Details about punitive measures used by the *natu* assembly when its decrees were flouted are not abundant in Vaduvur (see Dumont 2000 on punishments among the Piranmalai Kallars). Whipping, excommunication, and exile from the *natu* were the most extreme penalties that the headmen had recourse to and were reserved for especially heinous crimes. For misdemeanours, the fulfilment of externally imposed religious vows and financial restitution are customary. Here, the *avataram* refers to a fine. It is a financial penalty in that the guilty would have to sponsor the materials used in worship (such as the oil for fuelling the temple lamps) for a specified duration. Not only were the guilty punished but the *natu* temple also benefitted.

2. Quoted in the Tamil Nadu Election Commission Website: http://www.tnsec. tn.nic.in/. The spending caps for election for other posts in the village were as follows. For ward member of a village *panchayat*, the cap was INR 3,750. The village *panchayat* is composed of a number of ward members (each representing a street) led by the president of the *panchayat*. Above the village *panchayat* is the *panchayat* union consisting of a number of village *panchayat*s. Above this is the district *panchayat* which consists of a number of *panchayat* unions.

The spending ceiling for election as a ward member in the *panchayat* union is INR 37,500 and for a member of a district *panchayat* INR 75,000.

3. It was reported by those in the house where I lived that a truck with crates of bottles of liquor was hidden behind one of their haystacks the night before election day, to be distributed the day after. Stealth was paramount because all electioneering has to stop two days before the elections and election officers might have been out monitoring.

4. See Beteille (1971) and Gough (1989, 1981, 1971, 1960) on comparable but also shifting economic dependencies, between Brahmin landlords and lower-caste labourers in Thanjavur in the 1950s, 1960s, and 1970s, which gave rise to and reinforced exploitations and social stratifications.

5. My mother.

6. Legal cases involving tenants and absentee landlords are notoriously fraught and rarely decided in favour of the landlord, given land reform legislation inaugurated in 1953 favouring cultivating tenants. That Govindasamy not only won this case by acting for the landlord but also immediately employed a Dalit crier to proclaim this victory throughout the village was deemed audacious. Secure in his position, especially given that the case was being fought for nearly fifteen years, the defeated litigant had already planted rice as normal, and it was ready to harvest. Right after the favourable verdict, Govindasamy hired a hundred labourers (many of whom were Dalits from Vadapathy) and proceeded to harvest the whole crop in a *single* day. This act created a sensation. Consequently, many of the Vadapathy Dalits not only knew Govindasamy but also respected him.

7. Something else that convinced Govindasamy to change his mind was Masilamani bombarding Govindasamy with calls and threatening to fall at Govindasamy's feet if he had to. Falling at someone's feet means subordinating oneself to an acknowledged social superior or debasing one's dignity. While acceptable as a sign of respect from juniors towards their seniors in terms of age, social status, or even knowledge and experience, it is anathema among socially equal men of the same age. Govindasamy did not want Masilamani to lose face, even to himself.

8. Kanthan is a poor man, overseeing the cultivation of lands belonging to one of his street-mates, Kumaran Vanniyar, who runs a travel agency in Chennai and frequently travels to Singapore and Malaysia. Additionally, he supervised the building of a two-storeyed house in Vaduvur for Kumaran's maternal aunt's family living in Singapore. In return for his assistance (also because Kanthan is a remarkably honest man) and to alleviate him from his relative poverty, Kumaran and his Singaporean aunt decided to finance his bid. When he lost, they did not blame or berate Kanthan but settled his debts. Kumaran also had another aim

prompted by his ongoing friction with Velayutham. Since Velayutham declared his candidature first, Kumaran saw sponsoring Kanthan's electoral bid as an ideal opportunity to get even.

9. On Serukkan Vanniyar Street, there are four lineages in total – three with the suffix Vanniyar and one with Kandiyar. With one being his own immediate lineage, the other two Vanniyar lineages consist of his more distant lineage-mates. Given the endogamous nature of the lineage system, the Kandiyar lineage is reckoned as Kanthan's affines.

10. Masilamani's elder sister is also married into this lineage.

11. *Natu*s have had turbulent histories of formation, friction, and dissolution and their boundaries have been constantly redrawn (Stein 1980).

12. Evidence of significant past associations is apparent even today. Vaduvur continues to be given foremost honours (*mutal mariyatai*) during the annual Panguni Uthiram festival at the Paruthiappar temple.

Conclusion
Ritual Remnants, Political Permutations

Pidari Amman's procession is no longer enacted. The goddess does not leave her temple. She no longer ventures forth to survey her kingdom and sanction her subjects.[1] She does not visit her husband, Kailasanathar, at his temple in Vadapathy. Nor does she re-enact the marriage that forms the foundation of the Vaduvur polity and fuels its productivity. This radically departs from the ritual's heyday where, as the headmen's advisor Sevu Vanniyar reminisced,

> the seven-tier chariot used to ferry the goddess was not dragged like those you see today. It had to be manually carried by twenty men. This Pidari was born in Thenpathy.[2] But she was married into Vadapathy. While she lives in Thenpathy, her husband, Kailasanathar, resides in Vadapathy. For the *natu* festival, Pidari was carried from her own temple to husband's one, the Kailasanathar temple. The men used to say that she was very light and easy to carry at her own temple and in Thenpathy. As they got closer to Vadapathy, however, she became heavier and heavier. At her husband's house, Pidari was almost impossible to bear.
>
> Each house along the procession route sacrificed a goat. A priest conducted the worship. Eight Dalits wearing a protective bracelet (*kappu*) played their instruments. Since they had to keep playing, they could not go home throughout the festival. So, they ate and slept at the temple. The goddess was set down at her husband's house, beautified, and left there for eighteen days. Meanwhile, there were ceremonies for the other deities at the temple. At the end of the eighteen days, she returned to Thenpathy. The chariot was initially heavy but becomes

lighter as they got closer to her own temple. At her own temple, there would also be a grand festival....

From their settlement in Vadapathy, a topless Dalit woman carried a pot of sprouted grains on her head to offer to the goddess. Many goats were sacrificed. Their blood was mixed with cooked rice and the sprouted grains, rolled into balls, and tossed into the branches of the trees. The balls had not fallen down but been caught by the spirits....

The remains of long-abandoned rituals are palimpsests. Older forms remain visible through the contemporary iterations superimposed over them. Ritual remnants are chronicles of transformations – from a time, now passed, when rituals had been protracted, enacted with pomp, and the requisite deities had been especially powerful, but also a problematic era when the lower castes were ineluctably subject to Kallar power and coerced to perform sometimes ignominious ritual tasks. In Vaduvur, ritual remnants also allude to political metamorphoses. Ritual abandonment or transformations are propelled by the charged and changed political conditions that generated and sustained them. Rituals themselves can and have been overwhelmed by material and political vagaries. Their residues therefore serve as accounts of how such vernacular polities were initially formed and made potent through rituals. They are the ghostly traces of older, fallen or declined polities that continue to haunt contemporary politics.

A local goddess such as Pidari Amman marrying a pan-Indian god like Shiva is often the basis for connecting a local cult with a pan-Indian tradition (Fuller 2004: 41–44). It renders an autochthonous goddess the local incarnation of the universal Shakti (Shiva's consort) and incorporates her into the mainstream Hindu pantheon. Such divine marriages do not simply constitute an orthodox Hindu order by subsuming the local Tamil tradition into a cosmic Sanskritic one. Shiva's marriage (and eventual sacrifice) to a vernacular goddess is also the foundation for renewing the power and fecundity of the locality itself (Shulman 1980a: 138–316; Fuller 2004: 43–48). In Vaduvur, the divine marriage is also a political union – constituting the polity, fuelling its productivity, and legitimating its purposes. Vaduvur's Pidari Amman marrying the pan-Indian Kailasanathar delineates a local religio-political territory – the separate villages of Thenpathy (Pidari's natal village) and Vadapathy (her husband Kailasanathar's abode) unifying to form the Vaduvur *natu*.

So far, this concurs with theorizations of ritual as forms of ideology that provide an alternative and an antidote to the uncertainties of everyday life. Ritual's highly formalized structure, Bloch (1992) argues, underpins its consistency in the face of dramatic socio-political transformations and its essential capacity to restrict debates and inhibit contestations. Ritual's archetypal capacity to demonstrate a transcendent order's power over earthly life's violent and volatile vitality explains its attraction for powerholders attempting to endorse, reinforce, and claim a permanence to their authority. Rituals confer authority because they represent continuity and traditionality by constantly referring to 'an original state and an anterior order' that is simultaneously 'superior and a resource for a future and better order' (Feuchtwang 1998: 38). Any tensions and contestations within the ritual are themselves highly scripted and part of the ritual form itself. Mystifying the hierarchies of power, ritual here is essentially conservative.

Pidari Amman and Kailasanathar's divine union, however, neither suppresses conflicts nor superimposes harmonious ideals over everyday realities. While it does produce a temporary union, their marriage is a reluctant, even fraught one. As the bearers approach her consort Kailasanathar's temple, Pidari Amman's chariot becomes heavier and heavier until it is almost unbearable. The goddess is clearly unenthusiastic about leaving her own territory to go to that of her future husband. The simmering tensions between virginity and domesticity as well as that between sovereignty and subservience are blatant. During the eighteen days in her husband's abode, Pidari Amman is no longer the ruler of her own kingdom. She has to be a submissive wife, which she deeply resents. Drawing upon Reiniche (1979) and Dumont (1980), Fuller (2004, 1988) identifies four criteria upon which hierarchies between superior and inferior deities within the Hindu pantheon are premised. These include (*a*) the extent of the deities' jurisdiction,[3] (*b*) the inclination to accept or refuse animal sacrifice,[4] (*c*) occupational relations such as guardian deity and great deity, with the latter ascribed superior status, and, finally, (*d*) kinship dynamics – wife–husband, progeny–parents, with the latter always being superior.[5] Within her limited jurisdiction, Pidari Amman is a sovereign. Based on the aforementioned criteria, however, she is definitely subordinate to Kailasanathar. Pidari Amman is reluctant to sacrifice her own autonomy. She resents being encompassed by and subject to her husband and universal ruler's sovereignty. This unwillingness is not hers alone. Kailasanathar himself is Shiva's ascetic avatar who has renounced all domestic entanglements. Marriage disrupts his cosmic meditations. So, he too is disinclined. Following her obligatory conjugality, Pidari returns to her own kingdom, freed from the weight of wifely deference. As she nears her home, Pidari's chariot becomes lighter and lighter. The goddess clearly relishes reigning in splendid isolation.

The divine marriage that represents and should renew the Vaduvur polity is anything but a harmonious ideal. It does not transcend but is itself inherently political and therefore tense.[6] Both deities loathe having to surrender their sovereignty even for a short-term cohabitation. Their union is but a temporary concession to the demands of generativity. Pidari Amman's eager anticipation of the festival's end and the dissolution of her obligatory merger with Kailasanathar is manifest within the ritual complex itself. Her chariot's heaviness and lightness when approaching her marital home or returning to her natal kingdom respectively demonstrate how she begrudges being simply a wife, encompassed by her husband's ritual cult and subject to his male authority. The eighteen days she spends in her marital home are to be endured. She looks forward to returning to her own temple and resuming her own state of singular and uncompromised sovereignty. The ritual marriage does not resolve but is itself mired in politics.

These politics would not have been visible if one were to only privilege this festival's ritual core – the divine marriage itself. Merely concentrating on Thenpathy's Pidari Amman marrying Vadapathy's Kailasanathar and them subsequently receiving worship as a married couple may allow one to perceive a perfectly unified Vaduvur *natu*. This does allow one to dispense with process and practicalities to grasp, however momentarily, the ideal and the ineffable. It makes the sublime seem possible and even attainable. In the process, we would also be missing much. Pidari's clear reluctance to surrender her sovereignty to conjugality and her comparative relief to return to her natal village and resume her unattached autonomy – these are only apparent if we consider what precedes and what ensues after the ritual itself. Only if we consider the seemingly trivial matter of her chariot's weight on her journey to and from her ritual marriage can we grasp how resistant the goddess herself is to subordination and incorporation and how much she values her own sovereignty. Grappling not just with its core but also its infrastructure puts an entirely different complexion on the ritual. The ritual may be intended to defy process. However, it is precisely the process that illuminates the fundamental concern of this ritual – not political union as much as sovereignty.

The tension between incorporation and autonomy also resonates throughout the polity that this ritual sacralizes – from the lineage to the street to the *natu*. Rituals may define the Vaduvur *natu* as a (tensely) unified territory, delineate hierarchies of power, and assert a mode of self-governance. However, as I have described throughout, the polity thus narrated is not an inert artefact of statecraft. It is a complex arena of contestations over precedence, order, and autonomy. The Kallars acknowledge the necessity of cooperation and even incorporation for the purposes of survival and generativity. Simultaneously, they also surface repeated resistance to and resentment of integration within a larger political order. Coalitions are not just contingent but also largely reluctant ones. Saturating their myths, rituals, deities, kinship frameworks, feuds, and everyday lives is an enduring scepticism of attachment, specifically political affiliation. The eternal struggle between the need for social coherence and an emphatic insistence on sovereignty forms the ordering force of their politics. Before that, however, we must first consider how these polities are birthed and bodied – as concatenations of processes of self-making and state-building.

Building Polities, Crafting Politics

What goes into making a polity? Who and what is the polity for? Who are included within and govern the polity? Conversely, who are marginalized and excluded from or coerced into the polity? What happens when the nation state and popular elections add yet another layer onto already sedimented polities? For these Kallars, making and unmaking kin is a means of making the self – a self crucially laden with rights in and to shared deities, communal territories, and, most of all, kinspersons. This is the foundation of all their polities. Genealogy is not simply anthropologists' illusions but a critical part of political constitution for interlocutors (cf. Bourdieu 1997; Schneider 1980, 1984). Lived genealogy – recognizing and classifying types of kin – is vital for crafting this polity and producing political value. Embracing but also fighting with kin, including but also marginalizing not-so-kin, and completely excluding non-kin or strangers is part of doing politics. Within these traditional polities, kinship is citizenship – but not for everyone. The citizen – the rights-laden self – is a male, higher-caste (Kallar), married head of a household. Women, especially wives and mothers, do not have direct rights but are subsumed by those of their husbands and sons respectively. Reduced to their conjugal status and their fertile function, they lose a sense of an autonomous self – exactly what the goddess Pidari herself resents. By virtue of their birth into the polity, sisters and daughters do have certain inalienable rights that not even their exogamous marriage can disrupt. Nevertheless, even these birthrights are only partial, not as complete or complex as those of their fathers and brothers. Non-Kallars, especially those of lower castes, are not ascribed even this circumscribed selfhood. Engaged with, if at all, only as functionaries and subjects, they only hover at the margins of the polity. Not vested with political rights, they are denied citizenship and dismissed as merely animal life.

The kinship that the Kallars espouse is neither open nor inclusive. Building kinship is a drawn-out process, and much does depend on everyday practices. Nevertheless, allied as kinship in this case is to caste endogamy, ritual obligations, landownership, and political rights, limits to entry and attachment are also a feature. Troubling the contemporary emphasis on the permeability, elasticity, and fluidity of kinship undertakings, I delineate how boundaries are made and where they are asserted and reinforced (cf. Carsten 2000, 1997). These edges may bend, shift, or even break over time but they are nevertheless created, sustained, and asserted. When and where they are monitored and defended, these borders are solid and hold firm. As much as Kallar kinship does embrace and bind together, this largely extends only to those recognized as kin. For others, especially those of the lower castes, lofty barriers are erected. If there is a possibility of contravention, such barricades are substantiated with coercion and palpable threats of violence. Genealogical categorizations are the basis of a discriminating kinship. Kinship discriminates – between kin and not-so-kin as well as between self and strangers – and marginalizes or excludes accordingly. These gradations are also what determine the type and limits of citizenship within the polity. Only universal and egalitarian for Kallar males, for all others, citizenship within these polities is differentiated, hierarchical, and exclusive. Given how they have successfully mobilized kinship and caste to win local electoral contests, the Kallars have captured (some of) the Indian nation state so that it too is made part of their political capital. Gendered discriminations and caste-based hierarchies resonate within democratic politics, continuing to compromise representation within the nation and access to its resources. Normative associations of egalitarianism with democracy can blind us to ongoing political realities which are not only less than ideal but also brutal. While the egalitarian ethos is certainly part of the political imaginary, this does not preclude the concurrent and pervasive espousal of hierarchical values (see Piliavsky 2023 on how hierarchy remains a compelling democratic value in India).

Discriminating between self and others and between one's own kin and strangers has been critical to curating the Kallar polity. In crafting their politics, they deliberately draw up impediments to restrict kinship with most fellow humans. However, these same politics involve forming and fostering kinship with meta-human deities. Persons and polities are made and unmade not just through their kinship, or lack thereof, with each other but also with their gods. Anthropology, like most social scientific modes of enquiry, tends to prioritize the social over the gods. The gods are merely symbolizations – products of human intellectual, social, and artistic activity. People might make culture and meaning *through* the gods – make and remake kinship with fellow humans through exchanges with the gods. Ramberg (2014: 214), however, notes that they are seldom recognized as making culture (kin, worlds, and meaning) *with* the gods themselves. Troubling secular conceptions of persons and kinship, gods themselves are made kin through exchange, petitions, and rituals. Tutelary deities parent their lineage, street, and *natu* congregants, paving the way for their subsistence and reproduction, promoting their specific interests against all others, disciplining wayward behaviour, and protecting them from harm. As offspring to their deities, devotees tender obedience, offer gifts (animal sacrifice) and variously fear, cherish, and neglect them. What characterizes these deity–devotee relations is a presumption born of intimacy – a security in their rights to their own gods and a surety of divine support even if devotees do not worship them as consistently and as assiduously as they should. Indeed, the characteristic irregularity of tutelary worship is premised upon the almost unconditional love and support of their own gods. Despite the interloping attractions to other Sanskritic gods, their own tutelary deities remain their source and sustenance.

Making connections between genealogy – recognizing and classifying humans via gender, kinship, and caste into histories and forms of relatedness – and theology – defining forms and functions of divinities – is key to forging kinship between humans and gods. This divine kinship imbues their polity with power and sacredness. Interpenetrations between ontology and theology underpin their political cosmology. The positions of temples and the processions of deities trace the territorial contours of the sacred polity. In structure and practice, these jurisdictions are part of inclusive cosmic polities, which are ordered and governed by tutelary deities who wield life and death powers over the population (Sahlins 2017). The exegeses about the relations between the deities of the local pantheon (the fractious divine marital union) and their contiguities with political circumstances (the tense political union between Thenpathy and Vadapathy) are not just mythical but also themselves moral claims. These claims, made specifically by the headmen, articulate a theory of an immanent divine that is not simply permeable to politics but is itself inherently political. They are based on the permeability of different domains – persons, lineages, castes, and deities – to each other. This, however, does not preclude the establishment of impermeability between other domains, specifically between Kallar men and Kallar women as well as between Kallars and the lower-castes, specifically Dalits (or 'untouchables'). Ultimately, relatedness between human politics and divine power is being claimed. Given that such myths resonate throughout and give shape to everyday life, not just the political but the mythical is also personal. Rituals (and their exegeses) are part of the materializations of an everyday and intimate political theorizing.

Entangled Polities, Unsettled Sovereignties

Underlying the narrative of conjugal cohabitation with which I began is a defiant or at least a begrudging sufferance of alliance, community, and polity. The presence of kinship-polities such as the lineage, street, and *natu* troubles understandings of politics that remain limited to the modern nation state. Their contemporary resonance alludes to forms of imagined political authority and moral community that both precede and persist alongside the nation state. Eluding bureaucratic governance, these traditional polities have, especially in the past, served as parallels and alternatives to the monarchic, colonial, and nation states. Nevertheless, recurrent narratives of reluctance, recalcitrance, and outright refusal constitute discourses on opposition, subversion, and especially the desire for and value attached to autonomy. Tutelary gods refuse to be housed in permanent temples and subject to regular rituals, choosing instead to bask in the sun, be soaked in the rain, and roam the peripheries of the polity – alone (Arumugam 2023). Kinsmen are unable to come together and cooperate long enough to enact a sacrifice they know to be vital for their subsistence and reproduction. Frequent and fierce quarrels over seemingly trivial issues. Feuds kept alive over generations that can threaten to erupt into violent skirmishes at any moment. Attempts to arbitrate serious conflicts that often fail because the local juridical bodies cannot even be convened in the first place. Averse gods forced into conjugality for the sake of political unity and generativity who would rather reign as single sovereigns. These repeated rupturing of cohesion and strident disavowals of cooperation – in the face of sustained subsistence pressures and competing but contradictory ethical obligations – cannot simply be dismissed just as symptoms of an ailing polity, with obstreperous political interactions. Rather, they are also vital signs of a vigorous politics. Difficulties in reconciling the tensions between defining and assembling an authority and being free from its coercions to act autonomously fuel this agonistic milieu. Animating this political imaginary is the struggle between two seemingly contradictory but equally compelling ethics – sociality and sovereignty.

Sovereignty has emerged as a provocative concept as the 'dominant fiction that states as entities comprehensively ruled a territory and a population' and that they 'represented a modern and rational form of unitary governance' became increasingly threadbare (Geertz 2004: 579). Questions regarding the nature, utility, effects, and limits of state power arose amidst a sensitivity to the porous nature of state boundaries and the tenuous grip of state power, particularly in post-colonial societies (Hansen and Stepputat 2005: 1–38). Even as the post-colonial nation state has become the primary and pre-eminent structure in the political system and imagination, its power is neither total nor singular. While it wields considerable power, the nation state also finds its powers restricted by having to act within a fraught milieu of other parallel and competing agencies. Informal sovereignties such as that of vigilante groups, insurgents, illegal networks but also global corporations and market forces themselves are reconfiguring sovereign power (Hansen and Stepputat 2005: 3). Drawing attention to the multiple, elastic, and co-existing imaginaries and exercises of sovereignty, this book showcases the continuing significance of local polities and vernacular politics to theorizing power.

In 'What Is a State If It Is Not a Sovereign?' Geertz (2004: 584) argues that with its 'comparative, morphological, ethnographic eye', anthropology is 'uniquely equipped to study and theorize the complicated historical layers of authority, power, and other forms of attachment that constitute states and politics' in most of the contemporary world. Departing from the overwhelming emphasis on territorial boundaries, formal rules, and external recognition of state power, Hansen and Stepputat (2005) document sovereign power in practice – as exercises of violence over human bodies and populations. Not simply restricted to nation states but also exercised by local communities, sovereignty is a tentative and always emergent form of authority. Simultaneously, Hansen and Stepputat (2005: 8) argue that 'the crucial marks of sovereign power' are 'indivisibility, self-reference, and transcendence' as well as a certain 'excessive' quality. Scrutinizing sovereignty entails grappling both with the practices of power, including the wielding of violence and coercion as essential components in social order, and with imaginaries of power and their ultimate source of legitimacy. The exercise of sovereignty, Gilmartin (2020: 1) argues, requires appeals to 'an ultimate source of authority conceptualised as standing apart from the everyday worlds of power and social interest whether cosmic power, sacred authority, disinterested reason, or popular will'. However, even while citing extra-political sources to sanction authority, sovereignty also requires 'a deep engagement with the political power (including violence)' vital to establishing social order. Mediating between its profane and sublime attributes, this book is an ethnographic scrutiny of sovereignty as made visible and vital in everyday life. In the process, also made visceral are the inevitable and irreconcilable tensions inherent to the operations of power and the exercise of governing.

Lineages, streets, and *natus* are, I argue, bodies of self-governance. They gained strength in the interstices of the segmentary state (Stein 1999, also Tambiah 2013 on 'galactic polities'). The monarchical state's sovereignty was often less tangible than that exercised by such localized bodies where much of the 'actual taxation and adjudication over life and death took place' (Hansen 2005: 172). The sovereignty claimed by the central state was more ritual in nature (Inden 1981). This meant that there was space for alternative, if hierarchically organized, networks of authority which sought to control violence, rights, and reprisals (Dirks 1993; Stein 1999). Even amid the relatively more comprehensive and greater penetrative powers of the Indian nation state, such rival powers do continue, albeit on a more constrained scale (Brass 1997: 275–279; Mosse 2001; Hansen and Stepputat 2005; Michelutti 2020).

Ordering access to and distribution of resources such as land, irrigation water, and agricultural resources, kinship-polities help to structure and govern the agrarian economy. Extracting taxes from residents within their orbits, they finance commons such as temples, land, groves, ponds, and, more recently, roads, hospitals, markets, electrical substations, and health-care centres. They mobilize labour and funds to serve public interests. Sponsoring, organizing, and performing spectacular rituals such as temple consecrations, deity processions, annual festivals, and sacrifices, they strive to secure the viability and fecundity of their jurisdictions. Kinship-polities propose and enforce rules and laws within their narrow ambit. When a patriarch dies, they determine the division of his properties among his heirs. They advise disputants, adjudicate conflicts, render judgments, and administer punishments. In so doing, these vernacular polities function as parallels, additions, and alternatives to the nation state and its bureaucratic arms like the police and courts. Given their comparatively limited jurisdiction and more parochial applicability, they do not challenge but do structure how nation state sovereignty is experienced in the everyday (Gupta 2012, 1995). In claiming a divine and an ethical dimension to power, they critique attempts to impose an abstract, self-contained, and secular politics. Going about routines of governance, they create other forms of collectivity and citizenship and forge alternative ideas about how power should operate.

Based on a scrutiny of Roman jurisprudence and Schmitt's (2005) political theology, Agamben (2005, 1998) offers a compelling definition for sovereignty. Sovereignty hinges upon the question of distinction – the power to differentiate between those who are within the political community and those who are without. Those who are included are acknowledged as laden with rights; they are political agents – citizens. Outside of the polity are those who are simply biological beings. De-culturalized, deprived of any civic potential, they are reduced to their animal state as bare life who can be punished and even killed with impunity. In her scrutiny of the implications of colonial and post-colonial law in India, Kapila (2022) takes this argument even further to argue that sovereignty emanates from the capacity to extract and dispossess subjects of their rights to legal protection, property, and even their own bodies. Engaging in predation in the name of protection, sovereignty is premised not so much on declaring exceptions but in the capacity to act out of arbitrariness and chance. Illegibility to authority paves the way for absolute vulnerability. The lifeblood of vernacular polities is making distinctions between political citizens, peripheral populations, and excluded beings based on caste, gender, age, marital status, and residence. These discriminations are vivified in prohibitions from entering temples, residential territories, enacting or even participating in sacrificial rituals, and attending assembly meetings critical to legislating, arbitrating, executing, and governing. These discriminations are literally made flesh in the withholding of claims upon meat from the sacrifices and fish from the village commons. In the past, *natu* assemblies and headmen jurors were able to excommunicate, punish, and even have those they convicted be killed. They had exercised the power of life and death over their population. Citizenship is a right, but only for the privileged few. Political subjectivity is made vital not just through assertions and impositions but also through marginalizations, prohibitions, exclusions, and predations. Sovereignty favours and fractures to assert, maintain, and nourish, if not extend, its powers.

To determine who is incorporated into the body politics is the power of the sovereign. But what if one does not want to be included in a political community? Exclusion is not always a matter of external imposition or coercion. What if one chooses to abstain, preferring illegibility so as to preserve autonomy (Scott 2009, 1998)? Vaduvur's agonistic ambience arises from the tensions between different domains and scales of sovereignty. Individuals and households refuse to be subject to their lineages, lineages resist being encompassed by their streets, streets and villages repudiate their *natus'* authority, traditional headmen disdain politicians and political parties – all these are manifestations of struggles with authority. This recalls classical anthropological analyses which strived to explain law, order, and leadership in acephalous societies (Fortes 1970; Fortes and Evans-Pritchard 1940). Such situations are characterized by a balanced opposition between different segments of a political system. Segments cohere to resist external threats, and once they are gone, break part into their customary internal divisions to once again war with each other (Evans-Pritchard 1940). However, the continued resonance of kinship-polities within Vaduvur is not oriented towards structure and function. Kinship-polities act as a viable (though limited) alternative and means to assert some measure of independence from the overarching Indian nation state. Frequent disputes here are neither aberrations nor ruinations. Instead, they are potent with a robust sense of the self and its worth and will against the overwhelming pressures of political incorporation. Pregnant with political possibilities, conflicts are embodiments of a characteristic core political value – sovereignty. They are strident assertions of autonomy against the threat of encompassment by any polity. Even in rituals meant to sublimate the self into and thereby forge the wider community, individual interests remain equally insistent. Again and again rituals are stalked by and often stymied by politics so that they are not enacted at all. Ritual disruptions, delays, and cessations are not so much instances of failure, of the rites themselves, communality, or transcendence, as the realization of politics, of individuals, households, and immanence. These Kallars may have found themselves forced to submit to more dominant powers. They also do concede to cohere when necessary. Nevertheless, they are loathe to subject themselves to authorities other than their own. Obviously, this is a privilege, not extended to Kallar women and non-Kallars in general. Nevertheless, to be 'their own king and their own minister', as the popular Tamil saying goes – brooking no interference from others – is the ideal. In this crucible ferments a creative tension between multiple and competing assertions of sovereignty which is the lifeblood that forges and fuels Kallar polities. The ceaseless churning produced as individual interests vie with communal imperatives gives life to their politics.

All politics, despite ideological (nationalist) or academic (theoretical) posing to the contrary, is local. This was also brought to bear, to the consternation of pundits, pollsters, politicians, and party leaders, during the 2024 Indian general elections. The voters did not find grand narratives centring a monolithic and confrontational Hinduism and the single-handed efforts of one leader as compelling. Eschewing totalizing and abstract national ideologies, their voting showcased the decidedly local, pragmatic, and pluralistic nature of their politics. While people's political calculus may still be framed by and fuel religion, caste, and class, even these general hierarchies are rooted in particular experiences and stem from their everyday realities. The crux of this book is precisely the grappling with how a distinct place, persons, and practices nurture an edifice for a specific politics. Visceral politics paves the way for exploring how the cosmos, polity, and nation appear as they nestle into a particular consciousness, and vice versa.

Intimate Political Theorizing

Genealogy, foundational to the kinship studies that was once a cornerstone of anthropology, has largely become relegated to the margins (Morgan 1871; Rivers 2011; Fox 1983). Critiqued, and largely rightly so, for assuming Euro-American folk theories of kinship to be monolithically meaningful and therefore universally applicable, classical kinship treatises also tended to privilege bio-genetic relations while ignoring symbolic and performative ones (Schneider 1984, 1980). Even when it resumed its ethnographic interest, kinship was largely unmoored from its hitherto genealogical anchors to focus on ordinary practices and everyday processes (Carsten 2000, 1997). Despite his commitment to the genealogical method – as a means to excavate contemporary circumstances to posit a counter-history of subjects, knowledge, and discourses – for Foucault, kinship has no place in the modern nation and its constitution. It has been replaced by bio-power, which is premised entirely on 'the capacity of its citizens for physical reproductive, rather than for social and imaginative, life' (McKinnon and Cannell 2013: 35). However, genealogy is not purely metaphorical but continues to be part of lived reality. Through her scrutiny of colonial laws, Chatterjee (2004, 1999) has demonstrated how the elucidation of genealogy and the contested definition of 'family' were pivotal for the formations not just of the colonial but also of the Indian nation state (also Moody 2008 on the political contestations underpinning love marriages in Delhi). Genealogy, as we have seen, is part of people's social lives – how they curate connections and build constituencies by also precluding certain solidarities (see Bear 2013, 2015; McKinnon and Cannell 2013). Using genealogy to forge a matrix of caste, gender, religion, and class that underpins, defines, and sustains political communities is how the Kallars in Vaduvur have ruled and asserted sovereignty. Genealogy, even more significantly, is also a large part of their political imaginary – how they conceive of, experience, practice, and theorize power.

When I ventured my intentions to discuss my interlocutors' political theories, a repeated response was, 'But what makes it theory?' They may be thoughts, but they apparently lacked the systematic framing, comparative scope, and the stereoscopic mediations between the particular and the general that constitute theories. Other dichotomies that once framed an ethnographer's position vis-à-vis her interlocutors – native–foreigner, insider–outsider, informant–anthropologist, and them–us – may have collapsed. The long tradition of dismissing the intellectual prowess of interlocutors has been disavowed. Today no one would dispute that interlocutors are just as rational, credible, and capable as those who have come to study their societies as part of their profession. However, the assumption of a differential capacity to theorize continues to frame distinctions between the ethnographer and her interlocutors. Interlocutors live their lives. Ethnographers theorize these lived lives by 'analysing of a set of facts in their relation to one another, or the general or abstract principles of any body of facts' (Nader 2011: 211). Being able to deal in abstractions continues to be seen not only as the hallmark of the scholar but also as that which eludes our interlocutors.

And yet I would often encounter critical reflections from the villagers which troubled an academic monopoly on theorizing. I asked several women in Vaduvur why they did not press their brothers for their share of the inheritance from their fathers' estates even as the law gave them the rights. Why did they instead settle for prestations during life-crisis rituals or token gifts on festive occasions (cir, varicai)? An old woman, Chinnappa, answered:

> Now my brother comes to my house at least twice a year [during Pongal and Divali] to tender his varicai. When he comes, I serve him tea and we talk. He formally presents and I receive his gift. I know that he will come again soon. An inheritance terminates a relationship. When the property is divided between brothers, they hardly talk after that. It simply stops. But with varicai, brothers visit their married sisters again and again ... to give gifts. These gifts mean that even after marriage, I am still a part of my natal family. Our relationship (uravu) continues.... It may just be a tray of fruits, flowers, and about INR 100. But that's not the point. We will always have that relationship....

She has never read Marcel Mauss, and yet her explanation uncannily echoed his reading of the productivity of the gift in constituting and nourishing kinship sociality. Abstracting from her own specific circumstances, she was offering a general explanation for the difference between inheritance and prestations and the significance of gifting in general. On another occasion, the headmen's councillor, Sevu Vanniyar, explained that 'the Vaduvur *natu* is to govern (*nirvakam*) corporate bodies (*niruvanam*) [temples]'. Without recourse to Arjun Appadurai or Nicholas Dirks, he clarified that the purpose of the polity is the government of the temples within its jurisdiction. Headmen have assumed the royal function – financing and administrating religious institutions and sponsoring rituals such as sacrifices to ensure a cosmic order that encompasses socio-political order (Raheja 1998). There was no need for me to abstract this rationale from the remains of now abandoned rituals or even refer to the ethnographic record. It was unequivocally and baldly stated. The actors themselves are well aware of the interpenetrations of sovereignty and sacrality in constituting their polity and fuelling its politics. These conceptual connections, ventured casually during our ethnographic conversations, reiterated the potential for theories to assume different shapes and forms – not just as explicitly oral and written discourses but also in more oblique modes such as metaphors, myths, rituals, and practices. It became possible to imagine theorizations occurring beyond the academy and Euro-American notions of what is valid as theory. In the process, re-examining our understanding of what theory itself is, questions about who makes theory, and who recognizes and authorizes it as such becomes inevitable. More than any other discipline, the intimacy actively cultivated with interlocutors during extended and immersive fieldwork makes anthropologists uniquely appreciative of their interlocutors' theorizing acumen.

Anthropologists have been engaging in lively discussions about the inseparability of theory from ethnography (Da Col and Graeber 2011; Ingold 2014). Ethnography is not simply an empirical method, a documentary exercise, or processes of observation, or even a mode of description. Maintaining the differences between observation, description, comparison, and theory is ultimately untenable. As Nader (2011: 211) argues, 'ethnography is never a description but a theory of describing'. To go even further, theorizing is always premised upon inter-subjective communication. Life-laden, event-rich, experience-near, and human-dense as anthropological theorizing is and must be, anthropologists have to confront 'the totality of human creativity in everyday life' of which our interlocutors' theorizing forms a vital part. Ethnography is theory, 'not of people but with people' (Da Col 2017: 3). However, theorizing goes on irrespective of anthropologists' involvement.

Ordinary people in the process of living their lives come to form deep reflections on how they live these lives. Ethnographic interlocutors may not articulate why and how they do the politics they do in fashionable philosophical language or systematized into consistent suppositions. Nevertheless, they are actively engaged in processes of theorizing their circumstances and the workings of power. They are not merely describing their experiences and thereby generating data with which ethnographers can then theorize. Instead, they are offering their own theorizations of ideas, relationships, institutions, and practices. They are asking anthropological questions. Who is part of the polity and who is not? What is the polity for? What forms of politics are necessary to nurture particular relationships and provide for human flourishing? Data is never absolutely raw; it comes processed, already constituting and articulating theory – someone's theory, theory from somewhere, and theory in the everyday. Theorizing here is not some esoteric practice or a monumental achievement but a process of arriving at ordinary and pragmatic solutions to concrete and particular problems. It is simply a way of thinking that emerges as people learn to inhabit the worlds they have inherited and account for the lives that they live. This is not to deny that much of life often goes on in the absence of theories to explain it. Even where people do formulate theories, it would be remiss to assume that they necessarily underpin or explain their experiences. Nevertheless, their theorizations are both explicitly stated and embedded in everyday practices.

At the heart of political theorizing in Vaduvur is genealogical thinking. Claiming and asserting genealogical connections between persons, between people and territories, between peoples and gods frames their political constitution. Distinguishing from and disclaiming kinship with yet others is also part of defining and policing political membership. The making of a descent-based, caste-bound, and gendered pedigree defines gradations of political subjectivity and thereby citizenship or the lack thereof. What is reiterated is that politics is not something set apart, but that which is fundamentally enmeshed in the ways in which one's being in the world is constituted and intimately engaged with. The political is theorized in terms of intersubjective negotiations with ordinary things such as one's kin, one's lived spaces, one's gods, and the Indian nation state. The state is merely one entity in a much broader political imaginary that includes kinfolk, headmen, politicians, the Indian nation state, lands, spirits, and gods. Concurrently, it discriminates against and excludes specific others, such as women, non-Kallars, and the lower castes, especially the Dalits. These intimate forms of citizenships and political exclusions would not be evident from the perspective of some high political theory. They can only be discerned through ethnography – as part of the most immersive, humanistic, and empirical of the social sciences. Ethnography encapsulates within itself an ongoing theorizing that is both abstract and intimate – at once engaged with critical scholarship and moored in the everyday experiences and reflexive analyses of our interlocutors. Anthropology, in its focus on the local and marginal and its commitment to extended periods of fieldwork privileging the everyday lives of ordinary people, is particularly well quipped to uncover and grapple with alternate visions of political life within a space monopolized by the nation state. Older practices remain alive and vital within contemporary bureaucratic apparatuses as they are nourished by other political imaginaries premised upon resilient assumptions about how the world works.

Along with its substance, what emerges from ethnographic scrutiny is also the varied permutations – not just academic, systematic, and transcendental – that theorizing assumes. Contemplating the mortuary complex of the Lòlop'ò community in Southwest China, Mueggler (2017: 29) argues that funeral rituals and songs – which disengage a deceased person from the social relations that defined them while alive and give them a whole new body – are ultimately about the construction and reconstruction of a social order. The work of making bodies, he argues, 'is the most engaged, rigorous, and conscientious form of thought about ... persons' (Mueggler 2017: 6). In actualizing and formalizing social relations, he argues, ritual work is akin to what we recognize as social theory. Elaborating in 'Ritual as Theory, Theory as Ritual', Puett (2020: 1106) argues that anthropologists have largely been using 'theory to uncover the mechanisms, symbols and structures underlying social ritual'. Departing from this implicit social functionalism, he enjoins us instead to see ritual itself as theory and ritual work as theorizing. What our interlocutors do with rituals is 'the work that anthropologists do with theory' (Puett 2020: 1107). Rituals are not simply descriptions or representations of a pre-given social world but active constitutions and reconstitutions of a social order. People are 'themselves interpreting and working with their social worlds precisely through the work of ... rituals' (Puett 2020: 1107). They are, Puett (2020: 1108) concludes, 'making arguments about a social world and the workings of ritual'.

Not performed in the modes that anthropologists have conventionally defined as theory, these forms of theorizing are intricately bound up with the practical and technical work of constituting and reconstituting social relations. This draws from ongoing discontents with framing theories simply as 'overarching systematic accounts of the world informed or conformed through empirical study' (Candea 2018: 8). It entails moving away from conventional understandings of theory as 'exclusively a question of explanation and representation' (Ojani 2022: 473; Latour 2005 on actor–network theory and Holbraad and Pederson 2017 on the ontological turn). Instead, as Candea (2018: 8) argues, theories are 'something else: conceptual techniques, recipes for innovation; in one word: heuristics'. The facts of experience are constructed, engaged with, and transformed by imaginative leaps into concepts. Accordingly, theories do not stand separate from but are immanent to and constituted by social and ritual practices. To look for theory exclusively in literary or verbal mediums is to miss much of the more fragmentary, contingent, and casual forms that theorizing takes in routine life.

This book centres ordinary people figuring out and making arguments about the workings of power through their performances of sacrificial rituals, funerals, kinship, routine cohabitation, feuds, conflict-arbitrations, ethical dilemmas, emotional demands, and popular elections, that is, through the course of their living their everyday lives. It offers formulations of political theorizing, which are actualized in ethical dilemmas about what is owed to and expected from one another. Inherent to routine living, these dilemmas also constitute and articulate political order and chaos. This is a political theorizing realized in collective deliberative practices and civic action and even more so by the contestations of and resistance to them – a political imaginary elaborated upon by political virtuosos (traditional headmen, village officeholders, local politicians). One that is also, albeit with varying degrees of expertise, part of the processes of sense-making by ordinary villagers. A political theorizing not premised so much on explicit verbal discourse or the printed word as on the performative. A political theorizing that is not universal, complete, or perfectly coherent but necessarily partial, fragmentary, and allusive. Political theorizing that is primarily local and is expounded upon mainly through ritual enactments, spatial practices, and routine actions but is nevertheless foundational to the understanding of politics as practised by agnatic kinsmen, village headmen, regional political parties, and indeed the nation state.

In this polity, a political imaginary is not only made material but expressed viscerally: in the flesh (shared fish and sacrificed animals), soil (dwellings and gardens), blood (kinship claims and murderous violence), marrow (caste reputations and agonistic feuds), and guts (gendered exploitation and caste atrocities). Instead of assuming an anemic impassivity, this theorizing throbs with life. Rather than being abstracted into an anonymous generality, this is a theorizing that still evokes its sources and expresses its specificities. Instead of being petrified into perfection, it is one that embodies how incomplete, tentative, messy, and even ugly experiences can be. Through viscerality, one sees a political imagination at work in all its multiplicity, paradoxicality, unruliness, profundity, and even banality as refracted through a specific time, space, people, and social milieu. At the heart of this imaginary is an understanding of politics as a way of being in the world.

Notes

1. However, the political resonance of the procession is not completely severed. As mentioned in Chapter 4, her subjects now come to see her (also Arumugam 2019a).

2. This is complicated by Pidari Amman's temple being located near the Vaduvur Agraharam which is part of Vadapathy. Her temple is located in Vaduvur's

centre, while her husband's temple, as befitting his ascetic avatar, is located in the Vaduvur *natu*'s northern borders. Pidari therefore straddles both Vadapathy and Thenpathy.

3. Territorialized kin units, rooted villages, and the local versus the transcendental, pan-Indian, and cosmic – these affect the nature and efficacy of the powers various deities are able to wield. Tutelary deities are specific to a locality with a narrow range of responsibilities oriented largely towards their localized congregation's fertility. Sanskritic deities are universal and omnipotent.

4. Refusing animal sacrifice denotes a superior position in the divine hierarchy. Since not all deities who accept sacrifice also accept meat offerings, the deities' diets – carnist and non-Sanskritic versus vegetarian and Sanskritic – further complicate this issue.

5. Theorizations of the interactions between the ritual and social in Hindu society have privileged the homologies between the representations of the Hindu pantheon and the caste structure. Hierarchical relations within the Hindu pantheon, specifically between the Sanskritic and village deities, Dumont argues (1980), correspond to relational ranking within the Hindu social structure. Such theorizations have been intensively critiqued – for their reliance on exclusively Brahmin scriptural sources and their privileging of Brahmin perspectives. By far the most extensive and erudite critiques have been over his underestimation of politics (Raheja 1998; Dirks 1994, 1993). For Dumont, material power is not only subordinate to but also encompassed by ritual authority. Heeding these critiques, Fuller (1988: 34–35) concedes that the south Indian Hindu pantheon does not mirror exactly caste society. Nevertheless, it is possible to extrapolate insights into hierarchy from the representations of Sanskritic and village deities. Drawing on the differential conceptions of the powers of Sanskritic deities (*sui generis* and absolute) versus village deities (relational and contingent), Fuller concludes that it is 'not Sanskritic deities but village deities –mainly worshipped by the low castes – who provide the model of and for a hierarchical world' (1988: 35).

6. The relationships among the deities in a pantheon, specifically between the local deities and the pan-Indian ones, are represented as being devoid of political content in and of themselves. Political relations are articulated on two rather different ritual fronts. First, the state deity is represented as sovereign, with the king serving as the deity's chief courtier. The monarch partakes of the divinity of the state deity in two ways, either as an 'incarnation' of this deity or as its 'regent' in the kingdom. The reign is therefore a joint one (Fuller 1992: 107). Second, rituals of worship at temples 'display and establish distinctions of rank' (Fuller 1992: 79). Calculations of high ranking include the right (and the capacity) to sponsor worship, precedence in receiving the sanctified offerings (*pracatam*) distributed after the worship, and the singling out for the receipt of honours (*mariyatai*).

References

Agamben. Giorgio. 2005. *State of Exception*. Chicago, IL: University of Chicago Press.

———. 1998. *Homo Sacer: Sovereign Power and Bare Life*. Stanford, CA: Stanford University Press.

Appadurai, Arjun. 1981. *Worship and Conflict under Colonial Rule: A South Indian Case*. New York: Cambridge University Press.

Appadurai, Arjun and Carole A. Breckenridge. 1976. 'The South Indian Temple: Authority, Honor and Redistribution'. *Contributions to Indian Sociology* 10(2): 187–211.

Arumugam, Indira. 2023. 'The Sacred Unbound: Insufficient Rituals, Excess Life, and Divine Agency in Rural Tamil Nadu'. *Hau: Journal of Ethnographic Theory* 13(1): 53–67.

———. 2021. 'Laying Out Feast-Offerings: Offering Meat, Feasting Together and Sharing with the Gods'. *Religions of South Asia* 15(3): 274–299.

———. 2019a. 'Gods as Monsters: Insatiable Appetites and a Surfeit of Life'. In *Monster Anthropology: Ethnographic Explorations of Transforming Social Worlds*, edited by Geir Henning Presterudstuen and Yamine Musharbash, 44–58. London: Bloomsbury Publishing.

———. 2019b. 'Coercive Gifts: Ritual and Electoral Transactions and Political Value in Village Tamil Nadu'. *Contributions to Indian Sociology* 54(3): 1–26.

———. 2015. '"The Old Gods Are Losing Power!": Theologies of Power and Rituals of Productivity in a Tamilnadu Village'. *Modern Asian Studies* 49(3): 753–786.

Babb, Lawrence A. 1975. *The Divine Hierarchy: Popular Hinduism in Central India*. New York: Columbia University Press.

Baker, Christopher John. 1976. *The Politics of South India 1920–1937*. Cambridge: Cambridge University Press.

Banerjee, Mukulika. 2021. *Cultivating Democracy: Politics and Citizenship in Agrarian India*. Oxford: Oxford University Press.

———. 2007. 'Sacred Elections'. *Economic and Political Weekly* 42(17): 1556–1562.

Barnett, Marguerite Ross. 1976. *The Politics of Cultural Nationalism in South India*. Princeton, NJ: Princeton University Press.

Barth, Fredrik. 1959. 'Segmentary Opposition and the Theory of Games: A Study of Pathan Organization'. *Journal of the Royal Anthropological Institute of Great Britain and Ireland* 89(1): 5–21.

Bayly, Susan. 2001. *Caste, Society and Politics in India from the Eighteenth Century to the Modern Age*. Cambridge: Cambridge University Press.

Biardeau, Madeleine. 2004. *Stories about Posts: Vedic Variations around the Hindu Goddess*. Translated by Alf Hiltebeitel, Marie-Louise Reiniche, and James Walke. Edited by Alf Hiltebeitel and Marie-Louise Reiniche. Chicago, IL: University of Chicago Press.

Bear, Laura. 2015. *Navigating Austerity: Currents of Debt along a South Asian River*. Stanford, CA: Stanford University Press.

———. 2013. '"This Body Is Our Body": Vishwakarma Puja, the Social Debts of Kinship and Theologies of Materiality in a Neoliberal Shipyard'. In *Vital Relations: Modernity and the Persistent Life of Kinship*, edited by Fenella Cannell and Susan McKinnon, 155–169. Santa Fe, NM: School of Advanced Research Press.

Beck, Brenda. E. F. 1972. *Peasant Society in Konku: A Study of Right and Left Subcastes in South India*. Vancouver: University of British Columbia Press.

Bell, Catherine. 1997. *Ritual: Perspectives and Dimensions*. Oxford: Oxford University Press.

———. 1992. *Ritual Theory, Ritual Practice*. Oxford: Oxford University Press.

Beteille, Andre. 1971. *Caste, Class and Power: Changing Patterns of Stratification in a Tanjore Village*. Berkeley, CA: University of California Press.

Berti, Daniela and Gilles Tarabout (eds.). 2009. *Territory, Soil and Society in South Asia*. New Delhi: Manohar.

Blackburn, Stuart. 'The Kallars: 'A Criminal Tribe' Reconsidered'. *Journal of South Asian Studies* 1(1): 38–51.

Bloch, Maurice. 1992. *Prey into Hunter: The Politics of Religious Experience*. Cambridge: Cambridge University Press.

———. 1986. *From Blessing to Violence: History and Ideology in the Circumcision Ritual of the Merina of Madagascar*. Cambridge: Cambridge University Press.

———. 1971. 'The Moral and Tactical Meaning of Kinship Terms'. *Man* 6(1): 79–87.

Bloch, Maurice and Jonathan Parry (eds.). 1982. *Death and the Regeneration of Life*. Cambridge: Cambridge University Press.

Bourdieu, Pierre. 1997. *Outline of a Theory of Practice*. Cambridge: Cambridge University Press.

Brass, Paul. 1997. *Theft of an Idol: Text and Context in the Representation of Collective Violence*. Princeton: Princeton University Press.

Busby, Cecilia. 2000. *The Performance of Gender: An Anthropology of Everyday Life in a South Indian Fishing Village*. London: Athlone Press.

Calasso, Roberto. 2014. *Ardor*. New York: Farrar, Straus & Giroux.

Candea, Matei. 2018. 'Introduction: Echoes of a Conversation'. In *Schools and Styles of Anthropological Theory*, edited by Matei Candea, 1–17. London: Routledge.

Carsten, Janet (ed.). 2000. *Cultures of Relatedness: New Approaches to the Study of Kinship*. Cambridge: Cambridge University Press.

———. 1997. *The Heat of the Hearth: The Process of Kinship in a Malay Fishing Community*. Oxford: Oxford University Press.

Champakalakshmi, R. 2011. *Religion, Tradition, and Ideology: Pre-colonial South India*. New Delhi: Oxford University Press.

———. 1996. *Trade, Ideology, and Urbanization: South India 300 BC to AD 1300*. New Delhi: Oxford University Press.

Champakalaksmi, R., Kesavan Veluthat, and T. R. Venugopalan. 2002. *State and Society in Pre-modern South India*. Thrissur: Cosmo Books.

Chandra, Kanchan (ed.). 2016. *Democratic Dynasties: State, Party and Family in Contemporary Indian Politics*. New York: Cambridge University Press.

Chatterjee, Indrani (ed.). 2004. *Unfamiliar Relations: Family and History in South Asia*. New Brunswick, NJ: Rutgers University Press.

———. 1999 *Gender, Slavery and Law in Colonial India*. Delhi: Oxford University Press.

Chao, Emily. 1999. 'The Maoist Shaman and the Madman: Ritual Bricolage, Failed Ritual, and Failed Ritual Theory'. *Cultural Anthropology* 14(4): 505–534.

Chibber, Pradeep. K. 2014. *Religious Practices and Democracy in India*. New York: Cambridge University Press.

Ciotti, Manuela. 2010. *Retro-modern India: Forging the Low Caste Self*. New Delhi: Routledge.

Clark-Decès, Isabelle. 2018. 'Towards an Anthropology of Gifting in Tamil Nadu'. *International Journal of Hindu Studies* 22(2): 197–215.

———. 2014. *The Right Spouse: Preferential Marriages in Tamil Nadu*. Stanford, CA: Stanford University Press.

———. 2005. *No One Cries for the Dead: Tamil Dirges, Rowdy Songs and Graveyard Petitions*. Berkeley, CA: University of California Press.

Cohn, Bernard. S. 1959. 'Some Notes on Law and Change in North India'. *Economic Development and Cultural Change* 8(1): 79–93.

Csordas, Thomas (ed.). 1994. *Embodiment and Experience: The Existential Ground of Culture and Self*. Cambridge: Cambridge University Press.

Da Col, Giovanni. 2017. 'Two or Three Things I Know about Ethnographic Theory'. *Hau: Journal of Ethnographic Theory* 7(1): 1–8.

Da Col, Giovanni, and David Graeber. 2011. 'Foreword: The Return of Ethnographic Theory'. *Hau: Journal of Ethnographic Theory* 1(1): vi–xxxv.

Daniel, Valentine E. 1982. *Fluid Signs: Being a Person in the Tamil Way*. Berkeley, CA: University of California Press.

Das, Veena. 2012. 'Ordinary Ethics'. In *A Companion to Moral Anthropology*, edited by Didier Fassin, 133–149. Malden, MA: Wiley Blackwell.

———. 2007. *Life and Worlds: Violence and the Descent into the Ordinary*. Berkeley, CA: University of California Press.

Deliege, Robert. 1999. *The Untouchables of India*. Oxford: Berg.

———. 1996. 'At the Threshold of Untouchability: *Pallars* and *Valaiyars* in a Tamil Village'. In *Caste Today*, edited by C. J. Fuller, 65–92. Delhi: Oxford University Press.

De Neve, Geert. 2008. '"We Are All *Sondakarar* (Relatives)!": Kinship and Its Morality in an Urban Industry of Tamilnadu, South India'. *Modern Asian Studies* 42(1): 211–246.

———. 2000. 'Patronage and "Community": The Role of a Tamil "Village" Festival in the Integration of a Town'. *Journal of the Royal Anthropological Institute* 6(3): 501–519.

Dirks, Nicholas. B. 1994. 'Ritual as Resistance: Subversion as a Social Fact'. In *Culture/Power/History: A Reader in Contemporary Social Theory*, edited by Nicholas B. Dirks, Geoff Eley, and Sherry B. Ortner, 483–503. Princeton, NJ: Princeton University Press.

———. 1993 [1987]. *The Hollow Crown: Ethnohistory of an Indian Kingdom* (2nd edition). Ann Arbor, MI: University of Michigan Press.

———. 1986. 'From Little King to Landlord: Property, Law, and the Gift under the Madras Permanent Settlement'. *Comparative Studies in Society and History* 28(2): 307–333.

———. 1982. 'The Pasts of a *Palaiyakarar*: The Ethnohistory of a South Indian Little King'. *Journal of Asian Studies* 41(4): 655–683.

———. 1979. 'The Structure and Meaning of Political Relations in a South Indian Little Kingdom'. *Contributions to Indian Sociology* 13(2): 169–206.

D'Souza, Dillip. 2001. *Branded by Law: Looking at India's Denotified Tribes*. New Delhi: Penguin Books.

Dundes, Alan. 1997. *Two Tales of Crow and Sparrow: A Freudian Folkloristic Essay on Caste and Untouchability*. Lanham, MD: Rowman & Littlefield Publishers, Inc.

Dumont, Louis. 2000 [1986]. *A South Indian Subcaste: Social Organization and Religion of the Pramalai Kallar*. New Delhi: Oxford University Press.

———. 1986. *Essays on Individualism: Modern Ideology in Anthropological Perspective.* Chicago, IL: University of Chicago Press.

———. 1983. *Affinity as a Value: Marriage Alliance in South India, with Comparative Essays on Australia.* Chicago, IL: University of Chicago Press.

———. 1980 [1970]. *Homo Hierarchicus.* Chicago, IL: University of Chicago.

Dumont, Louis and D. F. Pocock. 1957. 'Village Studies'. *Contributions to Indian Sociology* 1(1): 23–41.

Eck, Diana L. 2012. *India: A Sacred Geography.* New York: Three Rivers Press.

———. 1998 [1981]. *Darsan: Seeing the Divine Image in India.* New York: Columbia University Press.

Evans-Pritchard, E. E. 1940. *The Nuer: A Description of the Modes of the Livelihood and Political Institutions of a Nilotic People.* Oxford: Clarendon Press.

Farquhar, Judith and Margaret Lock (eds.). 2007. *Beyond the Body Proper: Reading the Anthropology of Material Life.* Durham, NC: Duke University Press.

Feuchtwang, Stephan. 2008. 'Centers and Margins: The Organisation of Extravagance as Self-government in China'. In *On the Margins of Religion*, edited by Frances Pine and Joao de Pina-Cabral, 135–152. New York: Berghahn Books.

———. 2004. 'Theorising Place'. In *Making Place: State Projects, Globalisation and Local Responses in China*, edited by Stephan Feuchtwang, 3–32. London: Routledge-Cavendish.

———. 1998. 'Historical Metaphor: A Study of Religious Representation and the Recognition of Authority'. *Man* 28(1): 35–49.

Flueckiger, Joyce Burkhalter. 2020. *Material Acts in Everyday Hindu Worlds.* New York: State University of New York Press.

Folch, Christine. 2016. 'The Nature of Sovereignty in the Anthropocene: Hydroelectric Lessons of Struggle, Otherness, and Economics from Paraguay'. *Current Anthropology* 57(5): 565–585.

Fortes, Meyer. 1970. *Kinship and the Social Order: The Legacy of Lewis Henry Morgan.* London: Routledge & Kegan Paul.

Fortes, Meyer and E. E. Evans-Pritchard. 1940. *African Political Systems.* London: Oxford University Press for the International African Institute.

Foucault, Michel. 1979 [1975]. *Discipline and Punish: The Birth of the Prison.* Translated by Alan Sheridan. London: Penguin.

Fox, Robin. 1983 [1976]. *Kinship and Marriage: An Anthropological Perspective.* Cambridge: Cambridge University Press.

Fuller, C. J. (ed.) 1996. *Caste Today.* Delhi: Oxford University Press.

———. 2004 [1992]. *The Camphor Flame: Popular Hinduism and Society in India.* Princeton, NJ: Princeton University Press.

———. 1988. 'The Hindu Pantheon and the Legitimation of Hierarchy'. *Man* 23(1): 1–39.

Fuller, C. J. and Veronique Benei (eds.). 2001. *The Everyday State & Society in Modern India*. London: Hurst & Company.

Fuller, C. J. and Haripriya Narasimhan. 2014. *Tamil Brahmans: The Making of a Middle Class*. Chicago, IL: University of Chicago Press.

Geertz, Clifford. 2004. 'What Is the State If It IS Not a Sovereign? Reflections on Politics in Complicated Places'. *Current Anthropology* 45(5): 577–593.

———. 1980. *Negara: The Theatre State in Nineteenth-Century Bali*. Princeton, NJ: Princeton University Press.

———. 1973a. *The Interpretation of Cultures*. London; New York: Basic Books.

———. 1973b. 'Deep Play: Notes on the Balinese Cockfight'. In *The Interpretation of Cultures*, 3–30. London; New York: Basic Books.

Gilmartin, David, Pamela Price, and Arild Engelson Ruud (eds.). 2020. *South Asian Sovereignty: The Conundrum of Worldly Power*. London: Routledge.

Gilmartin, David. 2015. 'Rethinking the Public Through the Lens of Sovereignty. *South Asia: Journal of South Asian Studies* 38(3): 371–386.

Gluckman, Max. 1956. *Custom and Conflict in Africa*. Oxford: Blackwell.

Gold, Anne Grodzins. 1988. *Fruitful Journeys: The Ways of Rajasthani Pilgrims*. Berkeley, CA: University of California Press.

Good, Anthony. 1991. *The Female Bridegroom*. Oxford: Clarendon Press.

———. 1983. 'A Symbolic Type and Its Transformations: The Case of South Indian Ponkal'. *Contributions to Indian Sociology* 17(2): 223–244.

Gough, Kathleen. E. 1989. *Rural Change in Southeast India, 1950s to 1980s*. New Delhi: Oxford University Press.

———. 1981. *Rural Society in Southeast India*. Cambridge: Cambridge University Press.

———. 1971 [1960]. 'Caste in a Tanjore Village.' In *Aspects of Caste in South India, Ceylon and North-West Pakistan*, edited by Edmund Leach, 11–61. London: Cambridge University Press.

———. 1960 [1955]. 'The Social Structure of a Tanjore Village'. In *India's Villages*, edited by M.N. Srinivas, 90–102. London: Asia Publishing House.

———. 1956. 'Brahmin Kinship in a Tamil Village'. *American Anthropologist* 58(5): 826–853.

Graeber, David. 2009. 'Debt, Violence and Impersonal Markets: Polanyian Meditations'. In *Market and Society: The Great Transformation Today*, edited by Chris Hann and Keith Hart, 106–132. Cambridge: Cambridge University Press.

Graeber, David and Marshall Sahlins. 2017. *On Kings*. Chicago, IL: Chicago University Press.

Gupta, Akhil. 2012. *Red Tape: Bureaucracy, Structural Violence, and Poverty in India*. Durham, NC: Duke University Press.

———. 1995. 'Blurred Boundaries: The Discourse of Corruption, the Culture of Politics and the Imagined State'. *American Ethnologist* 22(2): 375–402.

Habib, Irfan. 1999 [1963]. *The Agrarian System of Mughal India, 1526–1707*. New Delhi: Oxford University Press.

Hardgrave, Robert. 1979. 'When Stars Displace the Gods: The Folk Culture of Cinema in Tamil Nadu'. In *Essays in the Political Sociology of South India*, edited by Robert Hardgrave, 92–124. New Delhi: Manohar.

———. 1973. 'Politics and the Film in Tamilnadu: The Stars and the DMK'. *Asian Survey* 13(3): 288–305.

Hansen, Thomas Blom. 2005. 'Sovereignty beyond the State: On Legality and Authority in Modern India'. In *Sovereign Bodies: Citizens, Migrants, and States in the Postcolonial World*, edited by Thomas Blom Hansen and Finn Stepputat, 169–191. Princeton, NJ: Princeton University Press.

Hansen, Thomas Blom and Finn Stepputat (eds.). 2005. *Sovereign Bodies: Citizens, Migrants, and States in the Postcolonial World*. Princeton, NJ: Princeton University Press.

———. 2006. 'Sovereignty Revisited'. *Annual Review of Anthropology* 35: 295–315.

Harrison, Simon. 1993. *The Mask of War Violence, Ritual, and the Self in Melanesia*. Manchester: Manchester University Press.

Headley, Zoé. E. 2011. 'Caste and Collective Memory in South India'. In *A Companion to the Anthropology of India*, edited by Isabelle Clark-Decès, 98–114. Chichester: Blackwell Publishing Ltd.

Heesterman, J. C. 1985. *The Inner Conflict of Tradition: Essays in Indian Ritual, Kingship and Society*. Chicago, IL: University of Chicago Press.

Heitzman, James. 1991. 'Ritual Polity and Economy: The Transactional Network of an Imperial Temple in Medieval South India'. *Journal of the Economic and Social History of the Orient* 34(1): 23–54.

Hertz, Robert. 1960. *Death and the Right Hand*. Translated by Rodney and Claudia Needham. London: Cohen & West.

Hobbes, Thomas. 1981 [1656]. *Leviathan*. London: Penguin.

Hocart, A. M. 1969 [1927]. *Kingship*. Oxford: Oxford University Press.

Holbraad, Martin and Morten Axel Pedersen. 2017. *The Ontological Turn: An Anthropological Exposition*. Cambridge: Cambridge University Press.

Hoskins, Janet. 1993. 'Violence, Sacrifice, and Divination: Giving and Taking Life in Eastern Indonesia'. *American Ethnologist* 20(1): 159–178.

Howe, Leo. 2003. 'Risk, Ritual and Performance'. *Journal of Royal Anthropological Institute* 6(1): 63–79.

Hubert, Henri and Marcel Mauss. 1981 (1898). *Sacrifice: Its Nature and Function*. Chicago, IL: University of Chicago Press.

Humphrey, Caroline and James Laidlaw. 1994. *The Archetypal Actions of Ritual.* Oxford: Clarendon Press.

Hüsken, Ute. 2007. *When Rituals Go Wrong: Mistakes, Failure and the Dynamics of Rituals.* Leiden: Brill.

Inden, Ronald B. 1981. 'Hierarchies of Kings in Early Medieval India'. *Contributions to Indian Sociology* 15(1–2): 99–125.

Ingold, Tim. 2014. 'That's Enough about Ethnography!' *Hau: Journal of Ethnographic Theory* 4(1): 383–395.

Irschick, Eugene F. 1969. *Politics and Social Conflict in South India: The Non-Brahman Movement and Tamil Separatism 1916–1929.* Berkeley and Los Angeles: University of California Press.

Jaffrelot, Christophe. 2010. *Religion, Caste and Politics in India.* New Delhi: Primus Books.

Kapadia, Karin. 1995. *Siva and Her Sisters: Gender, Caste, and Class in Rural South India.* Boulder, CO: Westview Press.

Kapila, Kriti. 2022. *Nullius: The Anthropology of Ownership, Sovereignty, and the Law in India.* Chicago, IL: Hau Books.

Karashima, Noburu. 2001 [1984]. *History and Society in South India: The Cholas to Vijayanagar.* Oxford: Oxford University Press.

Karuppaiyan, V. 1990. *Kinship and Polity: A Study in Socio-Political Organization among the Upland Kallars of Thanjavur District in Tamil Nadu.* Madras: University of Madras.

Keane, Webb. 2018. 'Killing Animals: On the Violence of Sacrifice, the Hunt and the Butcher'. *Anthropology of This Century* 22. http://aotcpress.com/articles/killing-animals-violencesacrifice-hunt-butcher/ (accessed 22 January 2019).

Latour, Bruno. 2005. *Reassembling the Social: An Introduction to Actor-Network-Theory.* Oxford: Oxford University Press.

Leach, Edmund. 1961. *Pul Eliya, a Village in Ceylon: A Study of Land Tenure and Kinship.* Cambridge: Cambridge University Press.

Ludden, David. 1999. *An Agrarian History of South Asia.* Cambridge: Cambridge University Press.

———. 1985. *Peasant History in South India.* Princeton, NJ: Princeton University Press.

Maine, Henry Sumner. 1890 [1871]. *Village Communities in the East and West.* London: Murray.

Madan, T. N. 1987. 'Secularism in Its Place'. *Journal of Asian Studies* 46(4): 747–759.

Masilamani-Meyer, Eveline. 2004. 'Guardians of Tamil Nadu: Folk Deities, Folk Religion, Hindu Themes'. *Neue Hallesche Berichte* 5. Halle: Verlag der Franckeschen Stiftungen zu Halle.

Marriott, McKim. 1976. 'Hindu Transactions: Diversity without Dualism'. In *Transaction and Meaning: Directions in the Anthropology of Exchange and*

Symbolic Behavior, edited by Bruce Kapferer, 109–142. Philadelphia, PA: Institute for the Study of Human Issues.

———. 1968. 'Caste Rankings and Food Transaction: A Matrix Analysis'. In *Structure and Change in Indian Society*, edited by Milton Singer and Bernard Cohn, 133–171. Chicago, IL: Aldine.

———. 1959. 'Interactional and Attributional Theories of Caste Rank'. *Man* in India 39: 92–107.

Maunaguru, Sidharthan. 2020. 'Vulnerable Sovereignty: Sovereign Deities and Tigers' Politics in Sri Lanka'. *Current Anthropology* 61(6): 686–712.

Mauss, Marcel. 2000 [1925]. *The Gift: The Form and Reason for Exchange in Archaic Societies*. New York: W.W. Norton & Company, Inc.

McKinnon, Susan and Fenella Cannell (eds.). 2013. *Vital Relations: Modernity and the Persistent Life of Kinship*. Santa Fe, NM: School of Advanced Research Press.

Michelutti, Lucia. 2022. 'Divine Kinship: Towards an Ethnographic Theory of Political Theology'. *Political Theology* 25(2): 118–123.

———. 2020. 'Circuits of Protection and Extortion: Sovereignty in a provincial North Indian Town'. In *South Asian Sovereignty: The Conundrum of Worldly Power*, edited by David Gilmartin, Pamela Price, and Arild Engelson Ruud, 150–172. London: Routledge.

———. 2019. 'Caste and the Anthropology of Democracy'. In *Critical Themes in Indian Sociology*, edited by Y. Srivastava and J. Abraham, 195–208. Thousand Oaks, CA: Sage.

———. 2008. *The Vernacularisation of Democracy: Politics, Caste and Religion in India*. London: Routledge.

———. 2004. "We (Yadavs) Are a Caste of Politicians': Caste and Modern Politics in a North Indian Town'. *Contributions to Indian Sociology* 38(1): 43–71.

Michelutti, Lucia, Hoque, Martin Ashraf, Picherit Nicolas, Rollie David, Paul, Arild. E. Ruud, and Clarinda Still. 2018. *Mafia Raj: The Rule of Bosses in South Asia*. Stanford, CA: Stanford University Press.

Mines, Diane. P. 2012. 'Loss and Recognition: The Historical Force of a Goddess'. *Nidan: International Journal for the Study of Hinduism* 24(1): 1–15.

———. 2005. *Fierce Gods: Inequality, Ritual, and the Politics of Dignity in a South Indian Village*. Bloomington IN: Indiana University Press.

———. 1997. 'Making the Past Past: Objects and the Spatialization of Time in Tamilnadu'. *Anthropological Quarterly* 70(4): 173–186.

———. 1989. 'Hindu Periods of Death 'Impurity''. *Contributions to Indian Sociology* 23(1): 103–130.

Moody, Pervez. 2008. *The Intimate State: Love-Marriage and the Law in Delhi*. Delhi: Routledge.

Morgan, Lewis Henry. 1871. *Systems of Consanguinity and Affinity of the Human Family*. Washington D.C.: The Smithsonian Institution.

Mosse, David. 2003a. '*Rule and Representation: Transformations in the Governance of the Water Commons in British South India*'. *Journal of Asian Studies* 65(1): 61–90.

———. 2003b. *The Rule of Water: Statecraft, Ecology and Collective Action in South India*. New Delhi; Oxford: Oxford University Press.

———. 2001 'Irrigation and Statecraft in *Zamindari* South India'. In *The Everyday State and Society in Modern India*, edited by C. J. Fuller and Veronique Benei, 163–190. London: Hurst & Company.

———. 1999. 'Colonial and Contemporary Ideologies of "Community Management": The Case of Tank Irrigation Development in South India'. *Modern Asian Studies* 33(2): 303–338.

———. 1998. 'Making and Misconceiving Community in South Indian Tank Irrigation'. Draft paper presented at Crossing Boundaries, Conference of the International Association for the Study of Common Property, Vancouver, June 10–14. http://www.indiana.edu/~iascp/Drafts/mosse.pdf (accessed 15 March 2018).

Mueggler, Erik. 2017. *Songs for Dead Parents: Corpse, Text, and World in Southwest China*. Chicago, IL: University of Chicago Press.

Mullaly, Frederick S. 1892. *Notes on Criminal Classes of the Madras Presidency*. Madras: Madras Government Press.

Munn, Nancy D. 1992 [1986]. *The Fame of Gawa: A Symbolic Study of Value Transformation in a Massim (Papua New Guinea) Society*. Cambridge: University of Cambridge Press.

Nabokov, Isabelle. 2000. *Religion against the Self: An Ethnography of Tamil Rituals*. Oxford: Oxford University Press.

Nader, Laura. 2011. 'Ethnography as Theory'. *Hau: Journal of Ethnographic Theory* 1(1): 211–219.

Narayan, Kirin. 1993. 'How Native Is a 'Native' Anthropologist?'. *American Anthropologist* 95(3): 671–686.

Nicholas, Ralph W. 1981. '*Sraddha*, Impurity and Relations between the Living and the Dead'. *Contributions to Indian Sociology* 15(12): 367–379.

Obeyesekere, Gananath 1977. 'Social Change and the Deities: Rise of the Katagarama Cult in Modern Sri Lanka'. *Man* 12(3/4): 377–396.

Ojani, Chakad. 2022. 'Speculative Relations in Lima: Encounters with the Limits of Fog Capture and Ethnography'. *Hau: Journal of Ethnographic Theory* 12(2): 468–481.

Osella, Caroline and Filippo Osella. 2009. 'Vital Exchanges: Land and Persons in Kerala'. In *Territory, Soil and Society in South Asia,* edited by Daniela Berti and Gilles, 203–239. New Delhi: Manohar.

———. 2003. 'Migration and the Commoditisation of Ritual: Sacrifice, Spectacle and Contestations in Kerala, India'. *Contributions to Indian Sociology* 37(1 & 2): 109–139.

———. 2001. 'The Return of King Mahabali: The Politics of Morality in South India.' In *The Everyday State and Society in India*, edited by C. J. Fuller and V. Benei, 137–162. Delhi: Social Science Press.

———. 1996. 'Articulation of Physical and Social Bodies in Kerala'. *Contributions to Indian Sociology* 30(1): 37–68.

Ostor, Akos, Lina Fruzzetti, and Steve Barnett (eds.). 1982. *Concepts of Person: Kinship, Caste and Marriage in India*. Cambridge, MA: Harvard University Press.

Ortner, Sherry B. 1989. *High Religion: A Cultural and Political History of Sherpa Buddhism*. Princeton, NJ: Princeton University Press.

Ortner, Sherry B. and Harriet Whitehead (eds.). 1981. *Sexual Meanings: The Cultural Constructions of Gender and Sexuality*. Cambridge: Cambridge University Press.

Pandian, Anand. 2009. *Crooked Stalks: Cultivating Virtue in South India*. Durham and London: Duke University Press.

———. 2008. 'Devoted to Development: Moral Progress, Ethical Work and Divine Favour in South India'. *Anthropological Theory* 8(2): 159–179.

———. 2005. 'Securing the Rural Citizen: The Anti-Kallar Movement of 1896'. *Indian Economic Social History Review* 42(1): 1–39.

Pandian, M. S. S. 1992. *The Image Trap: M. G. Ramachandran in Film and Politics*. New Delhi: Sage Publications.

Parry, J. P. 2005. 'Changing Childhoods in Industrial Chhattisgarh'. In *Educational Regimes in Contemporary India*, edited by R. Chopra and P. Jeffery, 276–299. London: Sage Publications.

———. 1994. *Death in Banares*. Cambridge: Cambridge University Press.

———. 1985. 'Death and Digestion: The Symbolism of Food and Eating in North Indian Mortuary Rites'. *Man* 20(4): 612–630.

———. 1980. 'Ghosts, Greed and Sin: The Occupational Identity of the Benares Funeral Priests'. *Man* 15(1): 88–111.

Peters, Emrys L. 1990 [1987]. *The Bedouin of Cyrenaica: Studies in Personal and Corporate Power*. Cambridge: Cambridge University Press.

Piliavsky, Anastasia. 2023. 'Hierarchy as a Democratic Value in India: An Informal Essay'. *Current Anthropology* 64(5): 581–598.

———. 2020. *Nobody's People: Hierarchy as Hope in a Society of Thieves*. Stanford, CA: Stanford University Press.

——— (ed.). 2014. *Patronage as Politics in South Asia*. Cambridge: Cambridge University Press.

Pollock, Sheldon. 2007. 'Pretextures of Time'. *History and Theory* 46(3): 366–383.

Prasad, Leela. 2007. *Poetics of Conduct: Oral Narratives and Moral Being in a South Indian Town*. New York: Columbia University Press.

Price, Pamela. 2004. 'Kin, Clan and Power in Colonial South India'. In *Unfamiliar Relations: Family and History in South Asia* edited by Indrani Chatterjee, 192–221. New Brunswick, NJ: Rutgers University Press.

———. 1996. *Kingship and Political Practice in Colonial India*. Cambridge: Cambridge University Press.

———. 1989. 'Kingly Models in Indian Political Behaviour'. *Asian Survey* 29(6): 559–572.

Puett, Michael. 2020. 'Ritual as Theory, Theory as Ritual'. *Hau: Journal of Ethnographic Theory* 10(3): 1106–1108.

Radhakrishnan, Meena. 2001. *Dishonored by History: 'Criminal Tribes' and British Colonial Policy*. New Delhi: Orient Longman Ltd.

Raheja, Gloria Goodwin. 1998. *The Poison in the Gift: Ritual, Prestation and the Dominant Caste in a North Indian Village*. Chicago, IL: University of Chicago Press.

Ramberg, Lucinda. 2014. *Given to the Goddess: South Indian Devadasis and the Sexuality of Religion*. Durham, NC: Duke University Press.

Rao, Velcheru Narayana, David Dean Shulman, and Sanjay Subrahmanyam. 2003. *Textures of Time: Writing History in South India, 1600-1800*. New York: Other Press.

Reiniche, Marie-Louise. 1979. *Les Dieux et les Hommes: Étude des Cultes d'un Village du Tirunelveli, Inde du Sud*. Paris: Mouton.

Reynolds, Nedra. 1993. 'Ethos as Location: New Sites for Discussing Discursive Authority'. *Rhetoric Review* 11(2): 325–338.

Rivers, W. H. R. 2011 [1914]. *Kinship and Social Organization*. Abingdon; Oxford. Routledge.

Rosaldo, Renato. 1993 [1989]. 'Grief and a Headhunter's Rage'. *In Culture and Truth: The Remaking of Social Analysis*. London; New York: Routledge, 1–21.

Rudner, David. 1994. *Caste and Capitalism in Colonial India: The Nattukottai Chettiars*. Berkeley, CA: University of California Press.

Rutherford, Danilyn. 2012. *Laughing at Leviathan: Sovereignty and Audience in West Papua*. Chicago, IL: University of Chicago Press.

Sahlins, Marshall. 2017. 'The Original Political Society'. *Hau: Journal of Ethnographic Theory* 7(2): 91–128.

———. 2013. *What Kinship Is and Is Not?* Chicago, IL: Chicago University Press.

Sax, William. 2000. 'Conquering the Quarters: Religion and Politics in Hinduism'. *International Journal of Hindu Studies* 4(1): 3–60.

Schmitt, Carl. 2005 [1922]. *Political Theology: Four Chapters on the Concept of Sovereignty*. Translated by George Schwab. Chicago, IL: University of Chicago Press.

Schneider, David. M. 1984. *A Critique of the Study of Kinship*. Ann Arbor, MI: University of Michigan Press.

———. 1980 [1968]. *American Kinship: A Cultural Account*. Chicago, IL: University of Chicago Press.

Scott, James. 2009. *The Art of Not Being Governed: An Anarchist History of Upland Southeast Asia*. New Haven, CT: Yale University Press.

———. 1998. *Seeing Like the State: How Certain Schemes to Improve the Human Condition Have Failed*. New Haven, CT: Yale University Press.

Selby, Martha Ann and Indira Viswanathan Peterson. 2008. *Tamil Geographies: Cultural Constructions of Space and Place in South India*. Albany, NY: State University of New York Press.

Shah, Alpa. 2017. 'Ethnography? Participant Observation, a Potentially Revolutionary Praxis'. *Hau: Journal of Ethnographic Theory* 7(1): 45–59.

———. 2007. 'Keeping the State Away: Democracy, Politics and Imaginations of the State in India's Jharkhand. *Journal of the Royal Anthropological Institute* 13(1): 129–145.

Shastri, Nilakantha. K. A. 1975 [1967]. *The History of South India: From Pre-historic Times to the Fall of Vijayanagar*. New Delhi: Oxford University Press.

Shulman, David. 1985. *The King and the Clown in South Indian Myth and Poetry*. Princeton, NJ: Princeton University Press.

———. 1980a. *Tamil Temple Myths: Sacrifice and Divine Marriage in the South Indian Saiva Tradition*. Princeton, NJ: Princeton University Press.

———. 1980b. 'On South Indian Bandits and Kings'. *Indian Economic and Social History Review* 17(3): 283–306.

Singh, Bhrigupati. 2012. 'The Headless Horseman of Central India: Sovereignty at Varying Thresholds of Life'. *Cultural Anthropology* 27(2): 383–407.

Singh, Bhrigupati, and Naisargi Dave. 2015. 'On the Killing and Killability of Animals: Nonmoral Thoughts for the Anthropology of Ethics'. *Comparative Studies of South Asia, Africa and the Middle East* 35(2): 232–245.

Somanathan, T. V. 2003. 'Land Reforms in Tamil Nadu: A Case Study Based Analysis' In *Land Reforms in India: An Unfinished Task*, edited by M. Thangaraj, 21–46. New Delhi: Sage Publications.

Spencer, Jonathan. 2007. *Anthropology, Politics and the State: Democracy and Violence in South Asia*. Cambridge: Cambridge University Press.

———. 1997. 'Post-Colonialism and the Political Imagination'. *Journal of the Royal Anthropological Institute* (3)1: 1–19.

Srinivas. M. N. 1952. *Religion and Society among the Coorgs in South India*. Oxford: Clarendon Press.

Stein, Burton. 1980. *Peasant State and Society in Medieval South India*. New Delhi: Oxford University Press.

Subramanian, Ajantha. 2009. *Shorelines: Space and Rights in South India*. Stanford, CA: Stanford University Press.

Subbarayalu, Y. 1973. *Political Geography of the Chola Country*. Madras: State Department of Archaeology, Government of Tamil Nadu.

Tambiah, S. J. 2013. 'The Galactic Polity in Southeast Asia'. *Hau: Journal of Ethnographic Theory* 3(3): 503–534.

Taussig, Michael. 1987. *Shamanism, Colonialism and the Wild Man: A Study in Terror and Healing*. Chicago, IL: University of Chicago Press.

Thune, C. E. 1989. 'Death and Matrilineal Reincorporation on Normanby Island'. In *Death Rituals and Life in the Societies of the Kula Ring*, edited by F. H. Damon and R. Wagner, 53–178. DeKalb, IL: Northern Illinois University Press.

Thurston, Edgar and K. Rangachari. 1909. *Caste and Tribes of Southern India*. Vol. 4. Madras: Madras Government Press.

Trautmann, Thomas. R. 1981. *Dravidian Kinship*. Cambridge: Cambridge University Press.

Trawick, Margaret. 1992. *Notes on Love in a Tamil Family*. Berkeley, CA: University of California Press.

Turnbull, T. 1895. 'Account of the Various Tribes of *Cullaries*, in the Countries of Madura, Shevaguga, & Co.' In *Geographical and Statistical Memoirs of the Provinces of Madura and Dindigul*, Vol. 3, edited by B. S. Ward, 5–12. Madras: Madras Government Press.

Turner, V. W. 1996 [1957]. *Schism and Continuity in an African Society: A Study of Ndembu Village Life*. Oxford: Berg Publishers.

Uchiyamada, Yasushi. 2000. 'Passions in the Landscape: Ancestor Spirits and Land Reforms in Kerala, India'. *South Asia Research* 20(1): 63–84.

Valeri, Valerio. 1985. *Kingship and Sacrifice: Ritual and Society in Ancient Hawaii*. Translated by Paula Wissing. Chicago, IL: University of Chicago Press.

Van Gennep, Arnold. 1960. *The Rites of Passage*. Translated by Monika B. Vizedom and Gabrielle L. Caffee. London: Routledge & Kegan Paul.

Venkatasamy Nattar, N. M. 2005. *Kallar Carittiram* (*History of the Kallars*). Chennai: Carata Patippakam (Publishers).

Venkatachalapathy, A. R. 2006. *In Those Days There Was No Coffee: Writings in Cultural History*. New Delhi: Yoda Press.

Velayutham, Selvaraj and Vijay Devadas. 2022. 'Tamil Nadu Politics and Tamil Cinema: A Symbiotic Relationship?' *Society and Culture in South Asia* 8(1): 96–117.

Waghorne, Joanne Punzo. 2004. *Diaspora of the Gods: Modern Hindu Temples in an Urban Middle-Class World*. New York: Oxford University Press.

Washbrook, D. A. 1976. *The Emergence of Provincial Politics: the Madras Presidency 1870–1920*. Cambridge: Cambridge University Press.

Wink, Andre. 1986. *Land and Sovereignty in India: Agrarian Society and Politics under the Eighteenth-Century Maratha Svarajya*. Cambridge: Cambridge University Press.

Witsoe, Jeffrey. 2011a. 'Corruption as Power: Caste and the Political Imagination of the Postcolonial State'. *American Ethnologist* 38(1): 73–85.

———. 2011b. 'Rethinking Postcolonial Democracy: An Examination of the Politics of Lower-Caste Empowerment in North India'. *American Anthropologist* 113(4): 619–631.

———. 2009. 'Territorial Democracy: Caste, Dominance and Electoral Practice in Postcolonial India'. *Political and Legal Anthropology Review* 32(1): 64–83.

Yang, Anand (ed.). 1985. *Crime and Criminality in British India*. Tucson, AZ: University of Arizona Press.

Index